GLOBALIZATION AND THE MEANING OF
CANADIAN LIFE

WILLIAM WATSON

Globalization and the Meaning of Canadian Life

UNIVERSITY OF TORONTO PRESS
Toronto Buffalo London

© University of Toronto Press Incorporated 1998
Toronto Buffalo London
Printed in Canada
Reprinted in 2018

ISBN 0-8020-4220-1
ISBN 978-1-4875-7227-3 (paper)

Printed on acid-free paper

Canadian Cataloguing in Publication Data

Watson, William G.
Globalization and the meaning of Canadian life

Includes index.
ISBN 0-8020-4220-1

1. Canada – Civilization – Foreign influences.
2. Canada – Civilization – 1945– . I. Title.

FC95.4.W3 1998   971.064'.8   C98-930474-4
F1021.W3 1998

University of Toronto Press acknowledges the financial assistance to its publishing program of the Canada Council for the Arts and the Ontario Arts Council.

This book has been published with the financial assistance of the Donner Canadian Foundation.

To Scott, David, and Julia

Contents

PREFACE ix
ACKNOWLEDGMENTS xi

Part I: Globalization
1 Defining Moment 3
2 The Globalization Hypothesis 14
3 Four Hundred Years of Globalization 21
4 Convergence? 27
5 Home Truths 38
6 Are We There Yet? 46
7 Free to Choose 57

Part II: The Meaning of Canadian Life
8 False Premise 73
9 Governing Misperceptions 86
10 The American 'Governmental Habit' 91
11 'The Most Rugged Surviving Individualists' 104
12 The American Lead 113
13 Canadian Free Enterprise 121
14 The Unimportance of Being Different 131
15 Distinct Society? 143
16 Cement for a Nation? 158
17 The Rising Cost of Civilization 178
18 The Psychic Costs of Government 195

19 Virtually Canadian 214
20 Do Countries Still Make Sense? 237

NOTES 257
REFERENCES 289
INDEX 305

Preface

The race to the bottom – the idea that ever-deepening economic integration, or 'globalization,' as it is popularly known, will cause all the world's countries to become more and more alike in their tax rates, regulation, and public spending – is as close to an article of faith as can be found in the otherwise mainly unbelieving 1990s. The U.S. government, fearful that labour standards and environmental regulation will be driven to a lowest common denominator, is pushing hard, though so far unsuccessfully, to have national policies in these areas addressed by the new World Trade Organization, just as it insisted that they be included in the North American Free Trade Agreement (NAFTA) of 1994. Here in Canada, the decade-long drive for lower taxes and a streamlined public sector is widely attributed to the new, more competitive economic environment that followed the Canada–United States Free Trade Agreement (FTA), with the left invariably blaming the FTA and the right often as not citing its astringent imperatives as justification for the cuts. Even the free-trading *Economist* magazine, in explaining why public spending is expected to decline in real terms in Britain over the next few years, writes: 'Globalisation has led to international competition to offer low tax rates' (*Economist* 1996b).

For most developed countries, the prospect of policy harmonization with many of the world's most competitive economies is harrowing enough, but for a country such as Canada, which for at least three decades has vested so much of its identity in greater use of government than its principal trading partner, it threatens, at best, a near-death experience. If, as we have been told these many years, Canada is mainly its government, and if all governments are now to be the size of Singapore's or Malaysia's, then what will become of Canada in a new world without economic borders?

The two parts of this book address the two parts of this argument. The first – 'Globalization' – holds that deepening economic integration, which in fact has been going on for some time, does not bind national governments nearly so tightly as much popular commentary suggests. Both the facts of the last four decades and a good deal of economic theory suggest that there is still room for considerable diversity in national public policies. We Canadians therefore remain free, for the most part, to choose what sized government we should have.

The book's second part – 'The Meaning of Canadian Life' – argues that even if we *can* choose a larger government, we should think carefully before doing so. Government may be neither the wellspring nor guarantor of our identity, as is so often supposed, while such heavy reliance on the state as has become our habit may harm us, in ways that would be no less damaging if we lived as hermits economically and, in the famous phrase from 1911, had 'neither truck nor trade' with any other country.

Two final chapters argue that the main threat to Canada's continued existence is not the possibility that our governments will become smaller but the continuing intermingling of cultures and identities provided by the new communications technologies. But even here the threat may not be so great as is often thought, so that the nation-state – that sturdy, if sometimes distempered work-horse of the last two centuries – need not be put down just yet.

Owing at different times to its author's lethargy, fickleness, and attention deficit, this book has been nine years in gestation (if only three years in the writing). But the moment of its conception can be dated very precisely, and that is where, after some words of thanks, it begins.

Acknowledgments

Any book depends on the kindnesses of strangers (who often cease to be such in the process) as well as of friends and loved ones (who may cease to be *such* in the process). Writing this book has gained me several new friends and, I hope, lost me no old ones, though I have incurred many debts along the way.

I am very grateful to the Donner Canadian Foundation, which provided both a publication grant and the financial support that made possible the term away from my academic duties in which I was able to lay down a first draft. Both Devon Gaffney Cross and Adrienne Delong Snow provided enthusiastic and efficient administration and support. Tom Kierans and Angela Ferrante graciously offered the administrative auspices of the C.D. Howe Institute. Christopher Green, chairman of the Economics Department at McGill, generously acceded to my request for leave – despite the straitened circumstances that are most universities' lot these days. (He also bears the heavy responsibility of having taught the course, in 1970–1, that fired my interest in economics.) Fakri Siddiqui, chairman of Economics at Bishop's University, kindly provided me with an office in that university's Cormier Centre for International Economics during my term away from McGill. I am also grateful to Russ Mills and Neil Reynolds – publisher and editor, respectively, of the Ottawa *Citizen*, where I started as Editorial Pages Editor in January 1997 – who allowed me mornings off for six weeks in order to complete revisions of the manuscript. The *Citizen*'s marvellously talented illustrator, xii Acknowledgments

Robert Cross, kindly provided the diagrams that appear in chapter 19.

At the University of Toronto Press, Rob Ferguson took an early and enthusiastic interest and helped shepherd the book through the Manuscript Review Committee, whose members I thank for their careful reading. Because of them it is at least slightly less intemperate than it would have been. When Rob Ferguson left the Press to pursue a career elsewhere, Virgil Duff and Anne Forte provided able replacement.

Many people provided very helpful comments on either parts or all of a very dense (sometimes in both senses of the word) manuscript. At the risk of leaving someone out, I would like to thank Michael Bliss, Neil Cameron, Bob Catherwood (who bought my first newspaper column, became a good friend for seventeen years, and, sadly, did not live to see this book published), Tony Deutsch, George Grantham, Franque Grimard, Chris Green, Seamus Hogan, Alfred Leblanc, Mary Mackinnon, Desmond Morton, Chris Ragan, John Richards, Bill Robson, Daniel Schwanen, David Sewell, Michael Smith, Andy Stark, and Tom Velk.

Last, and most, I am grateful to my young sons, Scott and David, and to my wife, Julia. To be the dedicatees of this volume is small recompense for their patience and understanding during the many hours I have had to spend away from them, whether at the keyboard, in the library, or in absent-minded preoccupation, but that, as well as my thanks and my love, are all I have to offer.

PART I
GLOBALIZATION

1
Defining Moment

Tuesday, 25 October 1988, a little after 10 p.m. EST. Twenty-eight days before a federal election would decide the fate of the Canada–United States Free Trade Agreement. Just over two hours into the federal party leaders' English-language debate. It was the defining moment of a defining election. Or so people thought at the time.

Looking every bit the prime minister he once briefly had been, John Turner spoke calmly and confidently, his silver hair shining in the television lights, his clear, blue eyes locked onto Brian Mulroney's, his words flowing quickly and smoothly, with none of the baffled hesitation or full-diesel throat-clearing that had marked his return to politics five years earlier. Cupping his hands to show reasonableness, lifting his shoulders for emphasis, he began to explain why he thought another leaders' debate was necessary, one solely on the subject of free trade.

'I think the issues happen to be so important for the future of Canada. I happen to believe that you've sold us out. I happen to believe that once you enter ...'

'Mr. Turner, just a second ...'

Mulroney's baritone blared. He had just finished a long passage, in the hushed, unctuous tone he evidently still did not understand many Canadians loathed, but now he saw an opening and his voice rose to full volume.

Turner tried to continue ... 'Once any nation' ... But Mulroney insisted ... 'You do not have a monopoly on patriotism ...'

4   Globalization

'One sec' ... Turner tried to interrupt back, but Mulroney held the floor. 'And I resent the fact that, your implication that only you are a Canadian. I want to tell you that I come from a Canadian family and I love Canada. And that's why I did it. To promote prosperity. And don't you impugn my motives ...' It was all at full bore and from anyone the country trusted more would not have looked rehearsed.

'Once any country yields its economic levers ...'
'Don't you impugn my motives or any one else's!'
'Once a country yields its investment; once a country yields its energy ...'
'We have not done that!'
'Once a country yields its agriculture ...'
'Wrong again!'
'Once a country opens itself up to a subsidy war with the United States ...'
'Wrong again!'
'... on terms of definition, then the political ability of this country to sustain the influence of the United States, to remain as an independent nation, that is lost forever, and that's the issue of this election, sir.'

As Turner paused in his attack, Mulroney told a story about how his working-class father had been a nation-builder and how Ukrainians and eastern Europeans had rolled back the prairie and how they had been nation-builders, too. 'I today, sir, as a Canadian, believe genuinely in what I am doing' (which was not really the issue: Canadians were not yet so soured on Mulroney as to doubt that he believed in what he was doing). 'I believe it is right for Canada. I believe that in my own modest way' (an unfortunate choice of words, even then) 'I am nation-building. Because I believe this benefits Canada and I love Canada.'

Turner now for some reason felt obliged to establish his own patriot's pedigree and to withdraw the implicit charge of traitor. A man of the old school, he found that gutter politics suited him much less than it did his infamous Liberal Rat Pack. 'I admire your father for what he did. My grandfather moved into British Columbia. My mother was a miner's daughter there. We're just as

Canadian as you are, Mr. Mulroney.' (Which wasn't the point: the charge had been that Mulroney wasn't as Canadian as he.) 'But I'll tell you this. You mentioned 120 years of history. We built a country east and west and north. We built it on an infrastructure that deliberately resisted the continental pressure of the United States.' (By this he presumably meant the CPR, built before anyone had heard of 'infrastructure.') 'For 120 years we've done it. With one signature of a pen you've reversed that, thrown us into the north–south influence of the United States and will reduce us – will reduce us, I am sure – to a colony of the United States ...'

'With a doc ...'

'... because when the economic levers go the political independence is sure to follow.' Turner's eyes were in laser-lock with Mulroney's.

'Mr. Turner, with a document that is cancellable on six months' notice? Be serious.'

'Look ...'

'Be serious.' Mulroney was serving a dangerous brew of smugness and condescension.

'Cancellable?! You're talking about our relationship with the United States. Once that document ...'

'A commercial document that's cancellable on six months' notice.'

'Commercial document! That document relates ...'

'That is what it is. It's a commercial treaty. A commercial treaty.'

'It relates to every facet of our life ...'

'It's a commercial treaty.'

'It's far more important to us than to the United States.'

'Mr. Turner, please, be serious.'

'Well I have never been more serious in my life.' In fact, Turner sounded both convinced and convincing, though if a corporate lawyer from the right wing of the Liberal party were so dead set against a trade-liberalizing deal with the United States, it might be suspected that this was because he also had never been more dedicated to political necessity in his life.

6 Globalization

'Please, please,' Mulroney tut-tutted as he finally broke the laser-lock, looking away primly to the moderator, appealing for assistance – almost, almost rolling his eyes, as if the guest standing next to him at a garden party had made a spectacle of himself. But he took a deep draught from his water glass before the next question came. It dealt with the proposed 'national sales tax,' not yet referred to as the GST.

Viewing a tape of the exchange almost a decade later, it is surprising both how young the two men look – power ages even more quickly than it corrupts – and how well Mulroney performed in a round that everyone except Tory spin doctors awarded to Turner.[1] Mulroney was crisp. He was forceful. He certainly was loud enough. And he countered every accusation that Turner made, even countered them contrapuntally, as, Southern Baptist style, he chanted his denials to Turner's list of ways in which Canadian sovereignty had been surrendered. If he didn't think he had won the exchange, he probably regarded it as one he should have won, since Turner gave him the perfect opening for what in hindsight was obviously a set piece on patriotism.

In fact, an even better moment for Turner came at the end of the debate, in his own set piece, his closing statement. Mulroney had read his hurriedly, his eyes, in an amateur error, straying often from the camera. Turner also read, but he was calm, quiet, measured, and direct, the picture of sincerity. His delivery was almost, almost Reaganesque. Speaking about the Canada–U.S. free trade deal, he said:

There is virtually no area of Canadian life that has been left untouched. I believe in this country. I have faith in Canada. I don't believe my feelings are any different from yours. We have something special here, something we don't want to lose. We have a way of life, a way of looking at ourselves, a way of, a way of reacting to the world. Mr. Mulroney's trade deal will change all that. It will make us little more than a junior partner of the United States. I believe in a strong, sovereign independent Canada. I believe that we are now talented enough and competent enough and tough enough to make our own choices, for our

Defining Moment 7

own future, in our own way. I need your support on November 21st. You and I must not allow Mr. Mulroney to sell us out, to reverse 120 years of Canadian history, to destroy the Canadian dream.

The reference to 'the Canadian dream' was, in the context, unfortunately American. But even an economist who voted for the Tories and free trade can appreciate what a brilliant performance Turner's was.

What it wasn't, however, was the defining moment of the election campaign, for Turner and the Liberals lost. Replayed time and again in the following few days, the exchange propelled the Liberals to a twelve-point lead in the polls (Graham Fraser 1989: 470-1). It even made the network news shows in the United States, where its many instances of interruption and talkover were regarded as superior theatre to American presidential debates, which are essentially serial speechmaking, it being considered insufficiently respectful to subject presidents to the hectoring that is our prime ministers' daily fare in the House of Commons. But the Liberals' lead did not last, partly because several of Turner's subsequent appearances were not nearly so impressive, partly because the press responded to his success by turning its reptilian eye on his program and prospective cabinet, and partly, to give credit to Mulroney, because the Tories recovered quickly and mounted a full-scale blitzkrieg on free trade in the last two weeks of the campaign. In the end, of course, Turner lost, Mulroney won, and the Canada-U.S. Free Trade Agreement (FTA) became law. Five years later it was followed by the North American Free Trade Agreement (NAFTA), though by then both Turner and Mulroney were gone and the Tories had been reduced to two seats in the House of Commons, not so much a rump as a mole.

Though it did not turn the election, the television confrontation may have been a defining moment for free trade itself and for Canadians' understanding of the effects of economic liberalization. The Tories won the electoral battle, but there is every evidence that they lost the war of ideas. Popular support for free trade peaked in 1987, just after the FTA was negotiated. Since

8 Globalization

then, growing familarity with the deal apparently has bred contempt. In eleven soundings between 1988 and 1993, the Gallup Poll showed a plurality of respondents favouring the FTA only in December 1988 (44–38) and January 1989 (45–29), during the Tories' brief post-election honeymoon. By March 1990, opposition was back over 50 per cent, where it had been but two weeks before the 1988 election was called (Gallup Canada: 30 August 1993).[2] Moreover, at the one poll that counted, on election day, 1988, only 43 per cent of Canadians voted for the free trade party. Had the vote instead been a true referendum on free trade, it might well have lost.

Though most Canadians probably now are resigned to the FTA and even to NAFTA, they are just that – resigned: 'They accept it as a fact of life' (Gwyn 1995: 53). Free trade has formed a grim triumvirate with death and taxes, two other phenomena regarded as unpleasant, unwelcome, and unavoidable. Most Canadians very probably believed then and still believe now that closer economic relations with the Americans do put our country at risk. 'By opening Canada's economy to Americans,' Richard Gwyn writes, 'Mulroney ensured that it would become like America's. Under FTA, Canada's guiding economic rule has become the American one of the free market' (Gwyn 1995: 42). The Fraser Institute's Michael Walker argues that it would be possible to find 'thousands of [such] quotes by distinguished people' asserting that the FTA's result 'would be a kind of averaging down of social programs toward the U.S. level, one which Canadians would not find attractive, given our "kinder, gentler" approach to life' (Walker and Emes 1996: 8). As John Turner said, 'When the economic levers go, the political independence is sure to follow.'

Now, heading towards 2000, this belief is reinforced by the world-wide fascination with 'globalization' – the idea that because of changes in both policy and technology, businesses have almost completely free choice about where to produce goods or services. Parts now can be made in China or Malaysia or Puerto Rico and shipped 'just in time' virtually anywhere in the world. Accounting can be done by keypunchers in India or Ireland or the Philippines and zapped by satellite to the home office

Defining Moment 9

– if there is a home office, since these days home may be virtually anywhere, or anywhere that's virtual, and virtually everywhere is. In the era of globalization, there's hardly a closed economy left. Even Albania is open now, and North Korea cannot be far behind.

In such a wide-open economic environment, the question naturally arises, how can any country impose taxes higher than those imposed elsewhere? If it tries to, capital will flee to safer tax havens, whence goods will be shipped back to the high-tax country. But without capital what will happen to jobs and incomes? And if a country *can't* tax more than other countries, how can it have a bigger government and more generous social programs? It obviously can't. The nation-state may not literally disappear, but in a globalized world all nation-states will look more and more alike. The economic levers may not be surrendered, as John Turner feared, but they will start spinning on their own. Not just Canada, it seems, but all countries will be forced to reduce their public sectors to the scale of the Japanese or the American or, even worse, Singapore's or Malaysia's or Mexico's. As the twenty-first century nears, this 'race to the bottom' is widely thought to be the fate of the world's welfare states. The fear is that nobody, not even the United States, is 'talented enough, and competent enough and tough enough to make their own choices, for their own future, in their own way.' That's bad enough as it is, but what if you are a country that defines your distinctivness through your social programs? What then?

This book is about the many issues raised in that brief but intense exchange on the night of 25 October 1988. John Turner and Brian Mulroney obviously didn't cover all the ground just surveyed. But much of it was implied by what they said. The debate rested on several unspoken premises, some shared by both men, many shared by most Canadians, almost all shared by the Canadian left, a group that may have gone into hibernation in recent years, but, with our combined governments now spending almost half our annual economic output, is hardly extinct. Among these premises are the following.

§We *are* different from the Americans. §It is important, both for

10 Globalization

ourselves and for the world, that we continue to be different from the Americans. §In large part, our difference is either caused by or sustained by our greater use of government. §We have always used government more than they have. §The economic liberalization brought about by the FTA, NAFTA, and the new World Trade Organization will require us to use government less than we would like. §This forced reduction in our use of government risks taking us below the critical threshold where we effectively become identical to the Americans. §The damage will be done both by trade agreements' direct prohibitions on specific kinds of government intervention and, even more effectively, by limits that we impose on ourselves as the increasing openness of our economy forces us to harmonize our tax rates, and therefore our social policies, first with the Americans and then eventually with most other countries in what is quickly becoming an essentially borderless world.

The economist John Maynard Keynes wrote of the constant 'struggle of escape from habitual modes of thought' (Keynes 1936: viii). This book challenges the modes of thought just listed, which have become habitual in late-twentieth-century Canadian life. Its practical purpose is modest: to banish the metaphor of the Canadian Pacific Railway (CPR) – 'we used government to build the railway, so we should use government to ...' – from discussions of contemporary public policy. It will have succeeded if those who propose policies feel at least marginally more obligated to justify them on their merits, rather than on appeals to how 'we have always done things more through the public sector than the Americans,' or how 'we are more compassionate and caring,' or how a market-oriented policy would be 'the American way of doing things' and therefore not permitted in Canada, however useful it might be. A main reason for eradicating this manner of thinking is that in Canada patriotism invariably is the first refuge of the self-interested.

The first part of the book, 'Globalization,' will please Canadians who still believe that our principal and preferred means of distinguishing ourselves from the Americans should be to tax ourselves more than they do, for it argues that in fact economic

Defining Moment 11

integration places many fewer restrictions on governments than is commonly believed. It obviously does limit them in at least some ways. Countries that sign free trade deals cannot raise their tariffs to whatever level they wish. And they may have to treat foreign and domestic investors the same way, even if they treat neither very well. Trade agreements may go beyond this if, for instance, governments agree to live by minimum standards for social policy or harmonize the way they collect sales taxes – forms of explicit harmonization typically proposed more by those on the left of the political spectrum than those on the right. Beyond what the language of trade treaties requires, freer economic relations may also create indirect pressures for policy harmonization, as John Turner warned. In particular, increased competition from foreigners may cause local interests to lobby hard for changes in government policies.

Governments, however, need not and in recent decades generally have not succumbed to these pressures. Despite considerable integration of the world economy over the last five decades, there still are very striking differences in the levels of taxation and public expenditure even among countries that have become deeply integrated. Canada is an obvious example: our tax rates and public sector became most different from the Americans' over the last forty years, a period during which our integration into the American economy reached new heights – or depths, if you are of that political persuasion. There are also sound reasons in economic theory which, though inevitably less convincing than fact, help explain why trading with each other need not force countries to adopt their partner's fiscal and regulatory habits. It is true that an economy's becoming more open to foreigners may change who in it pays for public services. In particular, in a world of highly mobile capital, capital is unlikely to pay. But so long as those who do pay remain willing to, they can continue to buy more public services than their trading partners. Thus if Canadians really do want a larger public sector than the Americans have, nothing either written into the FTA (or the NAFTA or the WTO) or resulting from these agreements need prevent us from having it.

If this first part of the book might please the Canadian left, its

12 Globalization

second part, 'The Meaning of Canadian Life,' is intended to infuriate it, for it takes issue with most of the governing shibboleths of the Canadian identity debate of the last thirty years. It argues, among other things, that:

- We actually *aren't* that different from the Americans, both because in their practice of government they have not been true to their official laisser-faire ideology – far from it – and because, in Canadians' own pursuit of profit, many of us have been every bit as entrepreneurial as Americans.
- Whether we *are* different from the Americans little interests the world and should not matter to us. What does matter is that Canadian society offer as good a life as possible to the people who make it up. When that means adopting American-style policies, insisting we be different from the Americans will stand in the way of sensible change.
- The important differences that do exist between our two countries – that they are large and we small, that they are one society and we at least two, and that we are (in more than one way) colder – have little to do with the size of our government and very probably would endure even if it were not larger than the Americans'.
- The idea that Canadians run a more generous, tolerant, and humane society is actually of quite recent vintage. For much of this century, the Americans were more interventionist than we were. We were Canadian, of course, before our public sector was bigger than the Amercians, and we undoubtedly would be Canadian after it was dismantled, there being no reason why Canadians' sense of themselves should be defined in perpetuity by the ideological fashions of the 1960s.
- Though our larger public sector is supposed to be a unifying force, it is no accident that the dramatic growth of our governments over the last three decades has coincided with increasing national disunity. On reflection, it should hardly be surprising that government's very visible redistributive hand has strained interregional and interethnic harmony to the breaking point, if not beyond.

Defining Moment   13

- Our larger government imposes heavy economic costs, not because our trade is affected – our trade is at record levels – but because of the economically destructive effects of high taxation and the morally destructive effects of a society in which effort and reward are increasingly unrelated.
- In fact, the greatest threat to the nation-state comes from cultural, not economic integration, as new communications technologies such as satellite broadcasting make people more alike the world around. But even here, the danger of cultural assimilation may not be as great as is commonly feared.

In sum, the message of this book is contrarian. Contrary to what many globalization theorists argue, Canadians remain largely free to choose what-sized government we want. Integrated markets will not force all countries to become fiscally identical, and, in particular, we will not have to become like the Americans, if we do not wish to. We should not presume, however, every time we come to decide a problem of government, that to preserve our separate identity we need choose a different policy than the Americans have chosen. Our independence is expressed not in what we choose but in the act of choosing ('to make our own choices, for our own future, in our own way'). If, as this book argues, we do remain largely free to choose for ourselves, we should choose what is best for us, not what we are accustomed to choosing, or what we think our tradition requires us to choose, or, worst of all, what those south of us are not choosing.

2
The Globalization Hypothesis

On 1 March 1989, exactly one hundred days after Canada's great free trade election, the head of the Canadian Manufacturers' Association made one of the least politic public statements since Pierre Trudeau's 'Zap! You're frozen' ridicule of wage and price controls in 1974. In a letter to Finance Minister Michael Wilson urging tax relief in the upcoming budget, Laurent Thibault wrote: 'The Canada–US free-trade agreement that we fought hard for creates great opportunities but also makes it more urgent that we tackle the outstanding issues that affect our competitiveness ... Since Canadian taxes are already high compared to our major competitors, the burden of reducing the deficit must fall largely on cutting expenditures' (*Globe and Mail* 1989).

All through the election the Liberals and NDP had argued that even if no secret giveaways on social policy had been written into the agreement itself, increased competitive pressures on Canadian industry would lead to renewed calls for reduced taxes and therefore reduced spending on social programs. Our fiscal heritage, our ability to establish our uniqueness, for this continent, by taxing and spending more than the Americans was therefore being put at risk. And Thibault's pre-budget statement was the smoking gun. A prominent free trader either hadn't followed the election, which just couldn't be true, since his organization had taken a leading role in supporting free trade, or felt that, with the vote safely out of the way and the deal finally done, candour was now permitted.

Whichever was true, the free traders' argument of only three months earlier – that a country could have both free trade and distinctive taxation and spending policies – apparently was false, and the free traders, or at least one prominent free trader, clearly knew it. A hapless Thibault protested that in fact he hadn't drawn any connection between free trade and the need for spending cuts. But there it was in black and white. The letter prompted a flurry of editorializing, as well as justifiably angry denunciations from anti–free traders, who protested – for once, with good reason, apparently – that the electorate had been had.

The timing of Thibault's remarks may have been unwise, but from the perspective of the mid-1990s their substance is now conventional wisdom. These days, it is almost universally believed that globalization will cause tax rates and the size of government to converge the world around. Increasing economic integration will force convergence, and nation-states will be powerless to do anything about it. As the columnist Richard Gwyn has put it: 'To make our way in the global world we have little choice but to become more like much of the rest of the world. To exaggerate, but not by that much: In order to compete successfully with a South Korea, say, our wages, social systems, and taxation schedules cannot be too different from those of South Korea ... Many government policies are being decided now by the urgent need ... to create a market economy as efficient as those with which Canadian businesses are now competing directly. Hence all the privatization and deregulation, the downsizing of governments and public services, and the acceptance of the necessity of reducing taxes, especially those that inconvenience corporations' (Gwyn 1995: 78, 42).

The political economist Daniel Drache made the same case in a commentary on NAFTA: 'Social policy is on the table to an unprecedented degree ... With capital more mobile than ever, no Canadian manufacturing sector is secure ... Wages are much more vulnerable to competitive pressures than ever before. And the social wage is also shrinking. The entire industrial wage-setting mechanism has to incorporate wage pressures that are no longer primarily local but are now starkly global' (Drache 1993: 271,

273). At the Canadian Centre for Policy Alternatives, Bruce Campbell had the same view of NAFTA: 'What is set in motion is a lowest-common-denominator competitive process where different areas ... vie for absolute cost advantages, resulting in a downward spiral of standards, wages, taxes and so forth' (Campbell 1993: 34). Or as Maude Barlow, the tireless (often tiresome) St Joan of Canadian nationalism, and her colleague at the Council of Canadians, David Robinson, told the letters editor of the *Globe and Mail* in 1995, the year of Paul Martin's harshest budget: 'As we predicted during the free-trade debate, it is not possible to harmonize the economic systems of the continent and allow our social and environmental infrastructures to remain intact. As health-care budgets are slashed and services privatized, free-trade rules are allowing American health corporations to move into Canada. With cutbacks in social services, education and welfare, we are witnessing nothing short of the Americanization of our social programs' (Barlow and Robinson 1995).

These quotes are all from members of the Canadian left or – in Gwyn's case – centre-left, but even the editors of a recent series of books on 'Integrating National Economies' from Washington's prestigious Brookings Institution say much the same thing, if more circumspectly: 'As cross-border economic integration increases, governments experience greater difficulties in trying to control events within their borders ... The pressures from ... integration sometimes even lead individuals or governments to challenge the core assumptions of national political sovereignty ... National policies and behaviours may eventually converge to common, worldwide patterns (for example, subject to internationally agreed norms or minimum standards) ... [World federalism], now relevant only as an analytical benchmark, is a possible outcome that can be imagined for the middle or late decades of the twenty-first century' (Tanzi 1995: xviii, xix, xxi, xxii–xxiii).

In 'Bushism Found,' an influential article that appeared in *Harper's* magazine in 1992, Walter Russell Mead put it more starkly: 'Either the progressive systems of the advanced industrial countries will spread into the developing world or the Third World will move north. Either Mexican wages will move up or

The Globalization Hypothesis 17

American wages will move down' (quoted in Bhagwati and Srinivasan 1996: 164). For her part, *Financial Post* editor Diane Francis has written: 'As trade between [Canada and the United States] increases, as it has under free trade, Canadian politicians have less discretion to adjust taxation and monetary policies than before ... Canada's taxation and interest-rate levels are dangerously out of step with its neighbour's. Neither people nor their capital can be held captive in a jurisdiction like Canada's where taxes, as a proportion of GDP, are 10 per cent higher than those of its neighbour' (Francis 1993: 2, 3). In the same vein, historian Jack Granatstein, hardly a right-winger, writes that, in the 1990s, 'Canadians live with the realities of a prolonged recession and the effects of globalization. Governments in virtually every provincial capital and in Ottawa are hacking and slashing at programs and budgets, following the global agenda as defined in the Republican-dominated Congress in Washington' (Granatstein 1994: 281). And, finally, in May 1997, in a cover story entitled 'The Disappearing Taxpayer,' the redoubtable, dependably market-oriented *Economist* argued: 'As the world becomes more integrated, and as capital and labour can move more freely from high-tax countries to low-tax ones, a nation's room to set tax rates higher than elsewhere is being constrained' (*Economist* 1997: 21).

With all its many and varied adherents, the logic of this 'globalization hypothesis' seems unassailable. If businesses are perfectly mobile – if they can produce more or less anywhere – and if goods can be shipped across national borders without penalty, then any attempt by a national government to tax firms at a higher rate than other countries will cause them to pick up and move to those other countries. They will produce in the low-tax market and ship into the high-tax market.

For some products – software and some services, for instance – life without borders already exists. Satellite communications enable companies to sell financial and accounting services into many different countries. Keyboarding and even computer programming are commonly done in low-wage countries such as Ireland or India and 'shipped' back by satellite to the home office. Drainage of the Los Angeles Dodgers' baseball field in Chavez

18 Globalization

Ravine is controlled by a computer two thousand miles away (dodgers.com). It happens to be in the United States, but it could just as easily be in Toronto – or Tipperary. On a slightly lower-tech scale, in 1996 more than five hundred telemarketing firms operated out of Canada into the U.S. market (Morton 1996), while even the nationalist Toronto *Star* hired an American mail-order service, based in Virginia, to arrange mail-order subscriptions.[1] As the internet grows, an increasing number of 'cyberproducts' will be 'downloadable' from anywhere in the world (Slutsky 1996b). Goods that cross borders must still pass the muster of customs agents, but the electronic transmission of cyber-goods and -services takes place invisibly, instantaneously, through the ether, almost entirely out of reach of earthbound government regulators.

That will never be true for everything, of course. Cement probably always will be produced locally, since it's so heavy. The same for bottled drinks, another high weight-to-value commodity, even if large numbers of Canadians, inhabitants of one of the world's wettest countries, already buy their drinking water from France. Transportation costs will never be zero, not until we start 'beaming' things around the globe (as in 'Beam me up, Scottie'). But transportation costs have fallen sharply over the last few decades.[2] If they continue to fall, producing offshore will be possible for manufacturers of more and more goods. The transnational production even of ordinary goods and services is also made easier by satellite networks, which continue to render communications easier, faster, and cheaper. In 1866, it cost $5 per word – *per word!* – to send a cable between New York and London. That's $51 in 1994 dollars (United States, Bureau of the Census 1989, Series R16, E135). In 1918, a three–minute, station-to-station telephone call between Montreal and Vancouver cost $14.60, or $140 in 1994 dollars (Urquhart and Buckley 1983: Series T341). In 1945, the average Canadian made just over five long-distance telephone calls per year; in 1980, almost seventy (Globerman 1988: Table 4). In 1920, it took fourteen minutes to complete a telephone connection between New York and San Francisco; in 1970 less than twenty seconds (Richard G. Harris 1993: 767). Now

The Globalization Hypothesis 19

connection is virtually instantaneous and expense is minimal. Internet voice communication, which is on its way, may be essentially free.

In the past, governments could use tariffs – that is, taxes on imports – to force businesses to maintain a production presence in high-tax markets. High duties on imports often made it unrealistically costly to produce elsewhere and ship into the high-tax market, so businesses decided that they were better off operating in such markets, even if this did mean facing higher corporate taxes. In fact, a standard view of Canadian economic history is that high tariffs after 1879's National Policy encouraged American branch plants to set up here and produce for the Canadian market.[3] But in the new world economic order that is emerging, tariffs on trade between nations will not last much beyond the first quarter of the new century. This is the result not just of the FTA and NAFTA, which bring North American tariffs to zero by 2005, but also of the old General Agreement on Tariffs and Trade (GATT), now replaced by the World Trade Organization (WTO), under which average rich-country tariffs on industrial goods will be down to 3.8 per cent by the year 2000 (Fieleke 1995: 4).

In sum, a technological revolution *is* causing dramatic declines in the cost of organizing production across national borders that are themselves less meaningful economically as tariffs gradually disappear. In this new, globalized world, what is there to stop firms from moving to the countries that offer the lowest tax rate? Nothing, apparently. It seems that Laurent Thibault may have been right after all, despite his protestations.

In fact, he was almost certainly wrong. Even in a perfectly globalized world, both theory and evidence suggest, there is still substantial room for the distinctive exercise of national sovereignty. The next four chapters try to make this case. Chapter 3 argues that globalization, far from being new, has been under way for at least four hundred years. Chapter 4 then documents the limited extent of policy convergence in the Organization for Economic Cooperation and Development (OECD), Europe, and the United States over the last fifty years, even in the face of substantial economic integration. Chapter 5 looks at the experience of

Canada and the United States, the world's two most deeply integrated economies. Chapter 6 asks whether globalization really has gone as far as many people evidently think and describes some startling Canadian–U.S. data that suggest it hasn't. Finally, chapter 7 tries to explain why countries can still choose larger governments than their trading partners, even in the face of rising competitive pressures.

3
Four Hundred Years of Globalization

If 'globalization' means just-in-time, computer-managed production by companies that operate in many different countries, then it really is something new: electronic computers are only half a century old. But if it simply means deeper and deeper economic integration, it is just the continuation of a process that has been going on for some time. 'The history of the world economy since the Industrial Revolution,' writes English historian Eric Hobsbawm, '[has] been one of ... increasing "globalization," that is to say of an increasingly elaborate and intricate worldwide division of labour; an increasingly dense network of flows and exchanges that [bind] every part of the world economy to the global system' (Hobsbawm 1994: 87). Or, as the Canadian-British author and commentator Michael Ignatieff puts it: 'We have lived with a global economy since 1700, and many of the world's major cities have been global entrepots for centuries. A global market has been limiting the sovereignty and freedom of maneuver of nation-states at least since Adam Smith first constructed a theory of the phenomenon at the outset of the age of nationalism in 1776' (Ignatieff 1993: 12).

Canadians should know this better than most people. We have had to live with the vagaries of economic integration from the very first days of European settlement, almost four hundred years ago. And even before that, archaeological findings suggest extensive continent-wide trade among the Native peoples of North America, especially in copper, silica, flint, and obsidian, which is a volcanic glass prized for its cutting properties (R.C. Harris 1987: Plate 14). At the outset, much of the European part of our civilization was underwritten by the Hudson's Bay Company, whose commercial reach, despite the difficulty of transportation in the middle centuries of the second millenium, was easily as 'global' as any modern transnational corporation's.

In fact, one reason Canadian history supposedly makes such tedious reading is that while our southern neighbours were fomenting revolution and fighting screen-worthy civil wars, Canadians were worried about such things as the price of beaver-felt hats on European markets and whether the British Parliament would continue a preferential tariff rate for imperial 'corn,' by which, of course, in their baffling way, the British meant 'wheat.' While the Americans founded their country with a stirring declaration of the rights of man, we established ours by adopting a policy of high tariffs. As Carleton University trade expert Michael Hart puts it: 'When Sir John A. Macdonald uttered his immortal words, "A British subject I was born, a British subject I will die," he was not thinking of the Plains of Abraham or Queenston Heights, but of the tariff on ploughs from New York' (Hart 1994: 3). International markets clearly have been important to us for some time.

In fact, in the 1930s and 1940s, the economist Harold Adams Innis built a distinctively Canadian approach to economics based precisely on the wide-ranging international effects – one might even say the 'global' effects – of changing prices. He argued, for instance, that the rise of coffee-houses in England after the Puritan revolution had stimulated the demand for sugar in the West Indies and, as a byproduct, lowered the price of rum in the New World, thus producing social consequences of which the Puritans presumably would not have approved (Innis 1945: 96). We Canadians have also been 'a source of disturbance to the economies of other countries.' In the early twentieth century 'pulp and paper production supported by provincial governments facilitated the rapid growth of advertising in the United States, and contributed to the ... destruction of a stable public opinion' as more and more Americans came under the influence of publishers such as Wil-

Four Hundred Years of Globalization 23

liam Randolph Hearst, the Rupert Murdoch of his day (Innis 1945: ix–x). A more modest example of the effects of international markets is the career of Sir Joseph Flavelle, one of the Toronto businessmen whose turn-of-the-century success in selling bacon is why that city's nickname is Hogtown. Flavelle made his fortune largely because the U.S. McKinley tariff kept Canadian wheat out of the American market, thus depressing the local price of hog feed and enabling him to undercut Danish suppliers in the British market (Bliss 1978: 54). Neither Southeast Asia nor microelectronics was involved – though Flavelle's firm was heavily into research and development – but could anything be more global? Asia *was* involved in the success of Canadian builders of electricity and tramway installations, who in a ten-year period bracketing 1900 participated in projects in Minneapolis/St Paul, Detroit, Birmingham (England), Barcelona, Havana, Trinidad, Jamaica, Mexico City, Monterrey, Rio de Janeiro, São Paulo, and Shanghai (Bliss 1978: 68–9).

Commercial history may never have quickened the pulse of the teenagers who used to have to study it, but Canadian business people long since learned the central lesson of globalization – what happens in foreign markets can change their lives in crucial ways. By contrast, the novelty of such an idea to Americans is understandable. Until the oil crisis and the emergence of Asia as a world economic power, trade was a small part, invariably less than 10 per cent, of American economic activity. In 1966, imports accounted for only 5.5 per cent of U.S. gross domestic product (GDP), and by 1994 the figure had almost tripled, to 14.4 per cent (D. Gordon 1996: 187) Though not quite as momentous an opening to the world as Japan experienced after Commodore Perry arrived in the 1850s, such a change is a source of culture shock. But Canada's economy, while almost always protected to a degree, has never come close to self-sufficiency. Trade has always been its lifeblood, and in this century, even through Depression and war, it has never been as small a share of economic activity as the 14.4 per cent that has so profoundly shaken the Americans.

Similarly, the Canadian capital market has also always been open to – or, more accurately, dependent on – foreign investment.

Foreign investment played such a pivotal role in the nineteenth century that one theory of Canadian Confederation has the British colonies of North America coming together mainly so that their collective debts, incurred largely through railway building, would be easier to finance.[1] Nor were governments the only Canadian institutions that depended on foreign capital. As in the United States, private economic development in this country was largely financed by foreign, mainly British, capital.

Transnational investment on a large scale is therefore nothing new. In the 1870s existing British investments in the United States amounted to 20 per cent of U.S. GDP, while British sources accounted for more than 15 per cent of all new American investment (Dunning 1970: Table 10). As Stanford University economist Paul Krugman notes, 'On the eve of World War I, Great Britain's overseas investments were larger than its domestic capital stock, a record no major country has ever come close to matching' (Krugman 1996: 22).[2] Between 1905 and 1913 'the annual outflow of capital from Britain for investment overseas averaged close to 7 per cent of her national income ... and reached a phenomenal 9 per cent' in 1913 (Kenwood and Lougheed 1992: 27). By contrast, even in the late 1950s and early 1960s, its heyday as a source of capital, American foreign investment never exceeded 2 per cent of U.S. GDP (Dunning 1970: Table 3). One economic historian concludes: 'Never before or since has one nation committed so much of its national income and savings to capital formation abroad' (Edelstein 1994: 173).[3]

Instantaneous flows of capital, money market dealings of a trillion and more U.S. dollars a day – these *are* new, but catering to the needs and desires of foreign investors is not. Under the gold standard, when the world's financial centre talked people listened: 'London's influence over international capital flows was so powerful that no other centre could afford to ignore events occurring there. When Bank Rate was raised in London, many central banks had no choice but to respond by creating further stringency in domestic credit markets so as to minimize the loss of gold' (Eichengreen 1986: 16).

Even in terms of trade, the nineteenth century was accustomed

Four Hundred Years of Globalization 25

to the tumult and hard disciplines of rapid economic integration. Between 1980 and 1988, the supposed dawn of globalization, world trade grew at 4 per cent a year, outpacing world production of 2.5 per cent per year (Kenwood and Lougheed 1992: 287). In the last century, however, trade outpaced growth by even more, growing at rates between 29 and 64 per cent per decade, even as overall economic growth averaged 7.3 per cent per decade (Kenwood and Lougheed 1992: 78–9). In the hundred years before 1913, world trade grew by a factor of 25 (R.G. Harris 1993: 758), rising from 3 per cent of world GDP to 33 per cent. By contrast, for thirty years in this century international trade grew hardly at all. By 1948, it was not significantly greater than it had been before the First World War. The problem, of course, was the collapse of the international market resulting from Depression, war, and protectionism. In 1945, Harold Innis could look back and conclude sadly that since the 1850s 'free trade has rapidly receded' (Innis 1945: 134). His melancholy was soon made obsolete, however: during the next twenty-five years world trade in all goods quintupled, while trade in manufactures grew ten-fold (Hobsbawm 1994: 88, 261). And all before anyone had heard of 'globalization.'

Rapid changes in technology, widely thought to go hand in hand with globalization, are nothing new, either. As Krugman observes, 'We all know that technology is what has made a truly global economy possible, but it turns out that the key technologies were the steam engine and the telegraph' (Krugman 1996: 22). The same thought has occurred to MIT's Lester Thurow, though his candidates for the only two inventions that have truly 'revolutionized our industrial world' are the railway and electricity. Napoleon's armies and Caesar's moved at the same speed, but after the railway human transportation was utterly changed, while electricity transformed existence by making night 'usable'[4] (Thurow 1992: 1). All four inventions came in the last century, of course, not the current one, though Thurow does allow that the microprocessor 'could be a third major revolution' (Thurow 1992: 1).

Quite apart from anything that happened in the nineteenth century, both Canada and the world already have considerable experience with economic integration in the years following 1945, a period during which international flows of both goods and capital have consistently outpaced world economic growth. Industrial countries' tariffs have fallen from average levels well over 30 per cent in the first days of the GATT in the late 1940s to 5 per cent or less following the Uruguay Round of the 1980s. Moreover, much of the postwar growth in the world's trade occurred in the 1950s and 1960s (Richard G. Harris 1993: 758). Similarly, the big influx of U.S. investment into Canada took place in the first two decades after the war, and even though Americans' investment here has continued to grow, in recent years overall Canadian investment in the United States has risen to a level about two-thirds what the Americans own here.

To be sure, the internationalization of markets may have seemed more constricting in the early 1990s, as Canadians faced the fact that their growing public indebtedness had given control of the country's budget policies over to pimply-faced, twenty-something computer jockeys, as they were invariably described, who worked the foreign currency desks of the world's major financial institutions and to '"stateless legislators" in their wide suspenders' (Gwyn 1995: 78), who periodically threatened to call in the International Monetary Fund (IMF) to tidy Canada's balance sheet. But in fact Canada's first experience with IMF supervision of its affairs came in 1962, when the 'Diefenbuck' lost the confidence of the world's money managers, who, though less numerous, older, possibly better-complexioned, and certainly less familiar with computer screens, were nevertheless powerful enough to threaten the survival of a Canadian government (see Smith 1995: 437–45).

All in all, both Canada and the world already have had considerable experience with deepening economic integration – enough, surely, to see whether countries that grow closer economically do become more alike in their tax and expenditure polices. So what do the data say?

4
Convergence?

What *do* the data say? Unfortunately, reliable economic data (in some countries, *any* economic data) don't go back very far. Ideally, it would be possible to look at how different countries' public sectors have changed over the last hundred years. But the farther back you go, the fewer countries have available statistics and the more dodgy are the data that do exist. Figure 4.1 is about the best that the economics literature can offer. It shows what happened to public spending in six countries – the United Kingdom, the United States, Germany, France, the Netherlands, and Japan – from 1913 to 1987.

The number charted is a statistical measure of the difference in the six countries' government spending ratios – that is, the ratio of their public expenditures to their GDP.[1] It shows that the difference across countries is dramatically lower after the Second World War than before, which certainly is consistent with the globalization hypothesis: as transportation costs have fallen and trading and investment regimes been liberalized, public sectors apparently have been driven to conformity. However, if the tax rates of countries that trade with each other really do converge, the rapidly growing trade of the postwar period should have continued to narrow the spread in expenditure ratios. But it didn't. Virtually nothing happens to the spread between 1950 and 1987 – in fact, it is actually a little higher in 1987 than in 1950 – despite the continuing decline in transportation costs and substantial liberalization of trade and investment. The six countries are trading

28 Globalization

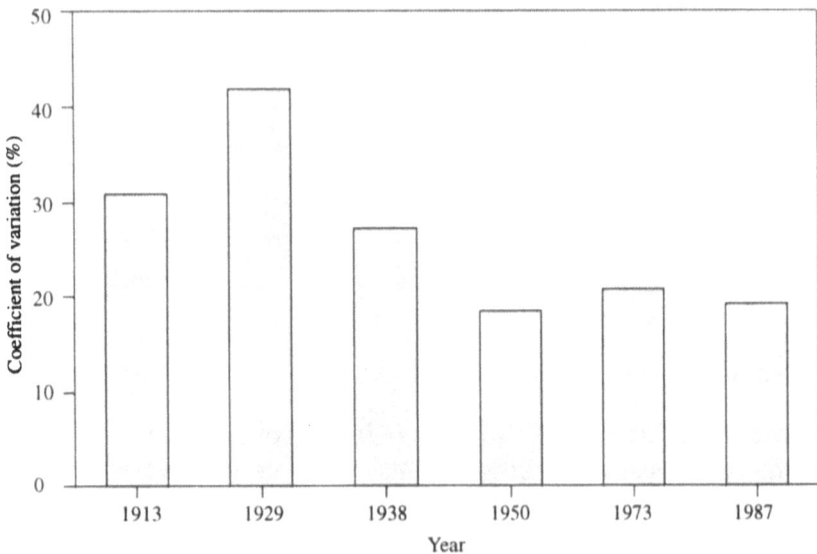

Figure 4.1 Spread in spending, six countries, 1913–87
Source: Calculated from Maddison 1991, Table 3.17.

with and investing in each other more than they did fifty years ago, but their public sectors are still as different as they were at mid-century.

THE OECD NINETEEN

Figure 4.2 shows the same measure of spread for another indicator of the size of government – the ratio of total tax revenues to GDP – for the nineteen member countries of the Organization for Economic Cooperation and Development (OECD) for which such data are available for the years 1955 to 1994.[2] The variation was 22 per cent in 1955 and 21 per cent in 1994, which suggests that not a lot has changed in almost forty years. Just looking at the endpoints gives a misleading impression, however. In fact, this measure of spread rose in the 1960s and 1970s, peaking in 1972 and again in 1979, at 26 per cent, after which it has declined. Its post-1979 decline is consistent with globalization theory: you would

Convergence? 29

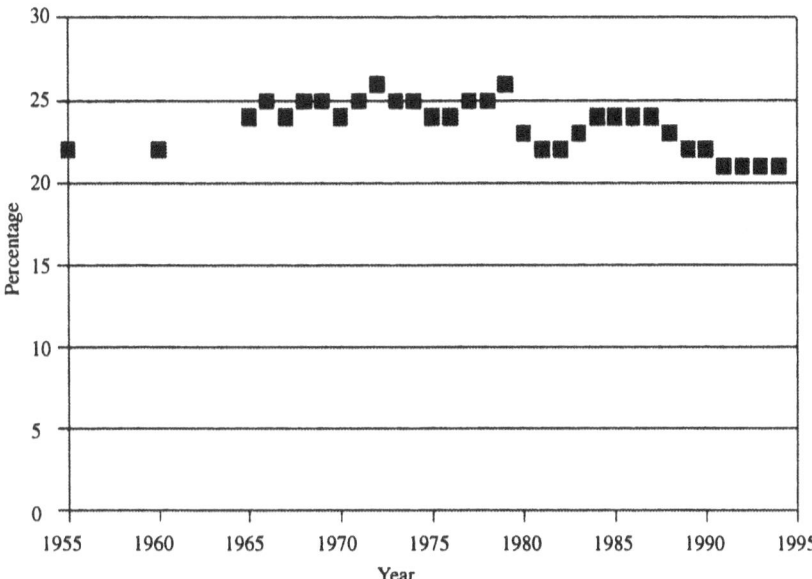

Figure 4.2 Spread in tax rates, 19 countries, 1955–95

expect less of a difference in national tax ratios as economies became more integrated. But the rise in the 1960s and 1970s is puzzling, for those decades were also a time of increasing integration. Moreover, the post-1979 decline in spread has hardly been steady. For instance, the indicator declined in the early 1980s, to 21 per cent in 1982, but then rose again to 24 per cent from 1984 through 1987. And, of course, the measure of spread is virtually identical to what it was four decades ago, despite quite dramatic economic integration over those forty years.

Figure 4.3 shows some of the raw data that went into Figure 4.2. The top line is the highest tax ratio in the nineteen OECD countries; the middle line, the average tax ratio, and the bottom line, the lowest tax ratio (which throughout the period was Turkey's). The spread between the maximum and minimum tax ratios is particularly interesting. Until 1990 or so, it moved in a direction that completely confounds the prediction of globalization theory. While economies were becoming more integrated, the tax gap was widening between the highest- and lowest-tax OECD countries. From less than 20 percentage points of GDP in 1955 it opened up to more than 35 points of GDP in the late 1980s. Despite considerable liberalization of industrial countries' trade, as a result of both the GATT and regional trade agreements, such as the European Community and the Canada–U.S. Autopact, the difference between the highest and lowest tax ratios did not shrink between 1968 and 1990 but grew, and grew by a lot.

After 1990, however, the gap began to close. Just why that year marked such a turning point is not clear. Perhaps globalization began to speed up in the 1990s, or maybe the statistical series is overly sensitive to changes in individual countries. From 1976 until 1992, when Denmark reclaimed this dubious honour, Sweden was the highest-tax OECD country.[3] But since topping out at 55.6 per cent of GDP in 1990, Sweden's tax ratio has fallen almost six points of GDP. Such a sudden turnaround is less likely the result of any new opening up of the nation's economy, which has been very open for some time, than of the debt-sparked crisis in Swedish fiscal policy that began in the early 1990s. And what explains Denmark, which also has a very open economy and yet in 1994 was levying taxes equal to 51.6 per cent of its GDP? Moreover, in 1994, the gap between the most- and the least-taxed OECD countries again began to widen after five years of narrowing. In sum, it is too early to tell whether the decline in the difference across countries since 1990 is a statistical fluke or the beginning of a trend that over time will eliminate such differences. Of course, even after its early-1990s dip, the spread in OECD tax ratios is still 29.4 points of GDP, and so even if trade is forcing countries to become more alike, they still have a long way to go before becoming identical.

Though the highest tax ratio in the OECD fell after 1990, this was not accompanied by any great change in the average tax ratio, as the middle line in Figure 4.3 shows. It rises, more or less steadily, from 23.4 per cent of GDP in 1955 to 38.2 per cent in 1992, an increase of 14.8 percentage points of GDP. Despite much media talk about how the anti-tax, Reagan/Thatcher revolution has swept the Western world, the average OECD tax rate fell in only

Convergence? 31

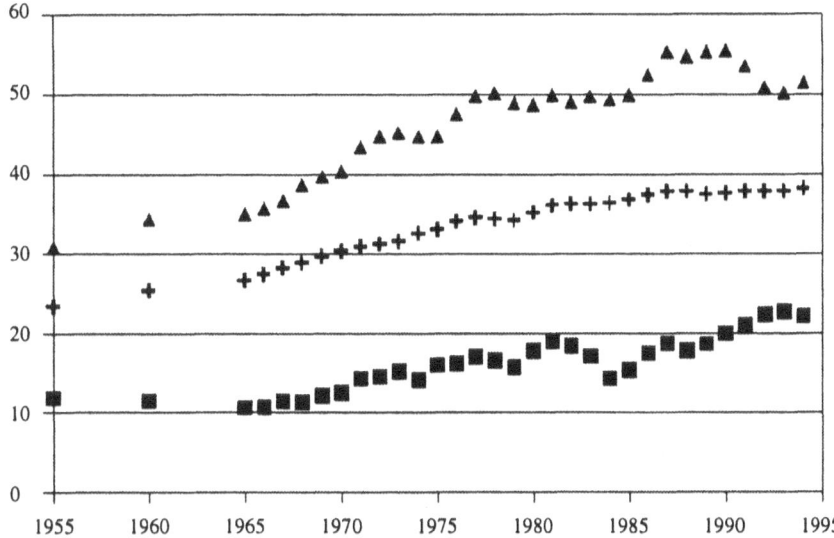

Figure 4.3 Maximum, minimum, average tax ratios, 19 OECD countries, 1955-94

four of the last twenty-nine years, and only once during the Reagan/Thatcher years.[4] To give the 'Iron Lady' and the 'Teflon' president their due, they may well have slowed the growth of taxes. Thus in the eleven years 1979-90 the average OECD tax ratio grew only 3.7 points, whereas in the eleven years before then it had grown 5.7 points. And, of course, Mrs Thatcher and Mr Reagan controlled only two of the twenty-three OECD countries. However, in the United Kingdom the tax ratio rose from 32.6 per cent in 1979, when Mrs Thatcher took office, to 36.4 per cent in 1990, when she left, while in the United States it was only three-tenths of a percentage point lower (27.0 versus 27.3) in 1989, when Mr Reagan was succeeded by George Bush, than it had been in 1981, before 'the revolution.'

The obvious conclusion from the middle line of Figure 4.3 is that, unless global economic integration began only in the very late 1980s, it is not in the least inconsistent with the continuing – in fact, never-ending – growth of government. In *Age of Extremes*,

32 Globalization

his magisterial history of our century, Eric Hobsbawm writes: 'From the eighteenth century until the second half of the twentieth, the nation-state had extended its range, powers and functions almost continuously,' which sounds as if it had stopped (Hobsbawm 1994: 576). The data suggest that, measured by taxes at least, it had not stopped. In his 1996 State of the Union address, President Bill Clinton declared that the age of big government was over – though, as wags suggested, what was likely to replace it was smaller government and lots of it. Whether big government really is gone remains to be seen.

THE UNITED STATES OF EUROPE

How about the European Economic Community? Europe has been liberalizing its trade and investment rules since the mid-1950s and in 1992 even went so far as to form a 'European Union.' With the deeper and deeper economic integration that Europe has experienced over the last four decades, you would expect to see a significant reduction in the differences across countries. And you do, though again this conclusion has to be qualified. Figure 4.4 shows how the spread in tax rates across the 'original six' members of the European Economic Community (EEC, or Common Market) – France, Germany, Italy, Belgium, the Netherlands, and Luxembourg – has changed since 1965.

The average spread is less than for the nineteen OECD countries discussed above. It ranges here between 7 per cent towards the end of the period and 17 per cent in the late 1970s.[5] For the nineteen OECD countries the spread was much larger, which is not surprising, since they included many more disparate countries than the European six, which are all among the richest of industrialized countries.

The spread first climbs and then falls, and it ends up not far from where it started out. The graph is a pretty good imitation of an upside-down 'V.'[6]

Why the spread in tax ratios behaved so differently before and after 1978 or so is both interesting and puzzling. The years following 1978 saw continuing liberalization for Europe, so the fact that

Convergence? 33

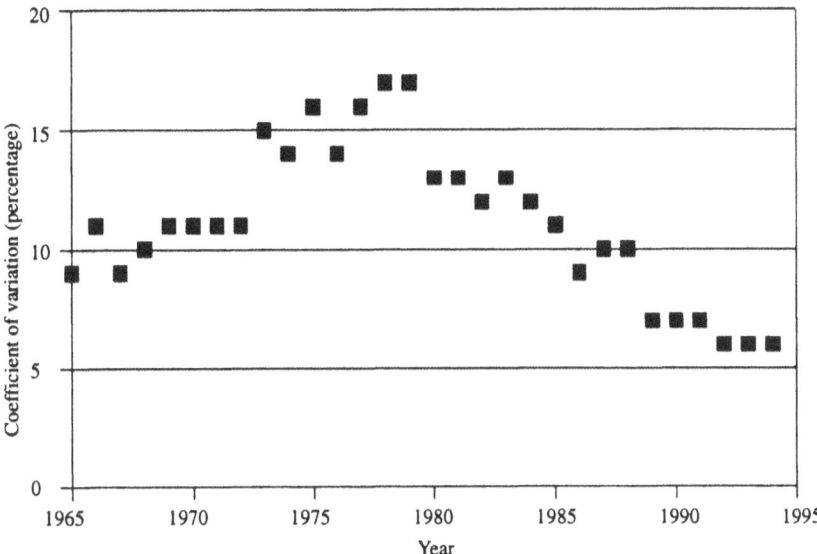

Figure 4.4 Spread in tax rates, original six members of the EEC, 1965-95

ratios moved closer together is consistent with the idea that closer trading and financial relations do lead to harmonization of tax and spending policies. But what about 1965 through 1977? These were also years of economic integration for Europe. A recent study estimates that between 1956 and 1973 trade among the original six countries of the Common Market grew at 3.2 per cent more per year than would have been expected without the advent of the community, which means that at the end of those seventeen years trade was 88 per cent higher than it would have been without integration (quoted in Helliwell 1996: 508 n.). To be sure, European liberalization has proceeded more quickly in some periods than in others, but the economic walls have not gone back up at any time and they have generally continued to fall. Yet despite relentless liberalization under both GATT and the EEC, these six countries became markedly less alike between 1965 and 1977. Where the globalization hypothesis would predict a fairly steady decline in the spread in tax ratios over time, there was instead a sharp rise, followed by an equally sharp decline.

In a recent review of policy harmonization in the European Union, economist André Sapir provides some clues as to what may have been going on. He argues that the EEC originally took an approach of 'benign neglect' towards policy harmonization, mainly because member countries were more or less similar to begin with, unemployment was low, and economies were growing rapidly. Other countries' less generous social policies may have harmed domestic workers by encouraging firms to migrate, but economic anxieties were not uppermost in people's minds (an argument admittedly easier to make from the safe distance of three decades). After 1973, however, both the entry of new members and the world economic slowdown caused by the oil crisis increased the political interest in restraining imports. Hence the desire to harmonize social policies so as to take away low-wage countries' cost advantage. By the mid-1980s, with low-wage Spain and Portugal entering the community and continuing 'Eurosclerosis' forcing drastic economic action, the EEC started the move towards even greater integration, which made the political pressure for harmonization of social policy irresistible for all but the very strongest politicians, such as Margaret Thatcher, who always favoured retaining national autonomy in matters of social policy.[7]

In brief, if Sapir is right, the tax/GDP numbers may be converging because European policies are converging, though as a result of explicit decisions to coordinate them. However, after reviewing various examples of harmonization, Sapir's conclusion is that 'in spite of the Social Charter and Maastricht, [which explicitly require the coordination of social policies], "social harmonization" remains a distant reality ... Differences in labour standards between member states remain substantial,' even though labour standards are the area on which the political and policy focus has been most intense (Sapir 1996: 565). The American economist Joel Slemrod arrives at the same conclusion regarding taxes on business, though these presumably would be among the first levies harmonized, given the high degree of business mobility these days. In 1992 a committee of experts commissioned by the ECC 'documented substantial differences among

Convergence? 35

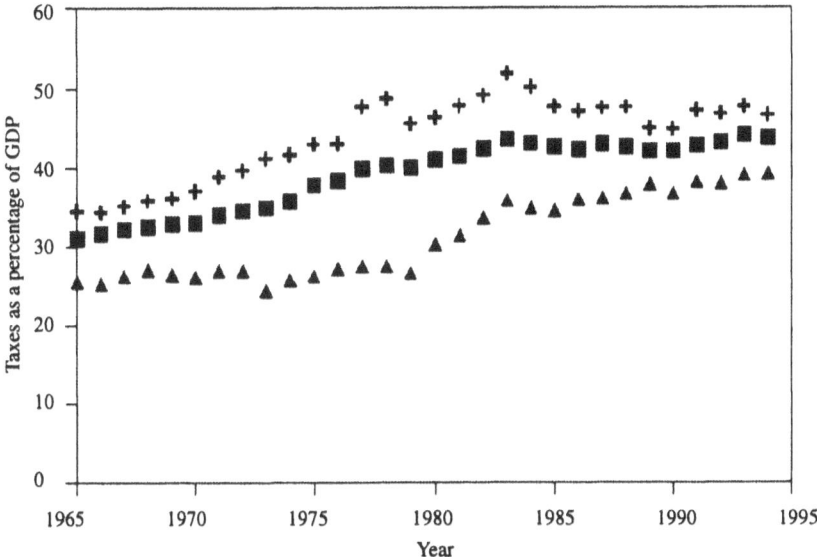

Figure 4.5 EEC maximum, minimum, and mean tax ratios, 1965–94

member states in both tax rates and definition of taxable income' and proposed that countries at least agree to move their corporate tax rates to within a 10-point band between 30 and 40 per cent, but in the end its proposals were not adopted. Slemrod concludes that Europe has failed to achieve 'any significant harmonization of business taxation' (Slemrod 1996: 287).

A final thing to notice about Figure 4.4 is that the values at the beginning and end of the period (9 per cent and 6 per cent, respectively) are not all that different, at least when compared to the 17 per cent at which the series peaked. But this only only adds to the puzzle. Both the modestly integrated Europe of 1965 and the substantially integrated Europe of 1992 tolerated roughly the same spread in tax ratios across the six original member countries.[8]

Figure 4.5 provides further detail on tax ratios in the 'original six.' As above, the top line shows the highest tax ratio among the six; the middle line, the average tax ratio; and the bottom line, the tax ratio in the country where it was lowest during the year in

36 Globalization

question.[9] By the end of the period the lowest tax ratio in the group had risen from 25.5 per cent of GDP to 39.3 per cent. As for the average tax ratio, it rose steadily throughout the period, falling in only seven of the twenty-nine years. Reagan/Thatcherites, however, will be pleased to note that five of these seven occasions occurred in the 1980s. Even so, average European taxes were higher at the end of that supposedly revolutionary decade than at the beginning.

THE AMERICAN ECONOMIC UNION

What many (though not all) Europeans would like to see emerge from their countries' continuing integration is a 'United States of Europe,' with Europe's member-states linked as closely as the states of the American union. Should economic integration that tight eventually occur, will the tax and spending policies of the former nation-states of Europe be perfectly harmonized? No, not even then, if American experience is any indicator.

The United States is the world's oldest continuing common market. Hardly anything there impedes the free movement of capital and labour among its states. It has a common language and culture, and its laws, when not actually identical across states, are generally very similar. If businesses or people dislike the tax rates they face in one state, they can pick up and move to a state that suits them better, and from where the federal constitution's guarantee of free interstate commerce allows them to ship their goods or services back to whichever state they have left without fear of discrimination.

Yet even within the United States, that prototype of the highly integrated economic federalism towards which the world itself may be evolving, there still are significant differences across states in tax rates. In 1992, state income taxes for the richest Americans ranged from zero in seven states to 10 per cent in Hawaii, 11 per cent in Montana and California, and 12 per cent in Massachusetts (or 'Taxachusetts,' as Republicans call it). Similarly, corporate income taxes for top earners ranged from zero in five states to 9.4 per cent in Alaska, 10.5 per cent in North Dakota, 11.5 per cent

Convergence? 37

in Connecticut, 12 per cent in Iowa, and 12.25 per cent in Pennsylvania. Even general sales taxes varied a good deal, from zero in five states to 7 per cent in Rhode Island and Mississippi. Gasoline taxes ranged from 4 cents a gallon in Florida to 26 cents in Connecticut and Rhode Island, while cigarette taxes varied between 5 cents a pack in North Carolina – where lots of tobacco is grown – and 50 cents in the District of Columbia, only four hours away by car (Tanzi 1995: Table 3.1). The net effect of all these differences in taxes was that per capita state and local government tax revenue varied between $1,323.61 in Mississippi and $3,841.16 in Alaska – in other words, over a range of almost 300 per cent (Morgan, Morgan, and Quinto, eds. 1995: 263). All in all, there is great variation in tax rates even among the members of the world's most highly integrated economic union. Considerable mobility of goods, services, businesses, and people has not eradicated these differences and does not look like doing so any time soon.

To sum up, despite continuing integration of both the world and European economies – a development that is supposed to make it much more difficult for governments to assert themselves fiscally – taxes have risen over the last twenty-five years in every one of the nineteen most industrialized countries. They have also risen on average – substantially. And they continue to differ by significant amounts within the OECD, across Europe, and among the U.S. states. While tax rates have become more similar in the 'original six' European countries over the last fifteen years, the degree of their spread is not greatly different than it was in the 1950s and 1960s, when, despite substantial trade and investment barriers, different countries' tax policies seem to have been fairly similar. Moreover, the harmonization of the 1980s and 1990s was preceded in the 1960s and 1970s by a puzzling – for a period of increasing economic integration – deharmonization. Perhaps economic integration may not be the ruthlessly levelling force that is so often claimed – a suspicion that the experience of the world's two most integrated economies conforms.

5
Home Truths

How about the situation closer to home? Does our own experience with taxation and public expenditure in Canada lead to any conclusions about economic integration and public policy? You would think it might, since over the last few decades we have become increasingly integrated with the world's biggest, richest economy. Figure 5.1 shows what has happened to taxes as a percentage of Canadian GDP since 1965. It is no surprise to anyone who lived through this period that this figure has gone up. From 25.9 per cent of GDP in 1965 it rose by 10.2 points, to more than one-third, to 36.1 per cent in 1994, and half that increase came during the supposed 'decade of greed,' the Reagan/Thatcher/Mulroney years. Average Canadian taxes fell in only two years of that decade, 1982 and 1988, and in each of those years by only four-tenths of one per cent of GDP (OECD 1995: Table 3.)[1]

How does our experience compare with what has gone on elsewhere? Figure 5.2 puts Canadian taxes side by side with taxes in the nineteen OECD countries examined above and in the 'original six' EEC countries.[2] Canadians frustrated by what they regard as punitive taxes may be surprised to learn that we are below both the OECD and the 'original six' average rates of taxation. Though we were pretty much on course with the OECD through the late 1960s and early 1970s and even exceeded its average for much of that period, in the late 1970s our average tax rate fell, while its continued to rise. During two of these years, from September 1977 to June 1979, Jean Chrétien was finance minister. His memoirs do tell how

Home Truths 39

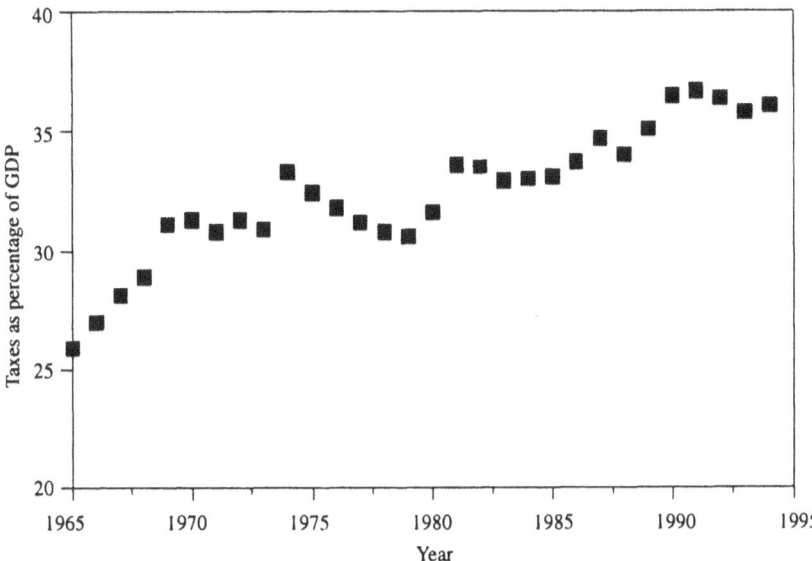

Figure 5.1 Canada's tax ratio, 1965–94

he cut taxes against the advice of his officials, but an overall tax rate may have fallen mainly because of decisions taken before he became minister (Chrétien 1985: 109–10).

In any case, our average tax rate began rising again at the beginning of the 1980s, the supposed dawn of the western world's tax revolt, and through that decade our taxes grew at roughly the same rate as the OECD average. However, because of our five-year hiatus during the late 1970s, we tracked the OECD at a lower level. As we saw above, European taxes also tended to grow more slowly during the 1980s, but by then what had been a relatively narrow gap between Canadian and European tax rates in the 1960s had widened to ten points. In 1994, the latest year for which OECD data are available, Canadian taxes were 36.1 per cent of GDP, 2.1 points lower than the average in the nineteen OECD countries and 7.7 points lower than in Europe's 'original six.'

How do our taxes compare with those of our major trading partner, the United States? Figure 5.3 shows that in the 1950s American

40 Globalization

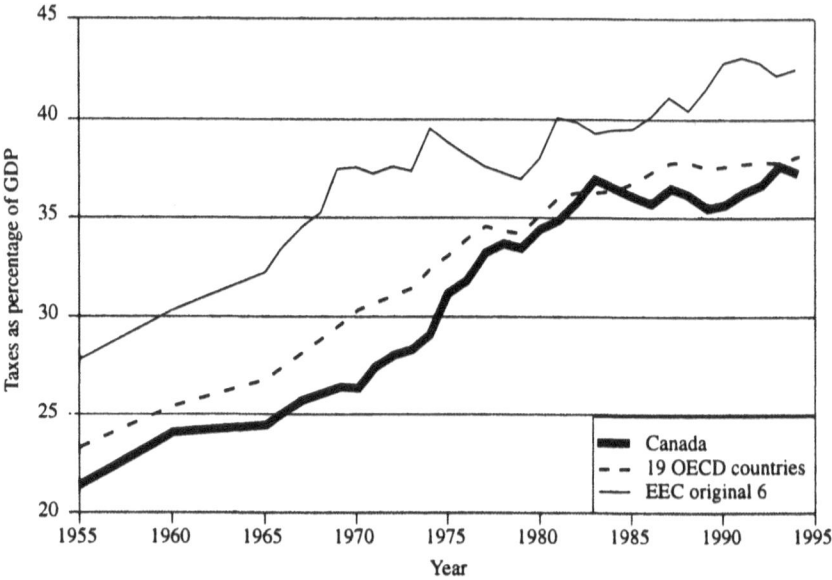

Figure 5.2 Canadian taxes in perspective, 1955–94

taxes were actually higher than ours. In the mid-1960s, during the Pearson era, we had essentially the same tax rate as the Americans, but in every year since then taxes have constituted a higher percentage of our GDP than theirs. Moreover, the gap between the two nations' tax rates has been rising. While their tax ratio has stayed more or less constant, bumping up against but never exceeding 28 per cent, Canada's has grown over time, to the point where in 1994 taxes were 8.5 points of GDP higher in Canada than in the United States. This gap was actually down slightly from the all-time high (for this data series) of 9.9 per cent in 1991. It is tempting to think of the difference as being what we spend on medicare – 7.1 per cent of our GDP in 1991. But we spend only 1.5 percentage points more of our GDP on publicly-provided health care than the Americans do. In 1991 they spent 5.6 per cent of their GDP on public-sector health care, mainly for the poor and the old.[3]

The change in the relative size of the Canadian and American public sectors is seen even more dramatically in Figure 5.4, which

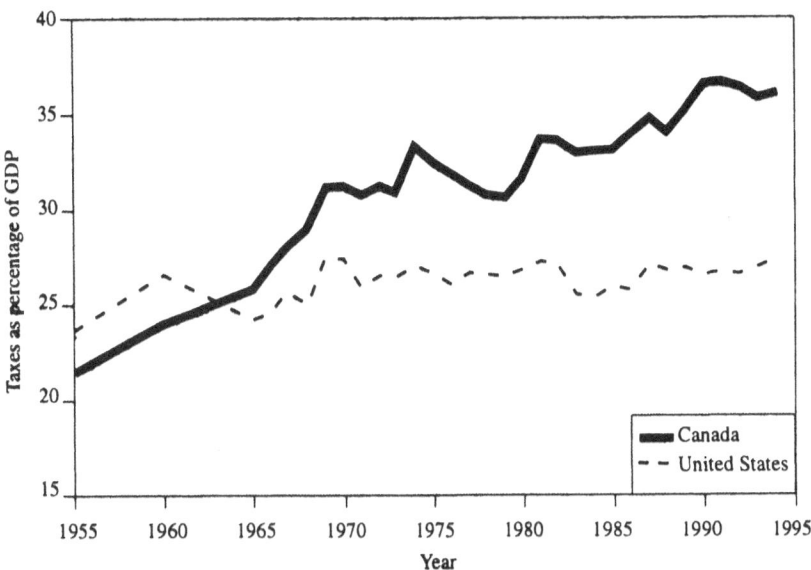

Figure 5.3 Canadian tax rates versus American, 1955–94

shows the course not of taxes but of public spending in the two countries over the last forty-five years.[4] Canadians raised on the dogma that this country defines itself mainly through its larger-than-American public sector will be surprised to learn that as late as the 1950s the Canadian and American public sectors were essentially the same size, at a little over one-quarter of each country's GDP. In fact, in some years in the 1950s the American was actually larger than ours in relative terms. Of course, the composition of public spending differed: the Americans spent more on the military than we did.[5] However, what's bought may not be crucial. People who are concerned about globalization usually worry about an economy's capacity to support its public expenditures through taxes. If the overall tax rate really is what counts, it may not matter much on what public money is spent. And in the 1950s our overall tax rate was for all intents and purposes the same as the Americans'.

From the end of the 1950s, however, what Canadians have

42 Globalization

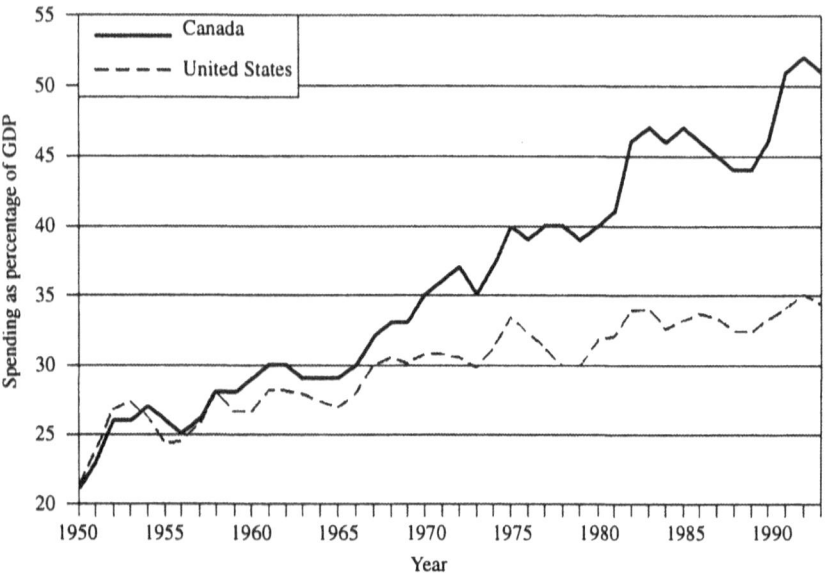

Figure 5.4 Spending/GDP, Canada versus United States, 1950–93

come to think of as the traditional pattern asserted itself: we have had the bigger government, by the metric of public spending at least. Despite a long-run decline in military spending, overall public spending has risen in the United States, from roughly one-quarter of GDP in the 1950s to just over one-third in the 1990s. But it grew much more quickly in Canada, from the same roughly one-quarter of GDP in the 1950s to over one-half of GDP in the 1990s. Despite the Mulroney revolution, despite downsizing, despite the attack on the welfare state, despite the terrible neoconservative 1980s, our three levels of government currently combine to spend virtually 50 per cent of GDP, which is not just a peacetime, but an all-time high. In 1992, they spent a grand total of 51.2 per cent of GDP (Perry 1996: Table 5). The pre-1990s high, recorded in 1944, when our public sector was busy liberating Europe, was 50.0 per cent. To be sure, almost ten points of what our governments now spend is on interest, which pays for *past* public spending, but it is public spending nevertheless.

The wisdom of raising taxes as high as we have, running deficits as large as we do, and allowing our public sector to grow so much larger than the Americans' will be debated below. What cannot be disputed is that we have done it. The numbers show that. And we have done it even though during this same period our economy became much more open to, even dependent on, foreign trade and foreign investment, particularly investment from and trade with the United States.

It may simply be an artefact of the two time series chosen, but the data suggest that the year 1958 was crucial. Two things happened then. First, Canadian exports hit a postwar low as a share of GDP: our trade with the United Kingdom had been severely reduced by its postwar economic difficulties, particularly its lack of dollars, which forced it to curtail its trade with countries, such as Canada, that wanted dollars in exchange for goods.[6] At the same time, our trade with the United States and with most other countries was still restricted by tariffs and other barriers. True, these had begun to fall as a result of negotiations – with the British and Americans from the late 1930s on, and with most other countries under the auspices of the GATT from the late 1940s on. But substantial barriers still remained. In the automotive sector, for instance, as late as the early 1960s our tariff on imports of cars and parts was 17.5 per cent. It wasn't until 1965's Autopact that autos and their components began to move across the Canadian–U.S. border tariff-free (see Wonnacott 1987).

Second, 1958 marks the last time in this century that, measured by the amount each country's governments spent, the Canadian public sector was actually smaller than the American. Since then, exports have nearly doubled as a share of our GDP, reaching 32.7 per cent in 1995. And yet over this period our government sector has become less and less like the American. Despite what the globalization hypothesis predicts, growing trade competition from the United States and growing dependence on U.S. capital have *not* kept us from building a distinctive public sector. Quite the contrary, the period of our closest economic ties with the Americans has also seen our greatest fiscal difference from them.

What happened in 1958 to send us on this different path? The size of a country's public sector depends on many things, including its demography, the growth rate of its economy, and its history and culture, so it is hard to say precisely. Politics, however, must have some effect on what happens, and 1958 is famous as the year of the Diefenbaker majority, the cleanest sweep in Canadian electoral history (until the Mulroney landslide of 1984). In their book *Derailed: The Betrayal of the National Dream*, David Bercuson and Barry Cooper (1994) date Canada's decline from the Diefenbaker government. Comparing Diefenbaker's with previous federal governments – especially Mackenzie King's, which they regard as having aimed, unambitiously, but sensibly and properly, at providing nothing more dramatic than capable government – they write: 'For the first time since Confederation, Canada had a prime minister whose chief objective was social justice and whose major aim was to mould a Canadian national character in his own image' (Bercuson and Cooper 1994: 77).

In their reading, Diefenbaker introduced the regional development grants and increasingly generous subsidies to the old and the poor whose further multiplication by Pearson and Trudeau created the public debts that have immobilized the current generation of Canadian politicians. At the same time, they argue, his desire to mould a national character initiated our forty-year self-absorption with the question of what kind of people we wish to be, a question whose answer, in many circles, has been that we wish to be a more governed, and hence, we naïvely trust, more civilized people than the Americans.[7]

Not everyone agrees that Diefenbaker is the villain of the piece. The philosopher George Grant's famous polemic, *Lament for a Nation*, painted Diefenbaker not as the initiator of Canada's decline but as the last genuinely Canadian political hero (see Grant 1965). In Grant's eyes, Diefenbaker's fateful refusal of the Americans' request that we allow Bomarc missiles to carry nuclear warheads – ultimately countermanded by Lester Pearson, the 'ambitious diplomat' who succeeded him – was the final death spasm of an independent Canada. Whatever Diefenbaker's personal or political faults may have been, he was for Grant morally preferable to the quisling Pearson – who now, of course, is widely regarded as having laid the foundations of modern Canadian distinctiveness by giving us medicare, the Canada Pension Plan, and other cornerstones of our European-style welfare state.

All this raises the question of 'The Meaning of Canadian Life,' however. For the moment, the subject is 'Globalization.' What we can conclude about globalization is that Canada's experience over the last four decades constitutes a compelling counterexample to the currently conventional view that greater economic integration among countries must lead them to pursue increasingly similar domestic policies. Canada became much more closely integrated with – some would say dominated by – the United States in the postwar decades and yet its public policies and the tax rates used to finance them became increasingly different from those observed in the United States. Despite globalization, despite economic integration, countries evidently do remain free to choose a separate course – the best proof of which is that this one did.

6
Are We There Yet?

When a theory apparently does not fit the facts, economists either fix the theory or fix the facts. 'Fixing the facts' sounds sinister but just means seeking reasons why the effects predicted by the theory may have been hidden by some aspect of reality. Maybe globalization really is forcing different countries' tax rates into conformity, but its effect is masked by other changes that are driving them apart. That would be significant in itself, since globalization is supposed to be an overpowering force, but investigating this possibility is a task best left to others more statistically inclined.

Fixing the theory means re-examining both the 'if' and the 'then,' both the premise and its conclusions. The theory under examination here is that if the world becomes globalized, then policy harmonization must follow. This chapter asks whether the 'if' is wrong. Maybe the world *isn't* quite as globalized as we think. If not, the fact that we have not seen the effects that globalization theory predicts is not surprising. They may be on their way but simply haven't arrived yet. The next chapter asks whether the 'then' part of the theory has to be fixed. Even if we do get perfect globalization, as seems bound to happen sooner or later, does that really require all countries to have more or less identical public policies?

FOOTLOOSE LABOUR?

In part, globalization theory depends on more and more people being mobile. One reason why tax rates supposedly cannot differ much across countries is that, if they do, workers will move from high-tax to low-tax countries. It's true that in 1993 one hundred million people lived outside the country of their birth; however, that was less than 2 per cent of the world's population (Lohrmann 1994: 10). In fact, labour may be less mobile now than in previous eras. Travel cost more in the past, but borders were much less significant. As John Maynard Keynes once observed: 'Before August, 1914, the inhabitant of London could secure forthwith, if he wished it, cheap and comfortable means of transit to any country or climate without passport or other formality, could then proceed abroad to foreign quarters without knowledge of their religion, language, or customs, bearing coined wealth upon his person, and would consider himself greatly aggrieved and much surprised at the least interference' (quoted in Friedman 1989). At century's end, of course, interference – whether by immigration authorities, customs officials, security agents, or police – is the rule.

Permanent migration was also easier then. Before the invention of the 'green card,' a social institution now so familiar as to have inspired a Hollywood movie of the same name, all that was needed to become a resident of the United States was the wherewithal to get there and a clean bill of health once arrived. The Nobel Prize–winning University of Chicago economist Milton Friedman notes that: 'Before 1914 ... anybody from anywhere in the world could present himself at Ellis Island in New York Harbour for immigration to the United States without having to go through long procedures in advance or qualify for an immigration quota' (Friedman 1989). In the first decades after Confederation, millions of Canadians availed themselves of this opportunity. In the 1880s alone, 19 per cent of the population simply picked up and moved, mainly southward (Colombo 1992: 156). In 1900 the U.S. census counted 1.18 million Canadian-born residents – almost one-quarter of Canada's population – among them Calixa Lavallée, the composer of *O Canada* (Thompson and Randall 1994: 52). For Canadians, the gates closed in 1930, nine years after they did for other would-be immigrants to the United

48 Globalization

States, even though Canadian restrictions implemented in the same year still let in Americans, as well as Britons and migrants from the white dominions (Bothwell, Drummond, and English 1987: 246).

Nowadays, of course, entry to both the United States and Canada, as well as to most other rich countries, is strictly rationed, and people must pass economic and other tests to get in. The result has been what was intended – a large drop-off in immigration. In the first decade of this century, 'the greatest period of mass migration in recorded history' (Hobsbawm 1994: 88), the rate of immigration to Canada was 24.6 per cent – that is, the number of new immigrants in the years 1901–11 equalled 24.6 per cent of the average population of Canada for that decade (McVey and Kalbach 1995: Table 4.2). By comparison, in the ten years 1981–91, when immigration again became a hot political issue, the rate was only 6.0 per cent, the lowest ten-year rate, not counting the 1930s and 1940s, since the 1890s, and the second lowest since numbers have been kept.[1]

In 1921, 22.3 per cent of Canadians had been born outside Canada (McVey and Kalbach 1971: Table 5.1), and in 1930 more than half the inhabitants of the Prairie provinces were foreign-born (Owram 1994: 103). In 1986, by contrast, only 15.7 per cent of Canadians had been born elsewhere (Colombo 1992: 168). The year that still holds the all-time record for immigration to Canada is 1913, at 400,870 new entrants. The average yearly immigration for the four years before the First World War was 348,688 (Overbeek 1980: Table 37), which is 66,000 more than in the next highest year, 1957, and almost 100,000 more than in 1993, the highest recent year (Department of Finance 1995: Table 2).

And, of course, this much larger immigration flow was on a much smaller population base. There were only seven million Canadians in 1911, compared to thirty million now. Needless to say, the numbers have fallen off so drastically not because people no longer desire to come here but because the borders have closed – even though ours are among the most open in the world. As far as labour mobility is concerned, it is hard not to conclude we are actually in a period of *de*globalization.

FOOTLOOSE CAPITAL?

By contrast, the world's capital markets have been *re*globalized in recent decades. In most countries, controls on capital flows that were introduced in the early postwar years have finally been removed, with the result that the legal and institutional environment may be returning to the greater openness of the last century. And, of course, this century's revolution in transportation and communications has made capital flows hypersensitive to even the slightest political and economic twitches within a country. A recent claim that 'every day, billions of dollars are transmitted between countries with a single keystroke' may be overstating the case – usually, several keystrokes are required – but its gist is correct: capital can move with great speed and on a startling scale (Banting and Simeon 1997: 26).

Still, economists keep running across surprising hints that capital may not be as mobile as many people think – or fear – but instead retains what should by now be an anachronistic fondness for its home country. In fact, in December 1996, the lead article in the prestigious *American Economic Review*, the journal of the American Economic Association, bore the iconoclastic title, 'Why Is Capital So Immobile Internationally?' (R.H. Gordon and Bovenberg 1996). As evidence of immobility, its authors pointed to the well-known fact that national investment and saving rates are highly correlated: countries that save a lot also invest a lot, though there's no reason in theory why the world's best investment opportunities should be found in countries whose citizens like to save. If good opportunities were randomly distributed around the world, high-savings countries typically would experience outflows of capital, while low-savings countries would experience inflows. There *are* inflows and outflows of capital, but not nearly so many as might be expected.

In some cases, this tendency of capital to stay at home seems almost pathological. In the late 1980s, 98 per cent of the equity capital held by Americans was in American firms. Lest that be ascribed to American know-nothingism or xenophobia, in Sweden the equivalent number was 100 per cent; in Italy, 91 per cent;

in Japan, 86.7 per cent; in the United Kingdom, 78.5 per cent; and in Germany, 75.4 per cent (Levi 1997: Table 1). Many of the domestic firms in which the nationals of these countries held stock would themselves have investments in other countries; still, in a globalized capital market, Americans probably should be holding more than 2 per cent of their equity in non-American companies. But even firms themselves are often reluctant to invest abroad. Overall U.S. foreign investment was only $130.8 billion in 1994, just 1.9 per cent of its GDP of $6.7 trillion (United States 1995).

Why doesn't capital move as much as it should? The authors of the *American Economic Review* study have a straightforward answer with a pretentious name, 'asymmetric information,' which simply means that foreign investors have less information about an economy than do domestic investors. For example, during the run-up to the Mexican devaluation in December 1994, 'domestic investors shifted large amounts of funds into foreign currencies prior to the devaluation whereas foreign investors started to liquidate their Mexican holdings in any quantity only in February 1995' (Gordon and Bovenberg 1996: 1060).

Foreigners can try to buy domestic advice but in doing so lay themselves open to manipulation by those giving the advice. This can lead to unfortunate experiences: 'Being poorly informed [foreign investors] are vulnerable to being overcharged when they acquire shares in a firm or purchase inputs and services. They also risk misjudging domestic markets and, as a result, investing real resources less efficiently' (Gordon and Bovenberg 1996: 1058). It's not surprising, therefore, that 'foreign subsidiaries in the United States report dramatically lower rates of return than do domestic U.S. firms, even after controlling for industry, age, and other such factors, as well as the possibility that profits are intentionally understated for tax reasons,' nor that 'foreign acquirers of publicly traded firms pay a much higher premium for firms than do domestic acquirers, even after controlling for industry, year, and the extent of competition among acquirers' (Gordon and Bovenberg 1996: 1060). In a perfectly globalized capital market, foreigners shouldn't be consistently burned.

Are We There Yet? 51

EVEN MINOR BORDERS STILL MATTER

Perhaps globalization enthusiasts are getting ahead of themselves. Many important forms of this phenomenon are only just getting started. Though electronic computers are a half-century old, we are really only a decade into the 'compunications' revolution, in which virtually all businesses and increasing numbers of private citizens are able to manage their affairs electronically.[2] We may be getting used to it very quickly, but the free and instantaneous flow of information round the world is in its infancy. Perhaps it will cause a similarly free and instantaneous worldwide flow of goods and services – even those that don't fit into fibre-optic cables – but that may take a while.

New evidence on North American trade flows, however, suggests that so long as even minor impediments to transportation, communication, and migration remain, they may cause the international flows of goods, services, capital, and people to be much less responsive to differences in tax regimes than might have been thought. And so long as these flows are less than perfectly responsive – so long as people and businesses don't pick up and leave at the drop of a new tax – there will still be room for differences in national policies.

The best example of just how powerful even relatively minor differences between countries can be is provided by the Canadian economist John McCallum (1993), in a study aptly titled 'National Borders Matter.' The former dean at McGill University, now chief economist at the Royal Bank, looked at 1989 trade flows among the ten Canadian provinces and the biggest thirty American states. If the Canadian–U.S. border did not matter, he argued, the volume of trade should be determined by size and distance. People would trade more with bigger states or provinces than with little ones, since bigger jurisdictions offer more customers and suppliers, and they would trade more with closer neighbours than with more distant ones. If only distance and size did matter in the choice of trading partner, Ontario and Quebec should trade ten times more with California than with British Columbia. Why? Because while California and British Columbia are about the same distance from central Canada, California's economy is about ten times bigger than British Columbia's.

What did McCallum find? It turns out that trade between central Canada and British Columbia is three times greater than that between central Canada and California. Since it 'should be' ten times smaller, that makes it roughly thirty times – thirty times! – larger than expected. McCallum got similar results for other pairs of provinces and states. On average, trade among Canadian provinces was twenty times greater than would be expected if only economic size and the distance between jurisdictions counted. The average for Quebec was even higher: it traded with other Canadian provinces twenty-four times more than would be expected, a dependence on the Canadian common market that should give pause to Quebec separatists. McCallum's overall conclusion? 'Even the relatively innocuous Canada–U.S. border continues to have a decisive effect on continental trade patterns' (McCallum 1993: 11).

Whether it will continue to have such an effect remains to be seen, of course. McCallum's study used trade data for 1989, the first year of the FTA, which by 1998 will eliminate all tariffs between the two countries and many administrative or 'non-tariff' barriers, as well. Once that has been done, North American trade patterns presumably will be realigned. Most economists' expectations are that, for Canada at least, there will be much more north–south trade and much less east–west trade as a result. In fact, the best-known computer simulation of Canadian–U.S. free trade predicted a 255 per cent increase in Canadian–U.S. trade as a result of the deal (R. Harris and Cox, 1983), and the dramatic growth in our trade with the Americans in the first half of the 1990s seems to be confirming that prediction. Between 1990 and 1994 trade with the United States – exports and imports combined – rose almost 40 per cent in real terms, compared with overall growth in the economy of just 5.8 per cent.[3] Though the latest data on state and provincial trade flows are too old to be of much use in judging the impact of the current trade boom, they do suggest that the east–west bias may be diminishing. Our 'overtrading' with ourselves was only 12 times in the early 1990s, not

Are We There Yet? 53

the twenty times it was in 1989. Still, even if this overtrading is eroded by the FTA, the erosion will have to be huge in order to eliminate it altogether. Cut east–west trade in half – or double north–south trade – and Canadians will still be trading with each other ten times more than they would if the border didn't matter.

The reason McCallum's results are so surprising is, of course, that the Canadian–U.S. border is as open as any in the world. No U.S. president visits here or Canadian prime minister goes south without reciting the ancient bromide about our two countries having the world's longest undefended border. What is less often emphasized is that it is also essentially undefended in economic terms, as well. Even before the FTA, average Canadian tariffs were less than 5 per cent, and average U.S. tariffs were even less than that. The great majority of Canadians live within 100 miles of the U.S. border. Millions of us do much of our shopping 'cross-border,' and after the Canadian dollar started dropping in value in 1992 millions of Americans reciprocated. True, Canada's Foreign Investment Review Agency, established in 1973, investigated a few high-profile U.S. takeovers of Canadian firms, while 1980's National Energy Policy actively discouraged foreign investment in the energy sector. But Canadian capital markets remain closely linked to New York; Canadian banks offer U.S.-dollar accounts; funds flow easily back and forth across the border; and U.S. investment in Canada, while not as great as in some earlier periods, is higher than it is anywhere else in the world, while Canadian investments in the United States are now two-thirds the value of U.S. investments here. The future of international economic relations very likely is typified by the Canadian–U.S. border, which, even before the FTA, was one of the world's most permeable. In brief, 'we have seen the future and it is us.' And yet, as late as 1989 east–west trade flows in Canada were twenty times larger than they would have been had the border not mattered.[4]

Economists in Canada and around the world are scrambling to explain McCallum's result, which flies in the face of recently conventional wisdom that, as the business guru Kenichi Ohmae puts it, we now live in a borderless world (Ohmae 1991). McCallum's data suggest that national borders do matter and matter a lot, even after tariff and non-tariff barriers have been minimized, as they were by fifty years of trade liberalization between Canada and the United States. There are many reasons why they matter. Businesses feel more at home doing business at home. Differences in legal systems raise the cost – and risk – of buying and selling outside the home jurisdiction. Nationals may benefit from 'institutional comity' – 'courtesy laws [that] enable individuals and firms that conduct business in one province to enjoy a favored status in other provinces '(Hartt 1992: 14). Local tastes may differ in ways that are hard for outsiders to understand: Canadian Tire was a flop in the United States, though it still does well in Canada. If these cultural and legal barriers to trade are now as important as tariff barriers used to be, it may be a very long time before even neighbouring nations trade among themselves as naturally and easily as do neighbouring Canadian provinces, or neighbouring U.S. states.

Further support for McCallum's argument is provided by data on European trade flows. Quebec separatists usually argue that if we did away with Canada as we know it, it could easily be replaced by something like the European Union. But while Europeans have been dismantling the economic barriers between their countries for four decades now, they still have some way to go to achieve Canadian levels of economic integration. Trade in goods between France and Germany, the EU's economic giants, amounts to U.S.$40 billion a year. That's obviously a tremendous volume, equal to the entire economic output of Canada's Atlantic provinces. Still, it's less than three per cent of French and German GDP. By contrast, Quebec's exports to Ontario are over nine per cent of Quebec's GDP, while Ontario's exports to its eastern neighbour account for almost six per cent of its GDP. And that's just trade in goods.

Trade in services adds half again as much to Quebec's exports and three-quarters again to Ontario's. More than seven times as many people (130 million) live in France and Germany as in Quebec and Ontario (18 million), yet the dollar value of the trade between them is only three times the value of trade between Quebec and Ontario (which is Can.$20 billion each way).

When Berkeley economist Jeffery Frankel conducted a study similar to McCallum's, he found that Europeans were only 1.6 times more likely to trade with each other than with other countries.[5] The continued dismantling of European trade barriers may change this, but intra-European trade will have to grow a good deal to become as important for Europe as intra-Canadian trade is for Canada. And, of course, the members of the European Union, France and Germany included, are much more integrated than most of the world's countries. It follows that globalization may have to create a truly impressive levelling of the institutional and regulatory differences across countries before flows of trade, labour, and capital will be as sensitive to differences in their returns across countries as they currently are within countries.

The future is a long time, of course, and perhaps globalization eventually will make all the world's economies as open to each other as Ontario's and Quebec's – or Pennsylvania's and New York's.[6] But we may be a while waiting. The Canadian economic union was formed as part of a political union. The European Union was formed by people who hoped that one day Europe might also be a political union. There are no such political motivations behind NAFTA or the Western Hemisphere Free Trade Area (WHFTA). Very few, if any Canadians – free-traders included – want economic integration with the United States to result in political integration. The United States itself probably doesn't want that: Canada's entry would upset the political balance in that country, and besides, as Richard Gwyn has pointed out, 'the United States already has all the financial, commercial, and industrial access northwards that it needs' (Gwyn 1995: 64).

In the same way, even though there is talk of a Pacific Rim Free Trade Area, no one wants to form a political union around the Pacific Rim. Nor is anyone pushing a NAFTA-EU political union, though the reduction of barriers between North America and the European Union proposed by both Canadian and American trade ministers probably would be a good thing. In the absence of political pressures of this sort, however, it is hard to see how economic integration will reach the advanced stage in the world at large that it has within the world's federal states, Canada and the

United States included. And if it does not, the more extreme predictions of the globalization hypothesis may never come true.

Then again, even if extreme globalization does become a reality, there are good reasons for supposing that nation-states will still be able to pursue a considerable measure of distinctiveness in their tax and spending policies. Just how is the subject of the next chapter.

7
Free to Choose

As the last chapter suggested, a second way to react when a theory apparently does not fit the facts is to fix the theory. A good way to begin is to be very precise about what it actually predicts. Does globalization *really* require all countries to have more or less identical public policies? Or is that a straw man? What is it, exactly, that globalization theory does predict?

CAPITAL CAN'T BE TAXED

The heart of the globalization thesis is the idea that 'the threat by transnational corporations to move production to plants in underdeveloped nations "tames" the governments, and workers, of developed states' (Gwyn 1995: 98). If businesses face higher taxes or more intrusive regulations than they would elsewhere, they will move and ship goods and services into high-tax jurisdictions from low-tax havens. In short, as economies intermingle, taxing capital becomes harder and harder. The resulting 'race to the bottom' in corporate tax rates bears especially bitter fruit because no one can win it: if every country chooses low taxes, no country will have gained an advantage. They might as well have kept their taxes high (Klevorick 1996: 460). But because 200–plus countries can't collude to keep capital taxes high and because their economies can't run without capital, governments must at the very least bring their capital tax regimes into line with what is offered elsewhere.

58 Globalization

So, have they? Apparently not. A recent book by Vito Tanzi, chief taxation and public finance specialist at the International Monetary Fund, shows that despite capital's increasingly footloose nature, different countries continue to tax corporations at quite different rates. Among the G-7 countries, revenues from corporate taxes averaged 3.1 per cent of GDP in 1971 but varied from a low of 1.7 per cent in Italy to a high of 5.2 per cent in Japan. In 1990, despite what everyone assumes has been a dramatic increase in corporate mobility, revenues from such taxes had actually grown, to 3.4 per cent of GDP on average, and they varied even more widely, from 1.8 per cent of GDP in Germany to 6.8 per cent in Japan (Tanzi 1995: Table 7.4). If globalization works the way people say, governments shouldn't even have tried to raise corporate income taxes, let alone succeeded.[1]

Tanzi's numbers tell essentially the same surprising tale about the tax rates that corporations face. In 1980, in a sample of ten industrialized countries, marginal tax rates on corporate income varied between 33 per cent in Spain and 61.7 per cent in West Germany (for any earnings retained by the firm). Eleven years later – eleven Reagan/Thatcher years later – they ranged from a low of 34 per cent in France and the United Kingdom to a high of 57.5 per cent in Germany (Tanzi 1995: Table 7.5). That's a slightly smaller spread – 23.5 points in 1991 compared to 28.7 points in 1980 – but it's still more than twenty points, though all the countries named are members of the European Union and compete face to face for the same investments.

Still other data presented by Tanzi show the combined effect of both corporate and personal incomes taxes on the income generated by corporations. Here rates ranged from 27.7 per cent in Japan up to 53.8 per cent in France (Tanzi 1995: Table 7.7). This difference, 26.1 points, admittedly is much less than the 57.7 percentage point difference observed in 1980, which was so wide it's a wonder that all French capital hadn't leapt the English Channel from its home, where the effective tax rate was 66.6 per cent, to the United Kingdom, where it was a mere 8.9 per cent. Still, 26.1 points is a surprisingly large gap in an era in which capital supposedly is as free as the birds.

Free to Choose 59

A recent review of capital taxation in the twenty-four OECD countries by American economist Joel Slemrod confirms Tanzi's results. In 1992 the statutory rate of tax on corporate income in manufacturing varied between 10.0 per cent in Ireland and 58.1 per cent in Germany – that is, by 48.1 points. (Canada's rate was 38.3 per cent.) As a proportion of GDP, corporate tax revenues varied between 0.9 per cent in Iceland and 8.2 per cent in Luxembourg (with Canada at 2.5 per cent). The effective tax rate on the next dollar of corporate income varied between zero in Greece and Sweden and 31 per cent in Turkey (with the Canadian rate at 19 per cent; Slemrod 1996: Table 1).

Slemrod's conclusions couldn't be starker: 'The divergences across countries are large no matter which alternative measure is chosen ... To be blunt, the prospects [for harmonization or coordination of corporate taxes] are not good ... There is a vast cacophony of tax rates and tax systems, and no consensus on which is the best' (Slemrod 1996: 299, 305). Nor did he find 'convincing evidence that world tax systems are moving toward harmonization at a zero capital income tax rate or any other uniform rate' (Slemrod 1996: 306). And yet corporate taxes, of all taxes, are supposedly most subject to the harmonizing pressures of globalization.[2]

WHO PAYS CAPITAL'S TAXES?

Though the data show that businesses do still remit lots of tax dollars to national governments, they may not actually pay these taxes, in the sense of being worse off as a result of them. When corporations are hit with higher taxes than they would face elsewhere, one obvious alternative is to move. But another is to get someone else to pay their taxes for them. There are three possible victims. Firms can try to pass taxes along to their customers, in higher prices for what they sell; to their suppliers, in lower prices for what they buy; or to their employees, in lower wages.

They can try, but of course they won't always succeed. Take raising the price of what they sell. In a country whose borders are open to imports, it just isn't possible to jack up the product price. If firms try to, foreign competitors will undercut them. The same goes for reducing what's paid for the inputs from suppliers. If national markets are truly open, suppliers don't have to accept the lower domestic price. They can take their business elsewhere and receive the going world price for whatever they used to sell at home.

Eliminating suppliers and customers as candidates to pay a firm's taxes leaves its workers. In fact, workers may well be stuck. If their employer does respond to higher taxes by cutting or slowing the growth of wages, they'll look around to see if some other firm will employ them at their old wage. But if the firm's higher taxes are the result of an economy-wide tax increase, they'll find that they can't escape: all other employers are also trying to get their workers to accept lower wages. They do have the option of not working at all, but if that's not a credible option, they'll probably take the lower wage, which means that firms will have succeeded in avoiding their taxes. They still send a cheque to the minister of revenue, but what they lose in higher taxes they make up in lower wages. The burden of the tax – what economists call its 'incidence,' – falls on the firm's workers. In the end, the firm doesn't have to move offshore. Queen's University economist Robin Boadway, one of the country's foremost specialists in public finance, argues that the main effect of globalization is that, whatever national tax rules may say, capital simply won't pay tax (Boadway 1995).[3]

Of course, if 'globalization' means that labour is more mobile, too, then workers won't end up paying capital's taxes. If a country's businesses do try to pass along higher taxes, the intended victims will head for countries where wages haven't changed. If they leave in sufficient numbers, wages will be driven up by the resulting scarcity and businesses will have been left to pay the higher taxes. Thus free-agent players for the Montreal Expos and Toronto Blue Jays baseball teams, who can auction their services on the open market, almost certainly don't pay Canadian income taxes. They are legally liable for such taxes, but their teams compensate them with higher wages. If they don't, the players would sign with teams in the United States, where taxes are lower. The teams might like to leave, too, but in this case they may be immobile, for their leagues may not let them.

Free to Choose   61

THE ECONOMICS OF THE FREE LUNCH

Economic theory offers a number of reasons to believe that even if both labour and capital were perfectly mobile, tax and spending policies could still differ across countries. Most have to do with what economists call 'rents' – which, confusingly, are not the same as what people pay their landlords. For an economist, a rent is anything you get for nothing – which isn't supposed to happen in a science built on the axiom that there is 'no free lunch.' But perhaps it does. Visitors to Vancouver marvel at the beauty of the natural surroundings: the snow-capped peaks; the tall, straight trees; the temperate climate; the absence of insects, the laid-back pace. If they are of taxpaying age, they also think to themselves: 'All this and they can't tax it.' But of course they can tax it. Because Vancouver is so magical, people will continue to live there even if tax rates are higher than they are elsewhere. If Moose Jaw, for example, had tax rates half what they were in Vancouver, people still might not choose it over Vancouver, for it simply doesn't offer everything Vancouver does. So, even though mobility between the two cities is quite easy – no passport is needed and there are many means of travel – Vancouverites might over the years consistently pay higher taxes than Moose Javians and there would be no tendency for that to change. Lunch – in this case the visual feast – isn't free after all.

THE BEST THINGS IN LIFE

What's true of cities can also be true of regions or countries. They can have advantages that make it possible for governments to tax their inhabitants more than people are taxed elsewhere. 'Imagine the best day of the year in Quebec,' a friend who moved to California once boasted, 'and then imagine three hundred such days in a year.' If people prefer California, Hawaii, Florida, or British Columbia's Gulf Islands because of the climate, then, all other things equal (that famous economists' phrase!), taxes can be higher in these jurisdictions than in places where the climate is not so beneficent.[4]

62 Globalization

Regional or national advantages needn't always be God-given. By all accounts Bosnia is a beautiful place when not at war with itself, but the absence of peace, order, and good government makes it hard for Bosnia's government to add high corporate taxes to the challenges faced by potential immigrants to or investors in that sad country. By contrast, jurisdictions where peace, order, and good government abound – our own, for instance – may tax their citizens more without fear that as a result everyone will wish to leave. Though Canadians envy Americans' lower tax rates, many of us would not move to the United States because we fear its greater urban violence (which may or may not be the result of its low tax rates: Japan and Switzerland have similarly enviable tax rates and much less violence).

What is true for people is also true for businesses. In Vito Tanzi's international tax data quoted above, the lowest overall tax rate on income originating in corporations was 8.9 per cent, imposed by the United Kingdom in 1979, the year Mrs. Thatcher took office, though responsibility for the levy it lay with the outgoing Labour government. The most obvious explanation for this extraordinarily low rate is the extraordinarily high aggravation faced by businesses operating in Labourite Britain, which was to commerce what Bosnia has been to civil society in general. It simply wasn't possible for the British government to tax businesses at more than an 8.9 per cent rate and still hope to attract investors. By greatly improving the climate for doing business in Britain, Mrs. Thatcher made it possible to tax British corporate income again – even if that is not the usual view of her program or purpose. Nevertheless, by 1985 the overall tax rate on corporate income generated in the United Kingdom had risen to 34.9 per cent, and by 1990, the final year of her prime ministership, it was 37.9 per cent (Tanzi 1995: Table 7.7).

Apart from offering a hospitable environment for doing business in general, some countries may provide unique advantages for specific industries. Even after the communications revolution, it's still not possible to get very far in finance without an office in New York, London, or Tokyo. Similarly, if you want to be at the frontier in computer technology, you probably need a presence in

California's Silicon Valley or on Route 128 near Boston. Many such industrial advantages occur essentially because of historical accident. Montreal is where it is because seventeenth-century explorers couldn't get around the Lachine Rapids. The Rapids are now a carnival attraction, conquered many times daily by tourist-filled speedboats, yet Montreal endures, if barely. Eighty per cent of U.S. carpets are made in Georgia because it was in Dalton, Georgia, in 1900 that a young woman named Catherine Evans discovered a new method of tufting (see Krugman 1991: 60–1). Bill Gates's garage was in Seattle, so Seattle is now a major player in the computer industry. For whatever strange reason the particle of sand may implant itself, the pearl takes on a life of its own.[5]

Once a successful industrial agglomeration such as Silicon Valley or London's financial district or Italy's ceramics region has formed, and firms pretty well have to be there in order to compete effectively, governments not only don't have to persuade businesses to invest, they can actually tax investors more than other jurisdictions tax them and businesses still will come. There is a danger, of course, that governments will so enjoy taxing firms that they tax them at a rate that more than offsets the competitive advantage had from being in the region, in which case the firms may decide to leave despite the pure productivity advantages of staying. ('If you over-tax it,' W.P. Kinsella might have written, 'they will go.') When that happens, governments destroy their region's competitive advantage. In fact, the American economist Ann Markusen has based an entire theory of regional growth on the idea that after different areas acquire temporary productive advantages, unions and other institutions seize the resulting rents, and when the productive advantage eventually abates the region is rendered uncompetitive by its excessive wages, taxes, and/or regulations (see Markusen 1983). She argues that, in effect, this is what happened to the U.S. northeast in the century or so following 1870.

For as long as an advantage remains, however, governments can still have higher taxes – even if people and businesses are very mobile – provided that their jurisdiction offers something to compensate for them. What's offered won't necessarily be in exchange for the higher taxes: Vancouver's North Shore mountains weren't made possible by higher taxes. (Imagine what they'd be if they had been built by government!) They'll be there whether or not Vancouverites pay high taxes.

But what's offered could be in exchange for higher taxes. Maintaining Vancouver's Stanley Park does require tax revenues. People may decide that even though taxes are higher because the park has to be maintained, because the park is maintained they are content not to move. So long as the cost of taxes is offset by benefits provided by the public sector, then, even though people obviously would prefer to get the benefit without paying the tax – a trick possible in circumstances discussed below – they may be content to stay and pay. Judging by polls, at least, the Canadian system of financing medical care out of tax revenues, so that taxes are higher here but everyone has health insurance, involves a tax-benefit tradeoff most Canadians are willing to accept.[6]

NO MORE ROBIN HOOD?

The idea that different jurisdictions can have different tax rates so long as they provide benefits to go with them may seem to eliminate the possibility of income redistribution – taking from the rich and giving to the poor. Thus in his best-selling book *The Work of Nations*, Bill Clinton's secretary of Labour, Robert Reich, wrote: 'Most of the Americans who emigrate to Canada have been relatively low-skilled ... ; most of the Canadians who come to the United States have been high-skilled ... Why? Both nations offer a similar array of job possibilities. But a pertinent difference is that Canada has a more equalitarian distribution of income and offers more generous social insurance than does the United States. Thus do unskilled Americans find in Canada a hospitable environment where they can enjoy greater income security; and thus do skilled Canadians find in the United States a hospitable environment where they can retain more of their earnings for themselves' (Reich 1991: 299).

Reich is probably wrong. If rich Canadians see themselves as receiving at least some benefit from compulsory redistribution, they may decide to put up with it. Rightly or wrongly, most of us in Canada think that we live in a more civilized society than the United States (an opinion of ourselves that sits uncomfortably with our belief that we are also more modest than Americans). Crime rates are lower; inequality is not quite so extreme; our cities are more presentable and less dangerous than those in the United States. If the money taken from rich Canadians and given to poor Canadians really is responsible for these differences, then rich Canadians, though they complain about their taxes, may well tolerate the tradeoff.

Of course, our (in fact, only slightly) greater-than-American redistribution may not be what makes our society better than theirs, if that conceit may be entertained for a moment. Maybe the causation goes the other way. Maybe it's our civilized nature that makes us less resistant to fiscal encroachments, rather than these encroachments that make us more civilized. Or maybe our living conditions are a freak of nature or history and, like Vancouver's North Shore mountains, have nothing to do with our fiscal policies. But even if they do not, the fact that they exist may cause rich people to stay, since the higher taxes they face are offset by what they regard as the greater pleasantness of life, however it may be explained.[7]

The more general point is that as long as governments give people something in return for their taxes, possibly including socially productive income redistribution, then some jurisdictions can levy higher tax rates than others and this need not cause people or businesses all to leave. At bottom, it seems, globalization need not require all countries to have the same tax rates.

THE SINCEREST FORM OF FLATTERY

But are we really home free yet? If high-tax jurisdictions really can sustain themselves by offering citizens useful things such as health care, education, and social insurance in return for higher taxes, and if they can even attract immigrants and investors because the tax-benefit deal they offer is such a good one, won't every jurisdiction want to imitate them, and, if so, won't they all end up with essentially the same levels of taxes and public benefits? Policy convergence that aimed at relatively high levels of public spending and taxation, rather than at the level of the lowest taxer and spender, might be convergence that tax-loving Canadians would find acceptable, but it would still be convergence. The data presented in chapter 3 showed that in fact all industrialized countries were increasing their tax rates over time, even though the world's economy was becoming steadily more integrated. Isn't convergence still our likely future?

Perhaps not. There may yet be natural advantages that one country will have and others won't that will allow it to impose higher tax rates and still not lose investors or immigrants as a result. Until an earthquake sends it into the sea, Vancouver presumably will always be a more beautiful place than Moose Jaw. Moreover, many of the man-made advantages that some countries enjoy took so many years to create and would be so hard for even the most eagre competitors to duplicate that they might as well be regarded as 'natural.' Italy's ruins, Britain's tradition of civility and stability, the United States's constitutional protection of private property: each of these national assets took time to establish. The new Russian constitution may claim to provide the same sorts of property guarantees as the American, but Russia doesn't yet have two hundred years of case law backing up its claim. However much it might like to converge with these other countries, it can't yet offer comparable surety to foreign investors, so its tax rates probably will have to remain lower than in these other countries, even if that means not providing all the public services its citizens would like.

VOTING WITH THE FEET

Natural and social advantages aside, a second reason why national differences in spending and taxation may persist even in a thoroughly globalized world is simply that people may want it that way, and may vote with their feet until they get it, which is the standard operating assumption in 'the economics of federalism,' a subdiscipline of economics in which, not surprisingly, Canadian economists have played a leading role.

Free to Choose 67

The economics of federalism invariably takes extreme globalization as a starting point. In good economist fashion, it simply assumes that capital, labour, and goods can move freely among the states or provinces of a federal country and are perfectly responsive to the slightest differences in their market prices. These are very strong assumptions, of course. People aren't perfectly mobile. Canadians don't just pick up and move simply because they can earn $500 more in another province. Past a certain age, people set down roots. Or they may not have the skills – language skills, for instance – to be mobile. Any number of studies show that, for perfectly understandable reasons, French-speaking Canadians move from province to province much less than English speakers do. If perfect globalization requires that all such differences among people are eliminated, we will never have perfect globalization.[8]

But even supposing that people were perfectly mobile, different jurisdictions within a country still can have different tax rates and spending levels so long as people have different tastes. Some may want higher taxes and a more comfortable social safety net. Others – risk-lovers, presumably – may like lower taxes and working without a net. In fact, federalism assumes that people will have different tastes. If not, why have provinces in the first place? Why not give all responsibilities to a central government? Lower levels of government, being 'closer to the people,' might be more responsive to their needs. But if everyone across the country really did have the same needs and preferences, it's not clear why a national legislature couldn't pick up on these just as well. If the argument is that smaller governmental units would be more efficient in providing public services, nothing prevents a central government from decentralizing its administration, as Ottawa has at least claimed to do over the last three decades.

Why fiscal tastes differ is another question, of course. A preference for high taxes and generous public spending, or for the opposite, presumably is not genetically determined. If labour were perfectly mobile within a federation, the members of each new generation would have to re-sort themselves across the federation – or, in time, across the perfectly globalized world –

according to their likes and dislikes. Risk-loving children born to risk-averse parents would move from deep social safety net countries to countries where taxes were lower and the consequences of economic failure more dire. The more timid children of risk-loving parents would migrate in the opposite direction.

We don't see massive human migration every generation, and yet we do see significant and apparently persistent differences in tax and spending levels across countries and regions. Assuming that they aren't genetic, maybe such tastes are learned. After a twenty-year study of the history of public expenditure and taxation in the Western world, Carolyn Webber and Aaron Wildavsky, U.S. specialists in the determinants of public spending, concluded that there were enduring differences across countries in the approach to government (see Webber and Wildavsky 1986). Because culture is essentially a black box, relying on 'cultural differences' to explain something is always disappointing to economists. To say that a thing is culturally determined is mainly to say that we don't know what causes it. Webber and Wildavsky came to this conclusion only after excluding most of the other, more traditionally economic influences that might affect people's decision whether to tax themselves more or less.

If your national culture does favour high taxes and a comprehensive social safety net, you should worry at least a little bit about whether this will not chase away the more risk-loving members of your younger generations. If a taste for risk isn't genetically determined, risk-lovers will be found even among the children of risk-averters, so you'll never be short of young risk-takers. But if such people help secure economic growth, and if in each generation high taxes chase away a good proportion of them, in the long run you may ruin your society. Reich may be right, after all.

The business community naturally argues that Canadian taxes are getting to that point. Though undoubtedly self-interested, they may also be right. The top marginal tax rates in some American states – New York, to pick an economically important example – are now over 50 per cent, but they do not come into play until taxable income reaches U.S.$250,000. By contrast, in Canada rates that high generally start at around Can.$70,000 (Slutsky 1995: 24).

FREE TO CHOOSE

The wisdom of running a large state sector is the subject of the rest of this book. The purpose of these first seven chapters has been to ask whether such an endeavour is possible. The answer would seem to be that it probably is, even in a world in which economic integration is getting deeper and deeper. The best evidence of this is that it has been done. The members of the European Union have been integrating for four decades and still maintain sizeable differences in their tax and expenditure rates. Canada and the United States have been integrating since the late 1930s, and yet their tax and spending rates are farther apart now than ever.

And if facts are not to be trusted, economic theory suggests why persistent differences in tax rates may be possible even in a world (albeit one we are not likely to see soon) in which businesses and people are perfectly mobile. If nations enjoy natural productivity advantages or are particularly desirable places to live or do business, then governments can tax their citizens and businesses more without fear of capital flight or brain drain. Similarly, if governments provide benefits that are perceived as being at least equal to the value of the taxes they require, then people and businesses may choose to remain, even if they do complain about taxation.

That Canadians are free to choose a large government may seem a strange message from someone who wants them not to. The point of freedom, however, is that it is not obligation. We are all free to jump out the nearest open window, to use John Irving's image, but that doesn't mean we should. Whether we need a large government – more precisely, a larger-than-American government – in order to act out our national destiny is a question that Canadians will probably never cease debating. Proponents of that large government should not be overly encouraged by this chapter's conclusions, however, for they are not unqualified. A country may impose higher taxes than its neighbours and competitors only if it possesses scenic or productive or social advantages that they don't also have, or provides public services, possibly even income redistribution, that its taxpayers judge worth the taxes they pay. But if taxes exceed benefits, then people and firms will leave, business will be lost, and the country very probably will languish economically.

And there is a final qualification. If it does things right, a government may not have to worry, even in a thoroughly globalized world, that citizens or businesses will escape taxation by moving elsewhere. But even if they don't leave, they may escape into idleness and/or tax evasion. If taxes rise too high and public services grow too generous, people may decide that it is better to enjoy the services without paying the taxes. They can do so either by cheating on their taxes or by devoting more time to non-taxable activities, such as leisure or work in the home. If enough people do this, tax revenues will fall and either the country's debt will rise or its public services will have to be trimmed. In the end, it may arrive at the same level of taxation and public expenditure as is observed in neighbouring countries without a single business or individual having emigrated because of taxation. Thus even if Canada sealed its borders, became an 'autarky,' and, like Albania in its communist incarnation, had as little as possible to do with other countries, it still would have to worry about the possibility that its government may be too large and its tax rates too high. Too large a public sector might cause non-economic problems as well, to a discussion of which we now turn.

PART II
THE MEANING OF CANADIAN LIFE

8
False Premise

Were Canadians *not* free to choose their tax and spending policies, the country's political life would be much simpler, for we would be spared what for us so often seems the ordeal of self-government. The precise details of fiscal policy could still be debated, since they might differ slightly from what was on offer in the economies with which we were most closely integrated. We could also continue to indulge our fascination with – or, if you prefer, pick the scab of – constitutional issues. And there would be other things for Canadian governments to decide: gun control, abortion, foreign policy, and so on.

But the grand ideological question of what sized government we wanted would have been answered for us. What we wanted would not matter. The overall levels of taxation and public expenditure, as well as their net redistributive effect on different income groups, could not differ greatly from what they were in our closest economic partner. And that, barring sudden movement of the world's tectonic plates, will continue to be the United States, the world's biggest economy, which for most of us is only just down the road.

The message of the first part of this book, however, is that, within limits established by our productivity, mobility, and preferences, we must continue to provide our own answers to the question of how large our government should be. We must choose for ourselves how high our taxes should be, what our governments should do, and what Canadians should do for themselves, acting privately, whether as individuals or as members of churches, clubs, charities, non-profit organizations, businesses, or whatever. But if we are free to choose, what should we choose?

Cast in such a general way, the question is likely to elicit a general answer. 'We should choose whatever sized government makes us best off.' Or, as an economist might put it, in his profession's prosaic way, 'We should use government when its benefits are greater than its costs.' If benefits are less than costs, however, then whatever activity is at issue should be left to the private sector, which may in fact decide it should not be done at all. In either case, the focus is on results. Government is – or should be – a means, not an end. Its purpose is functional, to improve the lives of those being governed. Governing may be an art, but government need not be an art form. Seekers after self-expression will find many other more satisfying ways of achieving it.

LIMITED GOVERNMENT

To say that the problem of finding the right size and nature of government is a practical one is not to say that it must be decided in ad hoc ways. An economist would add several working assumptions (what else?) to the idea that government should intervene only when the benefits of doing so exceed the costs. One is that in most cases people's voluntary interaction in markets, unaided by governments, does a good job of providing many of the right kinds and amounts of goods and services. Like you, I can decide on my own how many tomatoes, or toasters, or tap-dance lessons I need. I can also decide the best way to earn the money to finance these purchases. If I need help making my decisions, I can pay for it, as I do when I subscribe to *Consumer Reports* or employ an insurance broker or real estate agent or career counsellor. As John Maynard Keynes wrote: 'The important thing for Government is not to do things which individuals are doing already, and to do them a little better or a little worse; but to do those things which at present are not done at all' (Keynes 1926: 46–7).

Government intervention should therefore be limited to cases in which markets can be expected to fail. 'Market failure' occurs, to take but one example, when it is hard for private sellers to exclude people from consuming a good, as is the case with city streets, for instance. Private contractors might be hired to build and maintain the streets, but on its own no private company would supply city streets, since it is all but impossible to charge people for their use. But if a firm can't charge its customers for the services it supplies, it goes out of business. Private firms might supply a bridge, since with barriers and toll booths they can charge their customers: people who don't pay the toll can't cross the bridge. But city streets must be provided by some agency that has the power to tax – to take money from people whether or not they use the streets. The technological boundary between private and public goods is, however, moveable. Who knows what new scanning technologies will make possible in 2050 or 2100?

A second example of market failure involves 'externalities.' I may be happy with the gasoline that I buy from Imperial Oil, while Imperial Oil presumably is happy to sell it to me. But people who breathe my car's exhaust may not be so happy. Thus a free market for gasoline may cause too many fumes to be produced. If I had to compensate my fellow citizens for the unpleasantness or even harm of breathing my exhaust, I might not produce so much of it. Or I might find a way – with the help of Imperial Oil, which would have an obvious interest in doing the necessary research – to consume gasoline that produced fewer fumes. But in the absence of a system requiring me to pay compensation, I probably won't reduce my output of fumes unless a regulator who has the power to fine me tells me to.

Despite what people may think about them, economists have spent at least the last fifty years enumerating the many, many ways in which markets may fail. For that matter, in a 1926 essay titled 'The End of *Laissez-Faire*,' Keynes wrote that for fifty years before that 'the view of all leading economists [has been that] the maxim of *laissez-faire* has no scientific basis whatever, but is at best a mere handy maxim' (Keynes 1926: 26). The long list of potential 'market failures' that has been compliled includes 'asymmetric information,' in which the buyer has less information than the seller about the benefits or costs of, say, a cancer operation; 'natural monopoly,' in which the cost of providing extra output falls, so that the largest producer in a market has a decisive cost advantage; 'moral hazard,' in which insurance markets fail because people who are insured become more likely to suffer the contingency against which they have insured themselves; 'public goods,' the case, for example, of the street network from which it is hard to exclude people; 'negative externalities,' as in the pollution just described; or, finally, 'positive externalies,' such as the uncompensated benefits that one person's education may confer on his or her fellow citizens. There are many other examples, as well, and there is also the obvious problem that neither the market nor charity will produce a satisfactorily even distribution of income or wealth.

This isn't to say all economists now believe in government, however. Partly in reaction to this century-long enumeration of market failures, a profession in which contrariness is second nature and iconoclasm is rewarded has spent the last twenty-five years describing various ways in which governments, too, may fail. The fundamental problem is that politicians and bureaucrats may not always do best for themselves by doing the public good. Instead, they may be better off – for politicians, this generally means more likely to be re-elected – by pleasing only certain parts of the public. Thus policies come to be decided by interest groups, while laws and regulations intended to serve the public at large may end up mainly benefiting those being regulated. To subscribe to this possibility it is not necessary to believe in the venality of politicians: it may be that only interest groups and lobbyists have an incentive to petition governments on various issues, so that they are the only people governments hear, with the result, not suprisingly, that their views prevail.

Because of this likelihood of government failure, and despite the obvious possibility that markets may also fail, even fail often, most economists would subscribe to the rule, nicely phrased by columnist Andrew Coyne, that 'Governments should only do what only governments can do.' In 'The End of *Laissez-Faire*,' Keynes himself stressed that where the dividing line should be drawn was essentially a technical question: 'We must aim at separating those services which are technically social from those which are technically individual' (Keynes 1926: 46).

Of course, being experts on scarcity, most economists would also caution against the excessive use of goverment on the simple grounds that government, wise government at least, is itself a scarce resource. If Lincoln or Gandhi or Mother Teresa were to head the next government agency granted the power to regulate or tax, we could be reasonably sure that it would be run justly, but merer mortals will be in charge. When government was only 25 per cent of the economy, a shortage of wise administrators may not have been a problem. But with government either at or approaching 50 per cent of economic acitivity in many countries, the shortage begins to bind.

THE CANADIAN WAY

Of course, the idea that government should be limited in this way will strike many Canadians as being both 'ideological' and, an even greater sin, American. Canadians' instinct – you might even say their ideology – is to resist 'being ideological,' by which, of course, is meant resisting the American ideology that too much government can be a bad thing.[1]

The proposition that Canadians are not ideological is, of course, absurd. As the American economist Robert Higgs has written, 'Every sane adult, unless he is completely apathetic politically, has an ideology – in other words, a "somewhat coherent, rather comprehensive belief system" about how the world works' (Higgs 1987: 38). In spite of this, our supposedly non-ideological nature is 'one of those self-congratulatory myths which bind [this] nation together,' to borrow Desmond Morton's phrase. Canadians' desire to believe that they really aren't ideological may in part reflect a genuine conviction about the unwisdom of preconception in policy matters – even if preconception is often a useful thing, as in 'forewarned is forearmed.' But mainly it arises from a deep desire simply to be different from the Americans.

As even Alpha Centaurians must know by now, the American Declaration of Independence, a long, particularized indictment of the dangers of oppressive government, is intensely ideological. So is the American constitution, which carefully delineates a system of checks and balances designed to render the U.S. federal government, if not actually impotent, as the Articles of Confederation which it replaced had done, then at least infirm. The Bill of Rights that accompanied the constitution also severely limited the power of government to intervene in the lives of citizens. By comparison, our own constitution, as has been noted numberless times, contains almost nothing of a philosophical nature and proclaims only our desire for 'peace, order, and good government' – goals that in fact are not at all inconsistent with the more famous, uplifting, and fun-sounding American triad of 'life, liberty, and the pursuit of happiness.'

The last generation or two of Canadians, particularly Liberal Canadians, has taken great pride in being 'pragmatic,' a term intended to indicate a willingness to look with fresh eyes, much in the manner of an Alzheimer's sufferer, at each and every decision whether to use government to solve a given problem. The greatest living philosopher of Canadian pragmatism, Jean Chrétien, wrote in his autobiography: 'I have never been doctrinaire on issues. That is one of the great things about being a Liberal; you can base your decisions on the circumstances without having to worry about your established public image' (Chrétien 1985: 57). Whether despite or because of this extraordinary admission, never disavowed, his party subsequently made Chrétien its leader, and his country, its prime minister.

An equally 'pragmatic' soul-mate of Chrétien's, Joe Clark, argues that intellectual flexibility is not merely a hallmark of Liberalism, it is the Canadian way: 'The secret of Canada's success is that this is a very pragmatic country. Although our political philosophers range across the spectrum, and political parties like the CCF/NDP have struggled to build a national base, our public policy has not been based on philosophical differences ... Our standard is to judge problems on their merits, not as tests of principle, and then solve them ... Our domestic public policy – from Sir John's railway to medicare, to proposals for child care – has

False Premise 79

aimed at practical results, not philosophical victories' (Clark 1994: 247-8). Perhaps so, though the obvious danger is that an open mind becomes an empty mind.

As Margaret Thatcher, the greatest living anti-pragmatist, has warned, the problem with not having preconceptions is that without stars to steer by, governments end up more or less anywhere. Policy becomes a random walk, Brownian motion of the sort exhibited by molecules suspended in liquid. Or, as Yogi Berra put it, 'If you don't know where you're going, you may end up some place else.' In theory, pragmatism might cause its Canadian practitioners to favour a smaller-than-American public sector. In theory, if a careful review of American politics revealed that *Harper's Magazine* editor Lewis Lapham is correct and the U.S. Congress really has fallen under the thrall of various moneyed interests, so that more and more laws aim merely at securing private profits, this might lead Canadian pragmatists to argue that we should stop imitating America's galloping interventionism.

In practice, of course, 'pragmatism' hasn't led to wandering. Invariably it has led to recommendations for bigger government than is observed in the United States. In recent decades it has become a premise of Canadian public policy that while Americans 'ideologically' avoid using government, Canadians 'pragmatically' conclude that in many if not most instances more government will make for a better society. To hear Messrs. Chrétien and Clark, our predisposition towards the use of government is as Canadian as snow or maple syrup or the Rockies and comes, almost literally, with the territory. 'Canadians have always helped one another. With a population of only twenty-five million, things can't be done on a strictly competitive basis. If rates weren't controlled on the railways there would be no railways. If there were no marketing boards, our agricultural production would decline. If there were no quotas on imports, our clothing and textile industries would vanish overnight' (Chrétien 1985: 94). 'We were never a laissez-faire country, which simply followed the flow of events ... We established crown corporations, and a mixed economy, because we had too much geography for common services to be profitable. We established our social security system because we have too many extremes of climate and resources for citizens to cope on their own' (Clark 1994: 48, 247–8).

These two brief paragraphs contain many interesting propositions. Chrétien implies that only large countries – American-sized ones, presumably – can afford widespread competition in their economies. This is strange, since cossetting an inefficient textile industry or agriculture or railway sector might be thought a luxury that only a big, rich economy could afford. (Recall John Kenneth Galbraith's comment that had the American government been transferred to the United Kingdom in the years after the Second World War the Exchequer would have run quickly dry.) And is it really true that without controlled railway rates we wouldn't have railways? Controls usually keep rates down, as the Crow Rate did for almost a hundred years. How is it that low rates keep the railways in business? There's also an interesting prediction implicit in Chrétien's comments. If 25 million is too small a population for competition, how about 30 million? Or 40 million? Or 50 million? At Confederation we were only three and a half million and may therefore have required greater direction from government in many areas of our life, but will we never reach a size at which we, too, can begin to rely on competition? Or, no matter how large or rich we become, will we always cling to our interventionist habits because that is the Canadian way?

Joe Clark's argument implies that we will, unless, that is, we catch a break from global warming. Thus we have a generous social security system because it is cold here, even though central heating is now widely available. Or does 'extremes of climate' mean that we have a social security system because British Columbia has mild winters while the rest of the country doesn't? Or maybe 'extremes' refers to the fact that our climate is highly variable, that from the Rockies east we freeze in the winter and stew in the summer? Maybe the argument is that our tradition of sharing emerges from difficult pioneer experiences in harsh meteorological conditions. Maybe so. But so few of us are ex-pioneers these days! People no longer raise their barns with the help of their neighbours. In fact, they don't raise barns at all. They don't own barns. They live in cities in houses or apartments. If our social security system really is a legacy from pioneer days, might it not be time to reconsider it?

But carping at politicians is too easy. Never mind the details of Clark and Chrétien's arguments. They have been chosen only because they are so typical. 'We do things differently here.' 'We have a different tradition here.' 'We were never a *laissez-faire* country.' 'That's the *American* way of doing things.' Anyone who had a dollar for every time these and like platitudes have been uttered in Canadian seminar rooms, lecture halls, television debates, and newspaper editorials might almost be able to pay the taxes to which they have led. In Canada, the assertion that we mustn't do things in a particular way because we allegedly have never done them that way almost passes for serious policy analysis. Thus discussions of how to conduct twenty-first-century social policy are laced with references to how, in the nineteenth century, the CPR was built, in the Canadian way, with public assistance. How would most of us react to reading about nineteenth-century commentators who argued that 'if limited suffrage was good enough for 1785, it's certainly good enough for 1898'?

In some Canadians' minds, 'pragmatism' doesn't just come with the weather, it's now virtually in our genes. 'We Canadians believe in government,' writes Michael Ignatieff. 'Social democratic interventionism is ... in my bones' (Ignatieff 1993: 175). Richard Gwyn writes about our '*instinct* for being distinctive'; the '*natural* sense of the importance of fairness ... [that] is part of our *national DNA*'; 'our *inherently* collectivist, egalitarian, and liberal, or Red Tory, or social democrat' community; and, finally, our 'distinctive Canadian *aptitude*,' our 'special skill at public enterprise, which we regularly demonstrate by the excellence of our peacekeepers and by the unusual competence with which we stage public events, from Expo to the Olympics to G-7 gatherings' (which suggests that Gwyn did not attend the Montreal Olympics, remembered the world round for their unfinished stadium and undying debt; Gwyn 1995: 48, 83, 256, 63, emphasis added).[2]

Though ideologies obviously aren't transmitted genetically, many Canadians do see themselves as having a different tradition of government from Americans, one that is not nearly so mistrustful of government – though perhaps that is mainly a measure of our naïveté, our 'fond Canadian belief,' as Donald Creighton wrote, 'that public ownership or control invariably [means] greater public welfare' (Creighton 1976: 23). Many of us persist in seeing government as a means for securing both our independence and distinctiveness from the United States, whether by using it to string a railway to the west coast, to patrol our northern waters, or to secure our broadcasters airtime sufficient to fill with our own often pitiful imitations of American television dramas and sitcoms.

And at least some of us see our greater use of government as an end in itself, almost, almost a form of self-expression. *Globe and Mail* science columnist Stephen Strauss refers to this as the 'My-Country-Isn't-A-Country-It-Is-A-Health-Policy' syndrome (quoted in Granatstein 1994: 130). I govern – or am overgoverned – therefore I am Canadian. Because we choose to use government more than the Americans, we must be different from them. QED. (The possibility that we are essentially the same and merely insist on appearing different is altogether too demoralizing to contemplate.) Without government, without greater-than-American government, we eventually, inevitably will become Americans, whether only in fact or in name, as well. As Richard Gwyn has written, 'Without government ... we will neither have "peace [and] order," nor eventually, Canada itself' (Gwyn 1995: 64). For at least the last three decades, this line of thinking, 'the State or the United States' (in Graham Spry's famous phrase, the six most quoted words on the CBC), has been the governing premise of Canadian public life: only our greater use of government keeps us as we are, different from the United States. As historian Jack Granatstein has put it: 'The Canadian social system is one of the very few things that makes Canada different from the United States. ... The definitive struggle of the 1990s ... [will be] to preserve what remains of it ... in the face of attacks upon it ... and it is not too much to say that the survival of Canada as an independent nation depends on its outcome' (Granatstein 1994: 132).

The argument presented in the second half of this book, 'The

False Premise 83

Meaning of Canadian Life,' is that this fundamental premise of our recent national life is false, false in its entirety and false in its many implied parts. To wit:
§In many if not most important respects, we *aren't* much different from the Americans. §To the extent that we are, it may not be government that makes us different. Government may merely be a symptom of our differences, or even simply of our desire that there be differences. §Whether we retain any distinctiveness from the Americans may not be that critical, certainly not to the world and possibly not to us, either. §At times in our history, we haven't actually used government very much. At times, including some relatively recent times, we have used it less than the Americans. §For their part, the Americans have shown no great reluctance to overgovern themselves, and their official ideology of *laissez-faire* often provides only modest restraint on interest groups seeking favours. §Our greater use of government brings costs as well as benefits. Those who wish us to bear these costs, who most often are the people getting the benefits, inevitably refer to them as 'the price of being Canadian.' In fact, there may be no such price. We might well survive as Canadians without paying any tribute at all to those who have wrapped their own interests in the maple leaf. And yet the costs imposed on us in the name of retaining a separate national identity may now be so great as to threaten both our prosperity and our continued existence as a federation.

DO IDEAS MATTER?

Before starting out, it is well to ask whether in fact our idea of ourselves is as important or consequential as we are accustomed to thinking. There is a longstanding school of thought, frequented by Marxists and anti-statist, 'public-choice' economists alike, that ideas do not decide issues, interests do. In this view, what ordinary people or even political philosophers may regard as the appropriate role of government is almost never decisive. Rather, public decisions are made by whatever coalition of interests is most powerful at the time. From this perspective, Canada has a different-sized government than the United States mainly because our slightly different economy and demography have produced a slightly different constellation of competing interests and our parliamentary system filters these interests in a slightly different way than America's congressional system. But to ascribe policy differences to differences in national outlook, self-image, tradition, or even ideology is, according to this view, to mistake symbol for reality, shadow for substance, cloak for content. While it may be customary to dignify what are essentially power struggles among competing interests in philosophical or ideological language, this is merely the political equivalent of the 'fool 'em strip,' as loggers apparently call the thin line of forest they leave at the roadside to conceal from passers-by the true nature of what is going on behind. Dress-up – façade, ornament, diversion for intellectuals – is all it is.

Do the fish know they swim in water? Maybe the size of a society's government is solely the result of *realpolitik* – of the competition among powerful groups aiming to use government for their own ends. A public-policy economist who spends much of his life discussing the appropriate role of government is bound, however, to believe that ideas count for at least something. Passers-by do occasionally influence the outcome of things. Moreoever, the public opinion whose appeasement the Liberal party of Canada calls 'pragmatism' must come from somewhere – recall John Maynard Keynes's famous line[3] about how 'madmen in authority, who hear voices in the air, are distilling their frenzy from some academic scribbler of a few years past' (Keynes 1936: 383) – and it is difficult to believe that it does not have consequences, even if Robert Higgs's assertion that 'in the study of human action, nothing is more fundamental than an appreciation of what the actors believe' probably puts the case too strongly (Higgs 1987: 35).

Canadians may have accepted in 1988 the kind of trade deal their parents and grandparents refused in 1948 and their great-grandparents in 1911 in part because the constellation of interests in support of free trade had rotated. It certainly was true that the Canadian Manufacturers' Association – Laurent Thibault's outfit – was much more supportive of free trade in 1988 than it had been earlier. It may also be true that business still had a veto over whether a deal would be made. But its decision not to exercise its veto may not have been sufficient on its own to achieve a deal. What was also necessary was that the 'climate of opinion' – an imprecise term for what may nevertheless be an important phenomenon – had also changed. Many more Canadians seemed much less anxious about closer ties with the Americans in 1988 than they had been in 1911, or possibly would have been in 1948, had Mackenzie King not quashed the free trade deal that his officials had secretly negotiated with the Americans.

An economist would never dismiss the influence of *realpolitik*. As we have seen, despite the 'conservative' revolution supposedly inaugurated by Ronald Reagan and Margaret Thatcher, industrialized countries' tax rates rose during the 1980s, they did not fall. Still, ideas may have a separate and at times even important influence, as well. As we have also seen, the American analysts Carolyn Webber and Aaron Wildavsky, after an exhaustive study of the determinants of differences in the level of public spending across countries, could not exclude the possibility that there are enduring cultural differences across countries in people's view of the public sector.

There is a danger in swinging too far in the other direction, of course. Richard Gwyn believes that 'in the United States, most public debates are won by whomever demonstrates that their argument is based on efficiency and effectiveness. The winners in Canada are most often those who can show that their proposals are fair and equitable' (Gwyn 1995: 180), which is a wild exaggeration, as anyone who has watched a congressional debate can attest. Still, if the average Canadian really is less predisposed against the use of government to solve social problems than the average American, then maybe in Canada the burden of proof is on those who oppose using government, while in the United States it falls to those who favour its use. If so, it would be surprising if such differences had not contributed to the differences in the size and nature of government in the two countries. Ideas probably do have consequences. Exploring our idea of ourselves may therefore be important, even if, as is certainly true, base calculations of self-interest also enter into many, if not most political decisions.

9
Governing Misperceptions

What everyone knows often is not true. Everyone in Canada knows that we have always used government more than the Americans have and that, weather apart, this is the most important difference between our two countries. 'Americans are individualistic,' writes Richard Gwyn, 'have always been sceptical about government, and have always believed that each person should be free to pursue "life, liberty and happiness" in their own way ... We believe – within sensible limits – in collectivism and egalitarianism' (Gwyn 1995: 61, 51). As every schoolchild knows – or used to know, when schools still taught history – the United States was born in a revolution driven by the idea that gentlemen-farmers should be as free as possible to pursue their own interests and desires without interference from government. We, by contrast, emerged from our colonial status by evolution, not revolution, and, whether trapping furs, building railways, subsidizing manufacturing, or protecting our 'cultural industries,' have always depended more on government both to secure our economic, political, and cultural independence and to pursue the peace and order we cherish so dearly. Didn't John Turner, in his debate with Brian Mulroney, refer to 120 years of building infrastructure with government? Everyone knows these things, but are they true?

There's no doubt – the charts presented in chapter 5 showed it – that Canadians pay more of their income in taxes than the Americans do and spend a higher percentage of their annual output on public services of one kind or another.[1] 'But the fact that

Governing Misperceptions 87

we have a larger public sector than the Americans hardly means that they are a society run by *laissez-faire* (if 'run by *laissez-faire*' isn't an oxymoron). There is more to government than taxes and government spending. The United States is a famously litigious society, much more litigious, most of us believe, than our own.[2] In 1990 more than 756,000 Americans were lawyers, which is more lawyers than in all other countries combined (*Compton's* 1994: 'Law'). There are more lawyers in Washington, DC, than in all of Japan. Washington has twice as many law firms as churches and thirteen times more law firms than gas stations (Slutsky 1996a). All these lawyers earn their living arguing about laws, and, of course, laws are made by government – by legislators, by judges and juries, and by regulators with powers delegated by legislatures. Taken together, all of America's law-makers make lots and lots of laws. Assigning Vice-President Al Gore, a lawyer, to supervise regulatory reform, Bill Clinton, another lawyer, explained: 'I asked him to do it because he was the only person that I could trust to read all 156,000 pages in the Code of Federal Regulations' (quoted in *Newsweek*, 6 March 1995, 23).

This great mass of regulation reflects the recent explosion of law-making: 'The number of pages of law entered into the statute books during the relatively uneventful 1991–1992 [Congressional] session was two and a half times the number entered by the 1965–1966 Great Society Congress ... In 1936 there were 2,355 pages of regulations amplifying federal laws published in the Federal Register. By 1969 the number had risen to 20,464 pages; in the 1990s the register has been averaging about 60,000 pages a year (Stark 1995: 101).' As Republican Presidential candidate Steve Forbes emphasized during his 1996 campaign, the number of sections in the Internal Revenue code has increased from 103 to 698 over the last four decades, while the number of words in the code tripled between 1964 and 1993 (Slutsky 1996a). Eastman Kodak's tax return has doubled in weight over the last ten years, to 35 pounds (*Economist* 1996: 20).

Maybe there is an innocent explanation for this Niagara of law-making. Maybe federal fonts and margins are larger than they used to be. Maybe laws and regulations are drafted more carefully than in the past, though presumably that would be because they are more likely to be challenged in court, which is just further proof of litigiousness rampant. But it does seem unlikely that the twenty-five-fold increase in the number of pages of new regulations written per year since the New Deal or the three-fold increase since the late 1960s is purely the result of changing typography. Sixty thousand pages a year is a lot of pages by anyone's count.

Of course, not everyone thinks that governmental prolixity is a bad idea. Thus the American political writer Sidney Blumenthal took Speaker Newt Gingrich's 104th Congress to task for being the 'least productive first-year Congress in modern American history.' Its sin was enacting only eighty-eight public bills. By contrast: 'the notorious 80th, indelibly branded the "do-nothing Congress" by Harry Truman, passed three hundred and ninety-five in *its* first year, 1947. Not since paleolithic times – before air conditioning, before television, before jet travel – has a Congress fallen into comparable doldrums' (Blumenthal 1996: 5). Eighty-eight new laws means that even if Congress had met around the clock every day of the year, it would have passed a new law every 100 hours. To be sure, this is less than the 80th Congress, which legislated every 22 hours and 10 minutes, but in law-making as in wine-making speed usually is not of the essence.[3]

Law, whether statute, precedent, or regulation, is government. If the United States really is the most litigious society in the world, it can hardly be the *laissez-faire* jungle which it is in the imagination of so many Canadian intellectuals and CBC producers. Unfortunately, it is harder to measure the reach of law than to measure the number of dollars the public sector spends, so in assessing how important government is in a society, it is only natural to focus on the sorts of ratios – taxes/GDP, government spending/GDP, and so on – presented in chapter 3's tables, which did confirm that we Canadians currently tax ourselves more and spend more in our public sector than the Americans do. They also showed, however, that our tendency to spend markedly more than they do is a relatively new phenomenon, dating only from the late 1950s.

Governing Misperceptions 89

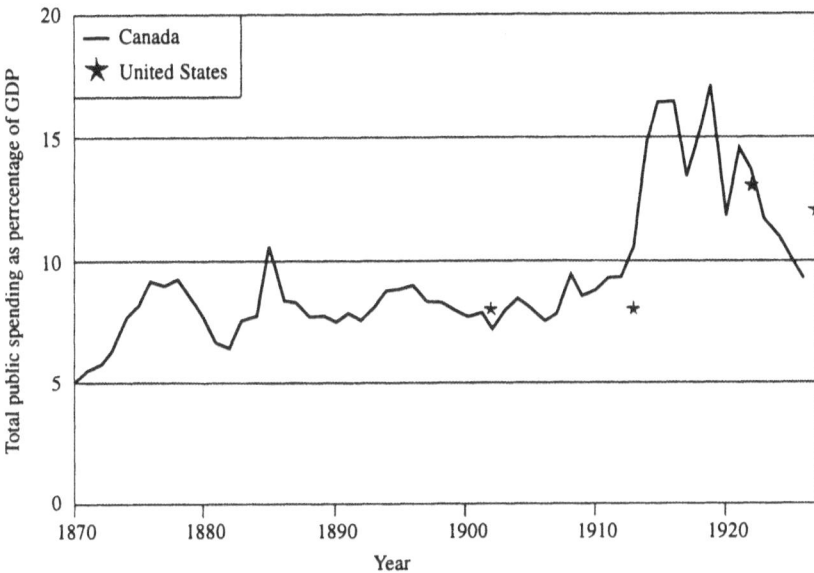

Figure 9.1 Public spending/GDP, United States and Canada, 1870-1927

But perhaps the 1950s were an aberration. Did we consistently outspend the Americans before 1950? As usual, the farther back you go, the less complete the data are.[4] Figure 9.1 shows what there are for Canada and the United States for the years 1870 to 1926. Unfortunately, it contains only four years of American data (indicated by the stars at 1902, 1913, 1922, and 1927). That's enough to draw some general conclusions, however. Before 1900, Canadian public spending exceeded 10 per cent of GDP only in 1885, the year of the Riel Rebellion and the Last Spike. It rose sharply with the First World War, but by the mid-1920s it was back under 10 per cent. Nor is Canada much different from the United States in this regard. In two years (1902 and 1927[5]) the United States outspent Canada, while in two others (1913 and 1922) the reverse was true. Containing as few American data as it does, Figure 9.1 is hardly conclusive, but it does strongly suggest that we Canadians haven't always had markedly higher government spending than Americans.

90 The Meaning of Canadian Life

Is that all there is to say about whether our governing perception about government is true – namely, that we have always used it more than the Americans? Not at all. There is ample historical evidence that: they have used government more than our national mythology assumes; that we have not always been so kind and gentle as we like to think; and that private initiative played a much greater role in the building of this country than it has been our habit to credit. The next three chapters are devoted to justifying these assertions.

10
The American 'Governmental Habit'[1]

Despite what we Canadians may think of them, despite their – by current international standards – comparatively low tax rates, Americans have a long history of government intervention in what their all-but-official ideology suggests should be private affairs. As the late Jonathan Hughes, Northwestern University economic historian, observed: 'There was no time in American history free of nonmarket controls over economic life' (Hughes 1991: 12). The reason is simple: 'The American distrusts the free market and accepts its decisions willingly only when they suit his needs ... Historically, Americans have proved to be more comfortable even with malfunctioning controls ... than with decisions of the marketplace that influential groups find repugnant to their interests' (Hughes 1977: 8, 10).

Hughes traced this tradition back to the colonial era. When still part of the British Empire, the American colonies relied on the common law and, as was true in this country until 1949, had final legal appeals heard in Britain. The common law allowed for extensive government oversight, if not overrunning, of the free market. The prices and quality of goods were often regulated; how many people practised a trade was often restricted; monopolies were granted; local governments engaged in various public undertakings; and international trade was controlled by tariffs, taxes, and restrictions, though control was exercised mainly by London, a sticking-point that proved fateful in the 1770s. In sum, 'during the colonial era virtually every aspect of economic life was subject to nonmarket controls' (Hughes 1977: 49).

Though the final locus of decision-making obviously changed after the American military victory over the British in 1781, Hughes argues that in the main the legal system carried over. The 'revolution' in fact wasn't. Even after 1789 the new constitution, with its accompanying Bill of Rights, did not overturn most colonial practices in respect of the regulation of business. As late as 1819 the state of New Hampshire lost a case before the Supreme Court in which it had tried to overturn a patent issued by George III (Hughes 1977: 78).

What *was* different after 1789, Hughes argues, was that the federal government had much less control in matters of regulation vis-à-vis the states than the British government had had vis-à-vis the same states when they were colonies. This changed in the 1880s, however, when Supreme Court decisions giving – or at least confirming – considerable regulatory latitude to both federal and state governments led to the establishment of the Interstate Commerce Commission, which the national government then used to regulate the railways.[2]

Of course, even before Washington's regulatory emancipation in the 1880s the U.S. federal government had hardly been supine. It had engineered western expansion by buying land (much of the west in 1803, Alaska in 1867). It had annexed or conquered what could not be bought (General Custer, it should be recalled, was a federal government employee). It had established rules for how settlement would proceed – rules later largely copied in Canada (Thompson and Randall 1994: 80). It had granted exclusive charters to settlement companies, given away large tracts of land at nominal prices to settlers, reserved still other tracts to the states for educational purposes, and, finally, as the frontier closed, established national parks. As if this weren't enough, in the first decade of the nineteenth century, Congress had established a national bank, the Bank of the United States, a jointly owned, private-public undertaking, which, though far from fulfilling the functions of a modern national bank, was intended to help regulate currency and fiscal matters. Though in the 1830s populist

The American 'Governmental Habit' 93

President Andrew Jackson effectively stripped its successor, the Second Bank of the United States, of its ability to influence money markets, a measure of federal control was reestablished in the 1860s, while in 1913, twenty-two years before the Bank of Canada came into existence, the Federal Reserve Act gave Washington, in theory at least, as complete control over its national currency as a government may have.

Nineteen thirteen was also the year in which the Americans amended their constitution to allow for income taxation. Such a tax had been imposed on a temporary basis during the Civil War, and Congress had enacted one again in 1894, though it had subsequently been ruled unconstitutional by the Supreme Court on the grounds that it set different tax rates for different citizens, thus violating the constitution's requirement of equal treatment before the law. Our own income tax was not introduced until 1917, during the First World War. Thus, in spite of our supposedly more interventionist traditions, the allegedly anti-statist Americans had both an income tax and a central bank, two necessary accoutrements of modern big government, before we did.

Another classic offence against *laissez-faire* doctrine is interference in international trade, whether by means of tariffs or by other trade barriers. Whatever its official ideology might ordain, the United States has always had an active – and when necessary protectionist – tariff policy. On 4 July 1789, the very first economic act the new Congress undertook was to legislate tariffs to both raise revenue and restrict imports. As Hughes says, 'America's own tradition of free trade ... was forgotten' (Hughes 1977: 43). That tradition, which had been short-lived in any case, had been embodied in a Massachusetts law of 1645 that allowed free entry to Massachusetts harbours to all trading vessels. But beginning a mere six years later this law had been superseded by imperial Navigation Acts, designed to control trade and integrate the colonies into the British mercantile empire. Towards the end of the colonial period, a number of these controls became the source of now legendary resentments on the part of the colonists, to the extent that George III's 'cutting off our trade with all parts of the world' is singled out in the Declaration of Independence as one of the reasons justifying the 'sundering of bands' between the United Kingdom and its colonies.

Even so, the strong affection for free trade at least implied by that document did not prevent the thirteen colonies, once independent, from imposing tariffs and other controls on their trade with each other. In fact, the disruption of internal American trade following 1781 was a main reason the thirteen states abandoned their original Articles of Confederation and replaced them with the 1789 constitution, which included a clause explicitly forbidding the imposition of tariffs on interstate trade.[3] But despite the restoration of free trade in the internal American market, the Navigation Laws adopted by the new country in 1792 and 1793 were not unlike those experienced under the British regime, even if the ultimate recipient of the tariff revenue was now Washington (Hughes 1977: 43).

As is always the case in trading nations, tariff policy has been source of continuing political controversy. In the United States in the nineteenth century, agrarian interests favoured free trade, while manufacturers often lobbied for protection – a pattern replicated in Canada, and for the same reason: in the mid-nineteenth century British manufactures were simply too competitive. In 1854, the United States did negotiate a free trade agreement with the British North American colonies, which were prevailed on by London to agree to it, mainly for geopolitical reasons. But free trade did not last long. The Americans abrogated the Reciprocity Treaty twelve years later, after the United Province of Canada had both raised its remaining tariffs in an unfriendly way (in 1859) and been perceived as being sympathetic to the South in the Civil War. In fact, the abrogation of the Reciprocity Treaty is commonly cited as a main reason why the colonies of British North America decided, as of 1867, to form their own free trade area. With the agrarian and Democratic South prostrate after its conquest by the Union armies, the northern manufacturing interests that held sway in the Republican party were not content merely to undo previous liberalizations of trade, however. They also hiked tariffs substantially across a wide range of manufactured goods, and did so with the express purpose of encouraging American industrial

The American 'Governmental Habit' 95

development. As Webber and Wildavsky (1986: 387) observe, high tariffs both 'subsidized manufacturing and ... linked nationalism to capitalism.'

A protective tariff was also the centrepiece of John A. Macdonald's National Policy of 1879, and it had exactly the same goals as the Republicans' tariffs: to encourage local manufacturing, raise revenue, and cement a sense of nationhood. But far from establishing Canadian uniqueness in our approach to policy, the National Policy tariff was both an imitation of and a strategic response to similarly high tariffs enacted for almost identical reasons by an at least equally activist American government. Both John A. Macdonald and Alexander Mackenzie, prime minister during the depression years of 1873 to 1878, had tried for a new free trade agreement with the United States. Mackenzie even got a draft deal in 1874 – negotiated by George Brown, founder of the Toronto *Globe* – but it fell through. Only when the approach to the United States had failed did Macdonald resolve 'on paying [the] U.S. in their own coin' and follow the American lead by turning to protection. Thus 'though Macdonald's development strategy has been hailed as the foundation of Canadian autonomy, the master stroke of nation building ... in reality, Washington dictated that Canada would have high tariffs through its own disinterest in lower tariffs' (Thompson and Randall 1994: 57). Macdonald's finance minister, Leonard Tilley, 'went so far as to import an assistant from the U.S. Bureau of Statistics to advise him on the drawing up the new Canadian tariff schedule!' (57).

WHOSE NATIONAL DREAM?

The second and more celebrated leg of the National Policy was the building of a transcontinental railway, and in fact the CPR still holds mythic thrall over Canadians. Whenever Ottawa sucks up its courage and withdraws another slice of the very high subsidies it pays the fewer than twenty thousand Canadians who still travel the country's railways, eloquent evocations of the country's railway-building history fill the (also generously subsidized) air waves. John Turner did not actually mention the CPR by name in his 1988 exchange with Brian Mulroney, but his reference to infrastructure – 'We built a country east and west and north. We built it on an infrastructure that deliberately resisted the continental pressure of the United States. For 120 years we've done it.' – can refer only to the railway. The decision to swing the main CPR line north of Lake Superior, rather than take the shorter, more southerly American route, clearly was an infrastructure decision that deliberately and explicitly resisted the continental pressure of the United States. And it was probably a reasonable decision, though for political and strategic, not economic reasons.

It is almost certainly true that private interests would not have built the railway on their own: 'Private enterprise never seriously considered building the C.P.R. without the financial assistance of the government' (George 1968: 741). In 1880, fewer than ten thousand Europeans lived in the Canadian northwest. Undertaking one of the world's greatest-ever construction projects to satisfy their transportation needs would have been one of the world's greatest-ever extravagances. As for a purely public railway, it was tried between 1873 and 1878 and was judged not to have worked: a royal commission reported in 1881 that the cost of the government-built portions of the railway was excessively high, partly because of widespread corruption and bid-rigging.[4] In the end, what we think of as that uniquely Canadian amalgam – private enterprise supported by public funding – got the job done.

But it *isn't* a uniquely Canadian amalgam. The Americans thought of it first. Far from being unknown, public support for railways, and before them roads and canals, was common in the United States, even if was often provided by state and local governments, Washington generally being reluctant to participate, on the perfectly sensible grounds that financial support for merely sectional interests would lead to sectional resentments. The Erie Canal, built in the 1820s, was a mixed public-private undertaking, while between 1815 and 1860 almost 70 per cent of all canal investment in the United States was financed by public sources (Hughes 1977: 70, 71). In the new technology's first decades, government participation in railway building varied from as low as 10 per cent in the midwest, to as high as 50 per cent in the South.

In total, in the years before the Civil War 'more than 25 percent of the total railroad capital stock ... had come from public sources ... mainly state and local governments' (Hughes 1977: 72). In general, 'the private element was strongest in the initial construction phases where the estimated profit potential was largest, and public participation tended to rise wherever profit prospects fell' (Hughes 1977: 71), which sounds very much like Canada's often-woeful experience with railway finance. It was not as if failure was completely unanticipated, of course: many private canal companies had also gone bankrupt, conveniently leaving governments to pick up the tab. The pattern was repeated, not invented, by the railways.

Though local governments were most active in railway construction, Washington was also a player, especially when it came to transcontinental railways. Like the CPR, the Americans' Union Pacific Railroad was massively subsidized. The federal government granted it 23 million acres of land and lent it $60 million, fully half the cost of its construction. In all, Washington ceded four transcontinental railways more than 100 million acres of land, ten per cent of the public domain at the time. Its total railway land grants were 131 million acres, with another 49 million acres given by the states (Hughes 1983: 286). By contrast, Ottawa gave the CPR 25 million acres; tax concessions; guarantees of temporary monopoly; and a $25-million grant (not a loan) that eventually equalled a little over 10 per cent of the company's capital expenditures (George 1968: 753).

That help for the Union Pacific and the lines that followed violated the principles of *laissez-faire* really wasn't an issue. The main American student of the profitability of the railways, Nobel Prize–winning economist Robert Fogel, reports that even though the idea of federal support for a continental railway was discussed in Congress for more than fifteen years 'the debate was never really conducted on the doctrinal level ... To all intents and purposes the necessity and inevitability of governmental intervention was [sic] accepted by everybody who favoured ... building' the railway (Fogel 1960: 27–8). The only real difference between the Canadian and American transcontinental railway experience was that the Americans went first: the Union Pacific was completed in 1869, three years before the first contract for the Canadian Pacific was signed and fully sixteen years before the Last Spike was hammered into place.

How did Congress rationalize a railway policy that seems so obviously contradictory to the United States's *laissez-faire* principles? In a phrase that would do Joe Clark or Jean Chrétien proud, Fogel refers to the congressional 'penchant for pragmatism.' *Laissez-faire* was not forgotten; it was merely set aside. In 1864 a correspondent in the *Atlantic Monthly* wrote that while all agreed that the political ideal was 'absolute non-interference of Government in all enterprises whose benefit accrues to a part of its citizens ... facts are not ideal, and absolute principles in their practical application make head only by a curved line of compromise with the facts' (quoted in Fogel 1960: 44). In this case, as in Canada fifteen years later, as so often when principle confronts expedience, the 'curved line of compromise' was with 'national necessity.' The railway was seen as 'necessary to defend our Pacific territories from foreign attack, to cope with insurrection and to aid in suppressing the Indians' (Fogel 1960: 20).

Apart from 'suppressing the Indians,' which Canadians now might not admit to having wanted to do, this all sounds very familiar. In fact, 'the decade of the 'sixties found both governments pushing forward the Pacific railway schemes for reasons both domestic and international, but political more than economic' (Irwin 1968: 222). Of course, from the American point of view, the fear was mainly of British incursions on the Pacific coast. Before California was ceded from Mexico in 1848, the plan was to have the Union Pacific end in Oregon, so as to 'make our claim to Oregon impregnable against any that Great Britain might put forth' (Irwin 1968: 222). But after cession, 'the railroad was urged to cement California's ties with the Union. It was feared that without the link that a railroad would provide, California might develop as a separate entity and eventually establish itself as an independent nation. While California never seriously threatened secession, it was quick to take advantage of the fear of this possibility to press its points' (Fogel 1960: 20). British Colum-

The American 'Governmental Habit' 99

bia played even harder to get, but the Americans' reasoning in the 1860s was essentially the same as Canadians' in the 1870s and 1880s.[5]

It might be argued that while Canadians had to subsidize their railways, the Americans at least had the choice of whether or not to adopt a *laissez-faire* approach. Robert Fogel's calculations do suggest that the Union Pacific was 'premature by accident': in reality it ended up being privately profitable even though investors had expected it not to be (Fogel 1960: 97). But what counts is that, when forced to choose between *laissez-faire* and government subsidy, Americans overcame whatever ideological reservations they may have had and chose government subsidy.

One clear difference, however, between the American and Canadian approaches to subsidizing transcontinental railways is that they stopped and we did not. After 1870, Washington's support for railways largely dried up. By contrast, subsequent Canadian governments, emboldened by the apparent economic success of the CPR and, even more important, impressed by the evident political popularity of the National Policy, subsidized a massive overbuilding of the transcontinental railway system, motivated, as Michael Bliss has stated, 'by the naive dreams of promoters and colonizing priests and other visionaries of Canada's northern wealth' (Bliss 1994: 49). The inevitable dénouement to investment premised on the vision of a rail-lined nation of 60 million persons was the bankruptcy and eventual nationalization of the unneeded capacity, a burden on the federal government not finally removed until Canadian National Railways was put up for sale in the mid-1990s.

The American historian Arthur Schlesinger, Jr, once argued that the costs of the French and British appeasement of Hitler at Munich included not just the Second World War but also all subsequent incorrect invocations of Munich's lesson that aggression must always be nipped in the bud, including the Americans' misinterpretation of the likely effects of the loss of Vietnam to communism (Schlesinger 1966: 99). Though Canadian economic historians have not yet taken the necessary sums, we may be nearing the point where whatever good was done by the initial investment in the CPR has been offset, perhaps many times over, by the imprudent public investments subsequently undertaken in its name, for our whole way of thinking about government and its appropriate role in our society is now conditioned by what we are accustomed to think of as the uniquely Canadian private-public partnership that built the transcontinental railway. Unfortunately, the mid–Great War bailout of the Canadian Northern created another enduring Canadian myth: the supposed wisdom – in this case born solely of financial necessity – of pairing private and public corporations in various industries. The three true lessons of our railway experience are, first, that purely public enterprise can be wasteful and inefficient, as was discovered between 1873 and 1880; second, that infrastructure can be a money pit, as was proved in the first part of this century; and, third, that where large public expenditures are involved corruption of one kind or another is bound to follow. Instead, the one lesson we do seem to have learned – and it is historically incorrect – is that public support for the transcontinental railway marked us for ever as distinct.[6]

THE WAY OF ALL DEMOCRACIES

Among the American public at large there may have been at the end of the last century a ritual appreciation for the virtues of *laisser-faire*, but there was almost no love for the modern managerial corporation. As business historian Alfred Chandler, Jr. (1977), argues, it 'had little political support among the American electorate.' Quite the contrary, 'the coming of modern business enterprise in its several different forms brought strong political reaction and legislative action' (497). The railways were one of the first industries to fall victim to this struggle. The (U.S.) Interstate Commerce Commission, established in 1887, was brought into being mainly to regulate them and their 200,000 miles of track, which accounted for most interstate commerce at the time (United States, Bureau of the Census 1989: Series Q288). As might be expected, regulation was introduced partly at the insistence of railway users concerned about free-market pricing of what was in many areas the only available source of efficient long-distance transportation. What's more surprising is that this assertion of federal regulatory control often met with only token resistance from the railwaymen who were to be regulated and in fact was often welcomed by them, if not openly.

The American historian Gabriel Kolko, a long-time student of this question, concludes: 'The railroads were a much more constant force for federal regulation than the shippers ... For the most part, [they] consistently accepted the basic premises of federal regulation since only through the positive intervention of the national political structure could the de-stabilizing, costly effects of cutthroat competition, predatory speculators, and greedy shippers be overcome' (Kolko 1970: 5). Kolko goes on to argue that traditional American free-market ideology had almost no role in the industry's thinking: 'Most railroad men approached the issue of regulation with purely opportunistic motives. The doctrine of *laissez-faire* ... inhibited very few practical executives; most ignored intellectual issues and concentrated on meeting immediate problems in the most expeditious manner possible. Insofar as railroad men did think about the larger theoretical implications of centralized federal regulation, they rejected the validity and relevance of ... the entire notion of *laissez faire*' (Kolko 1970: 4)

Federal regulation presumably was not the railways' first choice. But repeated attempts to organize rate-setting cartels had failed under pressure from defectors – including, on at least one occasion, Canada's own Grand Trunk Railway (Kolko 1970: 17). By the time the bill establishing the Interstate Commerce Commission was being debated before Congress in 1886, most railway interests supported it, though obviously not because they favoured price control in the public interest. As the director of the Union Pacific had written privately two years earlier: 'No matter what sort of bill you have, everything depends upon the men who, so to speak, are inside of it, and who are to make it work. In the hands of the right men, any bill would produce the desired results' (quoted in Kolko 1970: 37) The railways got their man when President Grover Cleveland appointed as first chairman of the commission a lawyer who 'had completely identified himself with the railroads' interests from at least 1882 on' (Kolko 1970: 47).

The idea that business people, even American ones, might trod on their own ideology in chasing after their financial betterment, or that regulatory agencies might be captured by the interests they are supposed to regulate, may offend the sensibilities of Canadians. But it shouldn't really be surprising that in the hurly-burly of democratic politics, principle often succumbs to self-interest. The most obvious fact of democratic life – in our own age, but in earlier times as well – is the incessant, inexorable grinding of interest-group politics. Ideas do count. But so do log-rolling, deal-making, and self-seeking, and *laissez-faire* principles do not prevent Americans from engaging in these activities. In Washington in the early 1990s, lobbying companies employed 125 people per member of Congress and were the largest single private-sector employer in the city. Nationwide in the same year, lobbyists were paid more than $3.2 billion in wages, salaries, and commissions – no doubt a small fraction of what they cost the U.S. economy (Slutsky 1996a). When a political deal can be struck that makes all parties to it better off, chances are it will be struck, even if it injures the public or offends against official virtues. As Jonathan Hughes (1977) put it: 'A history of American government limited to those laws which sprang pure from the brains of the nation's politicians with no special interests as their objects would be a very short history indeed' (10).

Perhaps the greatest tribute to the enduring radiance of American official ideology is that it so often blinds people to the true extent of private appropriation of public power. After a lengthy recitation of major federal legislation of the last twenty-five years, Hughes (1991) concludes: 'If we were Germans or Russians some deep-thinking scholar might pontificate about our love of *ordnung* or of a natural yearning to feel the weight of authority across our backs. But this mass of control legislation has come from the freedom-loving United States Congress, most of it *since* the Great Society epoch, in the regimes of successive presidents who promised, if elected, to get the government off the people's backs' (197). We Canadians presumably don't yearn 'to feel the weight of authority across our backs.' Still we are repeatedly told that only if our governments legislate feverishly can we distinguish ourselves from our unregulated southern neighbours. If Hughes is right that Americans 'simply continue along the familiar paths of group interests, always wrapped in the flag,' we will have to march at double time and furl ourselves even more tightly in our own flag in order to stay ahead.

11
'The Most Rugged Surviving Individualists'

In measuring our government and society against the Americans,' most Canadians probably do not think of such things as when we introduced the income tax or created a central bank or by just how much nineteenth-century railways and industrialists benefited from land grants or loans or tariffs. Rather, they think in terms of twentieth-century social policy, and their conclusion invariably is that, whether in the form of unemployment insurance or university tuition or medicare, Canadians' social policy is much more humane and interventionist than the Americans'. As historian Jack Granatstein (1994) has commented, 'Canadians' perception of themselves [is as] the kinder, gentler nation in North America' (132). That may be true now – though chapter 15 tries to raise doubts on this point – but it has not always been so.

As historian Doug Owram's 1986 book, *The Government Generation*, makes clear, as the twentieth century opened the dominant Canadian ideology was strongly individualistic, albeit in a particularly Canadian way: 'Individual choice was not so much an absolute principle [as in the United States] as it was a means to other more social ends ... The free will of the individual was the best way of achieving the end purpose, the uplifting of society to a more moral level' (8–9). Thus, in a highly topical turn-of-the-century example, prohibition of the sale of alcoholic beverages not only was doomed to failure, it was morally wrong. The reason? Paternalistic interference by the state 'may prevent individual action, which is the condition for having any morality at all.'[1]

Owram attributes this consensus view among English-Canadian elites to two streams of thought: Scottish idealism and Victorian liberalism, the latter typified by the writings of John Stuart Mill and Jeremy Bentham, the utilitarian godfather of modern neoclassical economics, whose works were widely and approvingly quoted in the debates of the day (and whose person is on display to this day in the University of London, propped up in a chair, encased in glass).

To be sure, as the young century unfolded and urbanization and industrialization created new social challenges, more and more Canadian commentators, including those in the fledgling social science departments of the country's few universities, took note of experiments with old age pensions and worker's compensation in Germany, Belgium, Britain, Australia, and New Zealand and wondered 'why Canada was so far behind other jurisdictions' (Owram 1986: 32). A main reason was that the Laurier government cast the nineteenth-century British constitutional tradition 'in more anti-statist terms than ... any other government in Canadian history' (34). Laurier himself warned in 1907: 'If you remove the incentive of ambition and emulation from public enterprises, you suppress progress, you condemn the community to stagnation and immobility' (35). Ronald Reagan himself couldn't have said it better. Thus when Laurier's Liberals introduced old age pensions, the scheme was voluntary and the only effective subsidy was that the government covered the plan's administrative costs, which were hardly burdensome, since the pension was paid only at age seventy and average life expectancy at birth was less than sixty years. As a result, between 1908 and 1927 the plan issued only 7,713 annuities (Guest 1980: 36).[2]

Owram (1986) summarizes Laurier's political philosophy as follows: 'The role of government was ... not to force action in any one direction but to remove barriers to man's own efforts to undertake personal and social improvement ... Man must be free to seek his own improvement and be responsible for his own destiny' (35). This is probably not the image most Canadians have of the high-browed, grandfatherly occupant of their five-dollar bill. Yet despite holding what today would be called 'neoconservative' views, Laurier was in power from 1896 to 1911. When late-twentieth-century interventionists argue that big government and comprehensive social polices are part of Canadian tradition, they mainly betray their belief that Canadian tradition starts sometime in the 1960s. True, they may dip back to the 1880s to cite public financing of the CPR as justification for today's interventionist nostrums. But if, inconveniently, the first seventy-five years of Confederation were typified by general public approval for the idea that people should not become dependent on the state and instead be self-reliant, that part of the Canadian experience is quietly erased from our historical memory. In fact, though pre-Depression notions about social policy may or may not be worthy of emulation, they are inescapably part of our tradition.

Tentative departures from the Laurier government's pure *laissez-faire* principles were attempted at times by Mackenzie King, first as deputy minister and then minister of labour. But King's efforts to settle a strike by threatening legislation against the Grand Trunk Railway were categorized by Laurier as 'a very unfortunate and dangerous precedent,' while his 1910 reforms to the Combines Investigation Act were denounced by a caucus member from Alberta – does nothing in Canadian politics ever change? – as follows: 'As a Liberal of the old school ... I regret very much ... to hear a young Liberal approach the subject of state control in so light hearted a manner because I recollect the fact that the progress of true Liberalism has been associated in the history of England with the diminution of state control' (quoted in Owram 1986: 39). But King's disagreements with his political hero, Laurier, were infrequent. In general, he 'retained his belief in the preferability of leaving the individual alone to work out his own destiny, wherever possible' (Owram 1986: 40). Social historian Dennis Guest notes that even in *Industry and Humanity*, the reformist tract that King published in 1918, he was 'assailed with doubts as to the possible adverse effects of social security protection on the habits of thrift and industry' (Guest 1980: 66).

It is true that such doubts were not universally shared in the years immediately following the First World War. In 1920 Stephen Leacock, in his day job a McGill University economist and leading Tory thinker, wrote: 'The obligation to die must carry with it the right to live. If every citizen owes it to society that he must fight for it in the case of need, then society owes to every citizen the opportunity of a livelihood. "Unemployment" in the case of the willing and the able becomes henceforth a social crime' (Owram 1986: 89).

As was not true of the Second War, however, the aftermath of the First eventually gave rise to a revulsion against 'Kaiserism,' as the aggressive use of state power often was referred to. As Owram puts it, 'new crusades ... in the name of great causes were not likely to appeal to an intellectual community that had always looked to social stability as the other aspect of reform' (Owram 1986: 112). Instead of using 'the sense of national purpose that had developed during the war to carry forward with postwar reconstruction ... the government relaxed most of its wartime powers and turned the country's domestic problems over to the provinces, their municipalities, and to the market place ... Following the war, the mood in Canada was to "get back to normal"' (Guest 1980: 69). Even so, by 1924 Leacock was writing in anguish: 'We are moving towards socialism. We are moving through the mist; nearer and nearer with every bit of government regulation, nearer and nearer through the mist to the edge of the abyss over which civilization may be precipitated to its final catastrophe' (Owram 1986: 111). In the year this was written, Canadian government spending on goods and services was 10.8 per cent of GDP.

What might have prompted Leacock's concern? 'With the important exceptions of mothers' pensions and old age pensions,' Dennis Guest has concluded, 'minimum wage legislation was the sole evidence of a welfare state in Canada in the 1920s' (Guest 1980: 74). The Old Age Pensions Act of 1927 did use the federal spending power to support provincial pensions for persons whose other income brought them less than $365 a year – but this was not an overly generous ceiling at a time when average annual earnings in manufacturing were $1,890 (Urquhart and Buckley 1983: Series E48).

Mother's pensions, paid to lone mothers in several provinces, had been resisted by a number of interests when they were first proposed. As late as 1932, Charlotte Whitton – social worker, future mayor of Ottawa, longtime Tory, and head of the Canadian Council on Child and Family Welfare, at the time 'Canada's most influential voice on social welfare matters' (Guest 1980: 56) – wrote in a report on British Columbia's mother's pensions: 'There is a grave danger of the development, as a matter of course, of a general tendency to reliance on social aid that the inquiry regards with grave disquiet as destructive of personal effort, and self-dependence, and so disruptive of the very basis of initiative, enterprise, and strength of character that must be the greatest resource of any people' (quoted in Guest 1980: 56). Today, of course, this reads like the most rockbound Republicanism. Whitton, 'a conservative idealist in an age of liberal technocracy' (Owram 1986: 315), was not opposed to state aid in principle but insisted that 'service must precede and accompany it, to the end that the family itself realizes that it, and each of its members, no less than provincial funds, must honestly and sincerely participate in the whole plan, which is the development of initiative, and self-reliance and independence at the earliest possible date, and to such degree and strength as to avoid future dependency' (quoted in Guest 1980: 56). In effect, what was wanted, in the language of the 1990s, was a hand up not a handout. It may surprise late-century Canadians to learn that Whitton's opposition to mothers' pensions 'marked the continuation of a traditional commitment by private welfare agencies to the values of individualism and localism ... The voluntary charity establishment, both in the United States and Canada, refused to define the one-parent family problem as primarily one of lack of income' (Guest 1980: 58, 52). This, too, is part of our forgotten tradition.

What the Great War did not achieve, however, the Great Depression did. As the English historian Eric Hobsbawm writes: 'The Great Slump destroyed economic liberalism for half a century ... The period 1929–33 was a canyon which henceforth made a return to 1913 not merely impossible, but unthinkable' (Hobsbawm 1994: 94, 107). Thus in 1934 Queen's University historian Duncan Macarthur could write: 'In all circles except the most reactionary it is now admitted that the principles of *laissez-faire* with their corollary of unrestrained individualism have failed to promote the best interests of the community. Some form of control of economic relationships is deemed essential and the state as the most effective agency of the larger community is being considered as the proper instrument for the exercise of this control' (quoted in Owram 1986: 171). Even so, the pace of change remained slow. Partly this was because Mackenzie King, prime minister for thirteen interwar years, was naturally – and in view of his unprecedented political success – sensibly cautious; partly it was because he had a political base in Quebec, which at the time was very conservative; but partly it was because of his own fondness for a traditional Liberal outlook on many matters.

Though by Duncan Macarthur's definition this would have made King 'most reactionary,' the historian Jack Granatstein (1994) argues that in 1935 the once and future prime minister still believed in 'orthodox economics' (126). As late as 1943, Bruce Hutchison could write: 'We Canadians can probably claim the distinction of being the most rugged surviving individualists ... The best Liberals, in their hearts, still believe in free trade, the play of natural economic forces, the sanctity of enterprise, and the evil of monopoly. They behold on all sides precisely the opposite ... but they hope that a better day will dawn, that the world will come to its senses, trade again, reduce government interference, abolish monopoly,' and he regarded it as 'the final tragedy of the war [that it] compelled a ministry devoted in theory to a minimum of government into complete and detailed control of the nation's economy' (Hutchison 1943).

In his twenty-three years in office, King many times displayed a reluctance to depart from this traditional *laissez-faire* liberalism, though whether his stubbornness was the result more of ideology or innate political caution is hard to say. At any rate, Jack Pickersgill, who worked in the Prime Minister's Office from 1938 to 1952, tells of how, in 1943, King was even reluctant to introduce family allowances – family allowances! – fearing that they would set English and French Canadians against each other because of the two groups' greatly different birth rates (Pickersgill 1994: 233).

110   The Meaning of Canadian Life

Pickersgill writes of King: 'He said no Canadian government would dare to start providing family allowances ... He felt family allowances would be a greater threat to national unity than any other measure he could think of except conscription' (233). There had been a long debate about family allowances in the late 1920s and early 1930s, with much opposition expressed (see Guest 1980: chap. 5), and it continued to be expressed in 1943.

George Drew, Conservative premier of Ontario and future federal Tory leader, denounced the proposed payments as shameless catering to French Canadians. The incumbent Tory leader, John Bracken, spoke against them outside the House, calling the plan 'a political bribe' (Smith 1995: 149). When the final division came, however, the Conservatives did vote with the Government, to the jeers of Liberal backbenchers (Pickersgill 1994: 236). Their decision followed a Tory caucus meeting in which forty-seven–year-old John Diefenbaker had led the fight for the allowances. In starting off the parliamentary debate for the Conservatives, he went so far as to proclaim that after the war against Hitler was over: 'The state must guarantee and underwrite equal access to security, to education, to nutrition and to health for all' (Smith 1995: 150). The mid-war popularity of interventionist social welfare policies was evidenced by Gallup polls which briefly put the Co-operative Commonwealth Federation (CCF), the forerunner of the New Democratic Party (NDP), ahead of the traditional parties. Mackenzie King responded by swiftly outflanking his political rivals, mainly by means of the Marsh Report – a hastily written facsimile of Britain's famous Beveridge Report – which in 1943 recommended comprehensive state-backed income security for Canadians.

Not everyone was enthralled by the prospect of a Canadian welfare state, however. Tory leader John Bracken's comment on the Marsh Report was that it risked the 'danger of a demoralized people being supported in idleness and rationed poverty' (quoted in Guest 1980: 116). There were also important dissenters outside politics. Charlotte Whitton held fast to the old idealistic individualism, warning in 1946 that the new dominance of interventionist intellectuals in Ottawa reminded her of events in Germany and

'The Most Rugged Surviving Individualists' 111

Italy after 1926 (Owram 1986: 328). In the same year the great University of Toronto economic historian Harold Innis echoed the nineteenth-century Liberal annexationist, Goldwin Smith: 'The opinions of the present writer are those of a Liberal of the old school as yet unconverted to State Socialism, who looks for further improvement not to an increase of the authority of government, but to the same agencies, moral, intellectual, and economical, which have brought us thus far' (Innis 1945: xvii).[3]

Even after the Second World War, Dennis Guest argues, King's government reverted to form and gave up on thoroughgoing reform. In his view, it never actually embraced the Marsh Report, while once the war was over its ardour for intervention cooled measurably. In April 1946, for instance, after making a formal prebudget presentation, the forerunner of the Canadian Labour Congress 'was sharply rebuked by Finance Minister Ilsley for its "costly" demands ... Ilsley's reply was that the government's priorities were for reducing taxes, balancing the budget, and retrenchment' (Guest 1980: 137). The King government did introduce shared-cost National Health Grants in 1948 to assist in disease control, the construction of hospitals, and medical research and training, but Guest argues that it did so mainly because the famous Montreal neurosurgeon, Dr Wilder Penfield, had warned Ottawa that he would have to close the Montreal Neurological Institute and move to the United States if Ottawa were not more forthcoming (Guest 1980: 141).

Louis St Laurent, King's successor, was also slow to expand the influence of the state. 'St. Laurent was not an advocate of the welfare state in any serious sense' (Creighton 1976: 207). In his memoirs, Jack Pickersgill tells how it took a three-year campaign to persuade the prime minister that self-employed fishermen should be eligibile for unemployment insurance, a measure that when it finally came before Parliament in 1956 was supported by all three parties. St Laurent's objections had been, first, that it 'would not be actuarially sound,' which was true, and second, 'that it might prompt costly demands from other groups,' which of course it did (Pickersgill 1994: 419).[4] Lester Pearson, in his memoirs, gently criticizes St Laurent for failing to authorize the building of the

South Saskatchewan dam because it had not passed a cost-benefit test – a comment which says much about both men. St. Laurent is infamous among arts groups, of course, for having taken six years following the Massey Commission's recommendation to set up the Canada Council, apparently because he was opposed to 'subsidizing ballet-dancing' (Creighton 1976: 187). Views such as these, though not necessarily his antipathy for ballet dancing, made St Laurent typical of his age. As Eric Hobsbawm (1994) has written, 'the great boom of the 1950s was presided over, almost everywhere, by governments of moderate conservatives ... The mood of the booming decade was against the Left. This was not a time for change' (283).

A conservative is bound to think that the strong correlation between fiscal caution and robust economic growth exhibited in that era may not have been accidental. In any case, Dennis Guest's verdict on the Liberals' policies in the 1950s is summarized by his appropriation of Liberal policy specialist Tom Kent's term for it: 'Our Conservative Decade': '[The government's] commitment to a comprehensive system of social security, despite the rhetoric of Mackenzie King during World War Two, was shallow. The foot-dragging performance on urgent social security matters which characterized the 1950's is compelling testimony to this fact' (Guest 1980: 142). As we have seen, in 'our conservative decade,' which followed many equally conservative decades, the Canadian and American public sectors spent essentially the same proportion of their respective GNPs. Yet this part of our social policy tradition is almost never talked of. Our 'social policy railway,' if that really is what holds us together, is a very recent construction.

12
The American Lead

So much in politics depends on the shrewd choice of adjective. 'Progressive' as applied to governments has become a synonym both for 'interventionist' or 'activist' and for 'good.' Good government obviously is desirable, but it is no longer so clear that interventionist or activist government is good government. Nevertheless, supposing that the old faith still held and Canadians did yet believe that 'that government is best which governs most – or at least a good deal,' there is ample evidence that by this standard American government has often been more 'progressive' than Canadian and that the United States has many times led Canada in social-policy innovations. Just as the actual railway was built on an American model adapted to Canadian circumstances, so our 'social policy railway,'[1] now widely regarded as being all that holds us together, was in many respects pioneered by the United States. Testimony to this effect is not hard to come by.

The Progressive movement itself, which swept across the United States in the 1890s and brought a sharp increase in the role of government, also had an important effect on Canadian politics and life. Robert Borden's 1907 Halifax Platform, 'an attempt by the Conservative leader to redefine the ideas which formed the core of Canadian political debate ... reflected the influence of American progressivism and other advanced social thinking at the time' (Bothwell, Drummond, and English 1987: 44). It was not until just before the First World War, by which time American

Progressivism had begun to wane, that 'the various loose strands of progressivism in Canada [began] to develop into a national force' (Owram 1986: 78).[2]

Similarly, the Canadian mother's pensions movement of the 1910s and 1920s took inspiration in part from a movement that had gripped the United States in 1911, after itself being sparked by a 'White House Conference on the Care of Dependent Children' presided over by Theodore Roosevelt in 1909 (Guest 1980: 49–50). Missouri and Illinois were the first North American jurisdictions to introduce such pensions, and though most American states and four Canadian provinces (Saskatchewan, Alberta, British Columbia, and Ontario) had them in place by 1920, Nova Scotia did not act until 1930, Quebec until 1938, New Brunswick 1943, and Prince Edward Island and Newfoundland 1949 (Jansson 1988: 97; Canada 1955).

A decade later, Canada's initial reaction to the Great Depression was also cribbed from the Americans. The immediate American response was the infamous Smoot–Hawley Tariff, a protectionist fiasco – by 1932, American imports were down to 2.3 per cent of GDP – which obviously made the Depression much worse: if no one could sell into the U.S. market, who could buy there? R.B. Bennett's government responded with its own protectionist offensive, boasting that it would use tariffs to blast its way into the markets of the world. 'The irony of Canadian anti-Americanism was never more obvious,' write the historians John Herd Thompson and Stephen Randall (1994) 'for these Conservative policies were the mirror images of Republican protectionism and nativism in the United States' (131).

Five years later, the 'Bennett New Deal' was indebted both in name and inspiration to Franklin Roosevelt's. Like Roosevelt's, much of it ran into difficulty in the Supreme Court. To be sure, while the U.S. Supreme Court judged many of the original New Deal's regulatory innovations to be beyond the power of *any* American government, our jurists merely found Ottawa's intitiatives beyond the power of Canada's federal government. The effect was similarly paralytic, however. It wasn't until a constitutional amendment in 1940 that Canada had national unemployment insurance, something the United States had put in place in 1935.³ Nor was the almost three-fold expansion of federal spending in the United States during the 1930s, from $3.1 billion in 1929 to $8.8 billion in 1939, matched in Canada, where Ottawa's spending rose by only 70 per cent in the same ten years, from $405 million to $681 million. Thompson and Randall (1994) point to the International Peace Garden on the Manitoba-North Dakota border as a striking symbol of the two countries' quite different approaches to the Depression: eight years after its dedication in 1932, the American side of the garden bloomed luxuriantly because Franklin Roosevelt's Civilian Conservation Corps had built a dam and planted a real garden; the Canadian side, however, remained 'untended prairie' (136). As Bruce Hutchison wrote in 1943, 'The reforms ... attempted by other nations, Canada has often resisted. It never went in for large expenditures on public works to relieve unemployment and never accepted the theory of deficit spending on its own account as a method of priming the pump' (90–1).

Nevertheless, there was eventually a Canadian New Deal, and it was intended to be radical: announcing it in January 1935, Bennett declared that it marked 'the end of *laisser-faire*' (quoted in Morton 1994: 205). He wasn't the only politician with a say, however. In 1935, as we have seen, W.L. Mackenzie King, who returned to the prime ministership in October of that year, still believed in orthodox economics. In his initial reaction, he could not decide whether the Bennett New Deal was 'Hitlerism, Fascism or Communism' (quoted in Thompson and Randall 1994: 135). Louis-Alexdre Taschereau, the *Liberal* premier of Quebec, was more precise, identifying it as 'a Socialistic venture bordering on Communism' (quoted in D. Morton 1994: 207). This initial reaction persisted. Bruce Hutchison wrote in 1943 that 'when the New Deal burst upon the world, Canadian Liberals and members of Mr. King's government deplored it as basically unsound ... They still believe it to be unsound. They still insist that they will not follow it, but step by step they have been following it' – though only out of wartime necessity, he believed.⁴

The historians Thompson and Randall (1994) summarize

Canadian experience in the 1930s as follows: 'In 1933, the United States and Canada lagged far behind western Europe in government acceptance of responsibility for individual citizens; by 1940, the United States had begun to catch up ... At the end of the 1930s, the United States was the more advanced welfare state, Canada the backward northern neighbor' (134, 140). In this they echo Bruce Hutchison, who wrote in 1943: 'Beside pre-war Canada Britain was almost socialistic, and the New Deal of the United States was wild radicalism ... We are still a very conservative nation by the definitions of these times – perhaps the most conservative nation under the democratic system in the world' (90).

Even after the Depression finally ended, the United States continued to be a hothouse for social-policy innovation. Mackenzie King apparently first heard of Britain's Beveridge Report, which proposed a significant increase in social security, directly from Franklin Roosevelt at their meeting in Washington, DC, in 1942 (Owram 1986: 288). In fact, Thompson and Randall (1994) argue that American radicalism in the 1930s set the stage for that country's conservatism in later decades, and vice versa for Canada: 'In the United States, the success of the New Deal mitigated demands for more radical change; in electoral politics, it incorporated most of the American Left into an amorphous coalition behind Roosevelt and the Democratic party. The bankruptcy of Canadian responses to the depression had the opposite effect and helped to build the Co-operative Commonwealth Federation, a third party ... that dedicated itself to social democratic solutions to the problems of industrial capitalism. These divergent directions would shape the evolution of the welfare states of Canada and the United States, but their effects lay in the future' (140).[5]

The historian David Bercuson and his political scientist colleague Barry Cooper agree that in 1945 'the United States was still far ahead of Canada in the variety of welfare measures that the average American citizen could call on' (Bercuson and Cooper 1994: 81). Lester Pearson's biographer, John English, makes essentially the same point: 'Until the Pearson government, Roosevelt's New Deal had made the United States North America's kinder and gentler place for the poor, the old, and the young' (English

1992: 393). A 1950 review of social security provisions by the International Labour Office demonstrates that several American policies were more 'progressive' than their Canadian counterparts. It's true we had child allowances and they didn't. We also, in two provinces, had hospital insurance, though conditioned on regular payment of a hospital tax, while they had it, strangely enough, only for visiting seafarers. On the other hand, while both countries provided assistance to the elderly, ours went only to needy persons over seventy while in the United States all retirees over sixty-five were paid according to a formula based on previous earnings, a system not adopted in Canada until the Canada Pension Plan of 1966, thirty-one years after Social Security. Similarly, though both countries provided assistance to the dependants of breadwinners who died, Canada did it with discretionary mother's pensions paid by the provinces while the United States used formula-driven Social Security benefits. Finally, though both countries gave money to needy blind persons, in Canada such people had to have been resident for twenty years, a condition not imposed in the United States (ILO 1950).[6]

Nor did American social policy languish after the Democrats lost the White House in 1952. The Congresses of the 1950s repeatedly made Social Security more generous. Amendments in 1950 'began a period of increasing benefits or adding to the system in each election year, demonstrating Social Security's great popularity' (Skidmore 1995: 22). In 1950, benefits were raised and coverage was extended to the self-employed. Benefits were raised again in 1952 and 1954 and coverage granted to self-employed farmers and some professionals. In 1956 disability benefits were introduced and women were given the choice of early retirement. In 1958 benefits were raised yet again and extended to the dependants of disabled beneficiaries. In 1960 disability benefits were offered to people under fifty. In 1961, men, too, got the opportunity to retire at sixty-two (Skidmore 1995: 21–2). After 1954, of course, this all took place under the direction of Senate Majority Leader Lyndon Johnson, whose political motto, borrowed from Franklin Roosevelt, was 'Tax and tax, spend and spend, elect and elect,' hardly the watchword of a nineteenth-century liberal.

There is anecdotal evidence, as well, that the United States was not the Dickensian wasteland that in so many Canadian imaginations it is thought to have been. Business guru Peter Drucker, who sat on the board of the first Blue Cross health insurance system in postwar New England, has noted in an offhand comment that in the 1950s many Canadians even regarded the Americans' health care system as superior to their own: 'Right after World War II, the Habitants came over in tremendous numbers to have their babies because we had hospitals then' (quoted in McLaughlin 1995: 17). Blue Cross negotiated premiums with the Catholic church, then Quebec's primary provider of health care. Incredible but true: Canadians going south for better health care.

As we saw in chapter 5, David Bercuson and Barry Coooper date Canada's modern reformist phase from the government of John Diefenbaker. But even George Grant concedes in *Lament for a Nation* that his political hero took inspiration from the populist democracy of turn-of-the-century Wisconsin[7] (Grant 1965: 14), while Diefenbaker himself once wrote a fawning letter to Huey Long, the Louisiana populist, saying that his 'attitude to wealth inheritance and distribution' – Long was a radical leveller – 'impressed me greatly, and was far in advance of [the] political thought' of the day (quoted in Smith 1995: 80). Even in the 1963 election campaign, 'when anti-Americanism was his ever-present text ... he compared his role as "underdog" to that of President Harry Truman in 1948. Just like Truman, he told whistle stop audiences, "Everybody's against me but the people"' (Thompson and Randall 1994: 228).

The reformist character of Lester Pearson's government was also shaped at least partly by events in the United States. Tom Kent – editor of the *Winnipeg Free Press*, co-drafter of the Liberals' 1958 election platform, and later Pearson's chief policy adviser and principal secretary, a man once accused by C.D. Howe, perhaps accurately, of wanting to import Fabian socialism into Canada – argues that in fact 'there was nothing remarkable about ... [Pearson's] policies. They embodied Canadian versions of the ideas that were in the air of a world where, for instance, [John Kenneth] Galbraith was just finishing the writing of *The Affluent*

Society (it was published that summer) and Kennedy was preparing the presidential campaign that, in its expression of a new, forward-looking spirit, struck responses in many parts of the world besides North America' (Kent 1988: 56). English (1992) puts the matter even more starkly: 'Canada's liberals looked southward again for the breath of new life ... In one of those fundamental shifts in American history between reform and retreat that Arthur Schlesinger, Jr., Kennedy's friend and biographer, has argued are the salient feature of American history, the liberal hour had once again struck, and the sound reverberated in Ottawa as loudly as in Washington' (238).[8]

The hour may actually have sounded more profoundly in Washington. There was a Great Society, after all, before there was a Just Society. U.S. spending on social programs went from $77.2 billion in 1965 to $146 billion just five years later (Bénéton 1985: 76). Perhaps not surprisingly, the number of families in the state of New York receiving assistance under the federal Aid to Families with Dependent Children program went from 1 in 30 in the early 1960s to 1 in 6 in 1970 (Bénéton 1985: 76). In another major exercise in social engineering, by 1978 28 per cent of the school-age population – more than 12 million school children – were subject to compulsory busing aimed at desegregation of the schools (Bénéton 1985: 74) . 'For the first time in American history,' writes the English historian J.R. Pole, equality became a major objective of government policy; and also for the first time ... governments not only made laws but constituted themselves instruments of egalitarian policy' (Pole 1978: 326).

When, because of the apparently slow speed with which the Great Society programs worked, disenchantment with them set in, new, more direct regulatory approaches were tried that aimed not at the traditional American goal of equality of opportunity but rather at equality of outcomes. These involved, to say the least, difficult compromises with – if not outright rejection of – classic American notions of equality. In particular, 'the criterion of race, which was initially rejected in the name of the universalist principles of United States society, later became respectable and was used to bring about equal representation of the races at the various levels of social life' (Bénéton 1985: 73). With the customary lag of a half-decade or so, programs such as pay and employment equity now have made their way to Canada, where the backlash against them by even such a moderate observer as journalist Richard Gwyn suggests they may also be at odds with traditional Canadian values, which in this case sound suspiciously American: 'Aside from being an American import, the "equality of results" doctrine that underpins employment equity programs ... has always run counter to the Canadian grain' (Gwyn 1995: 180).

Perhaps in the end Pearson and Trudeau did lead Canada further down the 'progressive' path than Kennedy and Johnson were able to take the United States. The two countries' public expenditure figures displayed in chapter 5 certainly suggest as much. But the examples just cited put paid to the notion that the United States, in its practice as opposed to its preaching, has always been more dedicated to *laissez-faire* than Canada. In fact, on many important occasions in our history, we have copied their interventions whole cloth.

13
Canadian Free Enterprise

Just as Canadians often overlook the fact that government has always been important, even crucial in the United States, so, too, do they forget the part played in this country's development by our own private sector. Canada was not built by bureaucrats or politicians. Private initiative may have been supplemented by government aid and, as was also true in the United States, may have sought out protective regulation whenever it appeared that such coddling might be forthcoming, but it was private initiative nevertheless. Even worse for kinder/gentler revisionism: private initiative was motivated mainly by profit – or in today's vernacular, by greed.

It could hardly have been otherwise. Despite an obsession for railway construction, for most of our history Canadian governments, like governments everywhere, were simply too small to have played the dominant role they do today. As we have seen, in the first sixty years following Confederation, war years excluded, government spending on goods and services by all Canadian governments never exceeded ten per cent of the country's national output. Providing goods and services isn't all that governments do, of course. They also transfer money among citizens. But until after the Second World War Canada's transfer economy, like most countries', was not at all developed. So it is not too great a stretch to measure governments by their purchases, net of their cash gifts.[1] And by this measure, government was tiny during Canada's formative years. It was not without influence, of course.

Government both caused the CPR to be built before its time and raised tariffs to a level that encouraged Canadian manufacturers in an era in which more manufacturing was thought desirable. But the country was built mainly through private effort: governments were just too small for the job.

Nor was it simply a case of the private sector having filled in, making time until the public sector reached a reasonable size. Quite the contrary, the Canadian private sector thrived. Our commercial past is crowded with self-made men and, very rarely, women who took every advantage of the profit opportunities they either ran across or created for themselves. Indeed, 'practical men seeking profit were the first to sail to the New World' (Bliss 1987: 17). From the very first days of European settlement, cut-throat competition (sometimes literally) has been a hallmark of Canadian business. Rivarly in the fur trade was so intense that for one period beginning in the 1690s the Hudson's Bay Company went twenty-eight years in a row without paying a dividend, despite its supposed monopoly of the trade (Bliss 1987: 83, 82). Nor was it just Europeans who appreciated profit: Samuel Hearne noted in his journal that the standard mark-up charged by Native middlemen to their own people was 1,000 per cent (Bliss 1987: 86 n), a pricing strategy that might well have been appreciated a half-century later by the 'classic amoralist,' Sir George Simpson, who headed the Hudson's Bay Company from 1821 to 1860. 'Utterly ruthless and utterly devoted to the interests of the Company,' Simpson was 'a believer in the view that everyone, native and white alike, had a price' (Bliss 1987: 197), a point he proved in the 1850s when, convinced that competition from Métis and American traders had rendered the company's trading privileges 'almost a nullity,' he suggested to its directors that its charter be surrendered to the crown in exchange for whatever compensation could be had. In a sense, therefore, Canadian dominion from sea to sea was made possible by ruinous, one might even say 'American-style' competition in the fur industry.

Entrepreneurship worthy of Americans also played a starring role in the National Dream. The money that built the CPR came from profits made in a leveraged and barely scrupulous buy-out of an American railway. Putting up only $100,000 cash, a four-man syndicate including George Stephen, president of the Bank of Montreal, bought out the Dutch bondholders of the St Paul, Minneapolis and Manitoba Railway for $5.5 million in the 1870s, partly with the help of a loan from Stephen's bank. With the end of the worldwide recession in 1878, the operation's worth grew to $20 million. There is even evidence that the Stephen group engineered the connivance of the railway's general manager in keeping the company's performance mediocre. At any rate, he later sued the syndicate for not giving him his allotted share of the business. The syndicate certainly did have the assistance of Minnesota's legislature, which for its convenience passed a law allowing the transfer of a railway's land grant when its ownership changed hands. In May 1879, just two years after the buy-out, the syndicate sold the greater part of its new railway's lands for $13,068,887. Over the next several years it floated stocks and bonds that fetched another $21 million on the financial markets. 'Catch them before they invest their profits,' Sir John A. Macdonald was advised in the summer of 1880, as his government looked for a private group to build the CPR, and catch them he did. It is ironic, in view of Canadians' perception of themselves as naive in the ways of business, that our iconic railway was built by sharp financial practices, with the help of an American legislature, in a triumph of what the *Manitoba Free Press* called 'Canadian sagacity,' if not over Yankee ingenuity then at least over Dutch common sense (Berton 1970: 307–36).

Stephen and his partner, Donald Smith, were neither our first nor our last clever businessmen, of course. We have had robber barons and plutocrats aplenty, enough to populate Montreal's famous 'Golden Square Mile' and to twitch the satiric pen of Stephen Leacock, in such works as *Arcadian Adventures with the Idle Rich* (Leacock 1991).[2] By 1900 the Bank of Montreal had 'assets and a volume of transactions as important as any bank in the New York money market,' while about fifty men, 'mostly English and Scottish Protestants in Montreal, either owned or controlled more than one-third of the railways, banks, factories, mines and other properties and resources which constituted

Canada's economic wealth at the time' (Westley 1990: 15, 17). Even our banks, nowadays regarded as ponderous leviathans, were aggressive in their early days: between 1881 and 1908 their failure rate was a swashbuckling 41 per cent, compared to only 22.5 per cent in the United States over roughly the same period (Naylor 1975: 119). Such a wide-open market created the possibility of great success, of course. Primarily as a result of mergers, 'by 1919 the Royal Bank had grown from 25 branches in 1894 to 662, including 74 international branches.'[3] By 1927 the Royal had 900 branches and was paying a 12 per cent dividend (Westley 1990: 189). Its success was due in large part to its president, Sir Herbert Holt, '*the* example of wicked business practices; indeed, he seems to have combined the ruthlessness of the nineteenth century entrepreneurs with the methods of the twentieth century financier' (Westley 1990: 202).

Not that our nineteenth-century financiers weren't also ruthless. Towards the end of the last century it 'was a standard technique of the brokerage firms of the day ... to get together and sell large amounts of a particular stock which they did not own in the expectation that the effect would be to depress its value, at which point the brokers would buy cheap and fill the sale orders they had already contracted to fulfill' (Naylor 1975: 211). The Montreal Stock Exchange's attempt to police itself against such practices is one reason the upstart Toronto Exchange, begun as an outlet for penny mining stocks, began gradually to overtake it (Westley 1990: 178–9). At the turn of the century, the Canada Life group of insurance companies, headed by Senator George Cox, originally of Peterborough, was notorious for what today would be called 'self-dealing,' even to the point of being investigated by a royal commission in 1906. One member of the Cox group, Sir Joseph Flavelle, a captain of Canadian industry and a patron of both the University of Toronto and the Toronto General Hospital, received a $50,000 loan from the Cox-owned Imperial Life Assurance Company, of which he was a shareholder, which was officially paid back one 31 December and then renewed the following 2 January, so that the transaction would escape the attentions of the Dominion Insurance Commissioner (Bliss 1978: 70).

In wartime some Canadians' unrestrained desire for profit took dangerous turns. During the First World War there were instances of inspection marks being erased on gun shells and of the use of fraudulent inspection stamps. On one Canadian shipment of 6-inch shells, holes in the casings had been filled with paint and British inspectors rejected 90 per cent of the lot (Bliss 1978: 271, 287). In his recent book, *Nationalism without Walls*, Richard Gwyn (1995) says the thing that most impressed the friends of an acquaintance of his who returned home to Italy for a visit was that 'in Canada, there's no point in trying to bribe the judges' (114). We may all be boy scouts now, but in the past many of our businessmen have been aggressive to the point of illegality – and beyond.

If in the last century the Canadian private sector knew how to make money, it also knew how to spend it. The grand houses the Montreal millionaries built for themselves in the area bounded by Dorchester and Pine, Bleury and Guy had 'lavish' interiors, with 'walnut or oak panelling and woodwork ... marble fireplaces, and ornate plaster cornices ... There were stables and often gatehouses and conservatories on the grounds [and] the grounds of one estate flowed into the next, so that the whole area was a huge park' (Westley 1990: 26). The children of the plutocrats entertained themselves in a style that would not have been out of place in Newport or New York. One daughter's dance cards from the late 1920s indicate that she 'attended forty balls in one season,' while thirty years later a scion of the Square Mile reminisced: 'Oh, the parties of the twenties! Never again can their like be seen in Canada. All the facilities were at hand. Houses were still large, and sometimes immense. Servants were taken for granted. Money was not worth thinking about. Everyone had time, and no one had worries. We dined and dined. Even among ourselves in our parents' houses there were "white ties," good food, and the ordered procession of wines' (quoted in Westley 1990: 150).

Which is hardly consistent with our self-image as the legatees of stodgy, self-denying, Presbyterian drones. But even today, we are better at capitalism than our view of ourselves as well-meaning underachievers would suggest. How else to explain our drastic overrepresentation among the world's billionaires. In 1995, according to *Forbes'* magazine, there was one Canadian (Kenneth Thomson) in the top ten, compared to only two Americans (Warren Buffett and Bill Gates), and we had three (Thomson, the Irving family, and Charles Bronfman) who were worth more than $2.2 billion, compared to forty-two in the United States, which isn't far from equivalent, controlling both for differences in the two countries' population and for the fact that one of the Americans was a Bronfman (Edgar Miles Bronfman, Sr). As Richard Gwyn (1995) has noted, in years in which the Canadian dollar was higher and real estate markets sounder, we did even better in this type of ranking (89). In the mid-1980s we placed three people or families in the world's twenty richest, not counting our head of state (Elizabeth II).[4]

To be sure, Canadian plutocrats may have specialized rather more in the exploitation of natural resources than their American counterparts – even if the greatest plutocrat of all, John D. Rockefeller, made his money in oil, the ultimate natural resource. But what of it? If Providence had not wished us to sell natural resources, She, He, or It would not have piled our plate so high with them, and instead would have given us more millions of people and fewer millions of acres. If we had the same ratio of the one to the other as, for example, the Japanese, we doubtless would be as little reliant on natural resources as they are.

Our unease at harvesting resources presumably stems from a belief that doing so is unchallenging: we merely gather rocks and chop down trees – 'hew wood and draw water,' as our ancient industrial motto puts it – while the Japanese and others must use their brains to survive. Yet the day is long past, if it ever existed, when our most valuable resources presented themselves on the ground like manna. Now they cower, often in the deepest, most fly-infested corners of our far-flung tundra. First they have to be found, and then they have to be dug up from far underground. Or they have to be carefully trimmed, artfully felled, and then floated or dragged or even now helicoptered to a computer-driven X-ray machine before being sawn into lumber in the most economical way possible. Harvesting resources has seldom been easy. Thus Michael Bliss contrasts what he calls 'the Martin Frobisher view of Canada as a rich land whose people would have been much wealthier if only its businessmen had been more enterprising' with the reality, first, that 'there has been no shortage of enterprise in Canadian history,' and, second, that 'it has been a harsh land, difficult to extract wealth from, and gravely handicapped by its small population and its peoples' and governments' great expectations' (Bliss 1987: 11).

Even if it *were* easy to market resources – which it usually isn't – if the world needs them, and we can make money selling them, why not do it? Others would in our place. No less an economic authority than Singapore's Lee-Kuan Yew has told us that doing what comes naturally is only, well, natural: 'Why should you bestir yourself in the same way as I have had to? We started off in the 1960s with a per capita GNP of about $1000US. Yours would have been $US7–8000. Your per capita GNP in 1991 – which wasn't a spectacular year – was around $US22,000. But last year ours was only $12,000. That's half yours ... What is life for? ... When you reach a certain level of life where you can afford to talk of leisure and recreation and the finer things of life, then your focus changes. I think that's natural' (Koller 1993: 106).What people do with their money once they've got it, not whether they came by it easily or with great difficulty, is the best measure of their worth. Only the very insecure or the very thick – and at times we are both – worry that they haven't exercised sufficient cleverness making their fortune.

It is also true that many of our plutocrats who did not make their fortunes in resources prospered because of protection afforded them by the National Policy tariffs. But, as we have seen, America's Republicans also favoured high tariffs and had them in place from the end of the Civil War on. The resultingly agreeable slope of the industrial playing-field has not dimmed their delight in their own entrepreneurship nor diminished their celebration of it nor our respect for it. As long as there have been governments, successful entrepreneurship has required their fastidious cultivation. Such skills may not be emphasized in the business schools, but they are business skills none the less. If our legislators repeatedly have spoiled their own market by making such favours too readily available, that is hardly the fault of our businessmen.

PRISONERS OF PRECEDENT?

The last four chapters were meant to demonstrate two things: first, that at many times in their history the Americans have used government as much, if not more than, we have, often in exactly the same way we have. Thus, if we seek distinctiveness from them, not being 'ideological' won't do it: for the most part, they aren't, either. In fact, on many occasions they have led us in interventions, at least some of which we have then come to think of as characteristically our own. Second, both *laisser-faire* ideology and the private sector have been quite important in Canada's history. These latter points have been elaborated in (as is most natural for a non-historian) an anecdotal way, but perhaps Figure 9.1, which showed how small Canadian governments were through much of the country's history, including its relatively recent history, will take the place of many words: for most of our history more than ninety per cent of our economic life has been conducted by the non-government sector.

None of this is to suggest that we haven't used government a great deal, that we haven't in recent years used it more than the Americans, or that they, at least in their national rhetoric, haven't been wedded to the market. But it seems clear that the period of our most marked distinctiveness, at least in terms of government spending, did not begin until the 1960s. It is also evident that, despite our famous longing for distinctiveness, we have always been acutely conscious of American precedents. How Congress had financed the Union Pacific was discussed at length in the House of Commons debates on the CPR contract. And we have often borrowed from them liberally, and Liberally, especially when America's presidents were powerful and attractive leaders like the Roosevelts and John Kennedy. But we have borrowed from them in conservative eras, too. Mackenzie King's and then R.B. Bennett's initial reactions to the Great Depression were scarcely more enlightened than Herbert Hoover's, while Brian

Mulroney's market-oriented reforms were widely criticized for supposedly having been inspired by his friendship with and obvious admiration for Ronald Reagan. If we *are* prone to borrow from the United States, presumably this is because we are the only substantially English-speaking country that lives right beside them. If we are more influenced by the United States than other countries are, what of it? Who else is in our position?

What our history has been and how much we are bound by it are separate questions, however. Even supposing it were true that we had, everywhere and always, used government more than the Americans, should this determine how we conduct ourselves in future? The CPR having been financed by subsidy, should public subsidy continue to be our principal tool of economic development? Canada having been built and peopled partly by the very visible hand of government, should that hand continue to manipulate our affairs as much as it does? Both precedent and precedent's accumulation – tradition – do and should count for something. A people gets used to organizing itself in certain ways, and many Canadians do seem more complacent about – or even welcoming of – government intervention than many Americans do. Of course, if tradition were the only consideration, we'd still be travelling back and forth between Winnipeg and Montreal by voyageur canoe. But the question here is not 'will we?' but *'should* we?' continue to do things in what so many of us think of as the distinctively Canadian way we did them in the 1880s? With the issue cast in these terms, the answer can only be 'no, not necessarily.'

Many things have changed since the last century, only the most obvious being that Canada is now geographically complete. The English historian Frederic William Maitland wrote that 'it is very difficult to remember that events now in the past were once far in the future' (quoted in Schlesinger 1995). The Canadians who in the 1880s built the CPR did not know whether what is now the western part of Canada would continue on as part of British North America. To ensure that it did, they may well have been justified in taking drastic action (probably the mildest way to characterize the construction of a transcontinental railway by a nation of 4 million people). But the question of political independence has long since been decided. Railway policy is no longer a part of national security.

In the debate over precisely what course of action 'no, not necessarily' will imply, we can expect to be told that we should persevere in what we think of as our traditional way, using government more than the Americans, so as to fulfil the important national goal of maintaining our distinctiveness. But this raises a batch of new questions. Are we as distinctive as we think? Is it really so important that we be distinctive? And what is the appropriate role of government in making us distinctive?

14
The Unimportance of Being Different

At bottom, how crucial is it that Canada be different from the United States? Not separate. Assume for the moment that we maintain our separateness from them. They have not challenged it, and few of us want to give it up.[1] So we probably won't have to. But to what extent should we consciously strive to use the legal separateness we now possess to be different from the United States?

Consider identical twins – an apt analogy, since, to our frequent distaste, the world at large thinks of us as largely indistinguishable from the Americans. Twins are separate beings but often are not very different. Being separate, should they strive to be different? They often do, of course, if sometimes in destructive ways. If one is an overachiever, the other may deliberately underachieve. Thus our lower income per capita does distinguish us from the Americans, but would we be so indifferent to this or so quick to discount wealth's importance if ours were the higher income? If one twin becomes richer and more famous, the other may stew in secret envy, a common Canadian syndrome as far as the Americans are concerned. Perhaps our greatest source of annoyance is that, despite our many virtues, the world, especially the American part of it, takes such little note of us. As columnist Jeffrey Simpson has put it, Americans 'know and care the square root of squat about Canada' (quoted in Thompson and Randall 1994: 3).

In fact, being different from the Americans should not concern us in the least. We should strive to be *better* than they are, in the sense of running a society that provides the greatest possible happiness for the greatest number of our citizens. All societies should try for that. That is what societies are for, presumably. But how different or similar to the Americans this leaves us is of little consequence. When they do things better than we do – technological innovation is a good example – we shouldn't shrink from copying them, even if this means abandoning what we may regard as our traditional interventionist approach to government-industry relations and opting for the less planned, more chaotic style of economic life that many analysts regard as the secret to American technological dynamism (see Porter 1990).

DIAGNOSTIC DIFFICULTIES

If we do become convinced that running a better society than the Americans requires us to use government more than they do, we obviously should not shrink from it. But whether greater-than-American intervention really is necessary depends on whether Americans' lesser use of government is what causes whichever of their problems we wish to avoid. A decent regard for the limitations of social science requires humility in making judgments about causality in questions this complex.

To take but one example, is violent crime in America's inner cities the result of too little government or too much? Too little, many Canadians would say, thinking of the Americans' free-spirited approach to gun control and less generous welfare payments. And yet, with greatly different gun laws, murder rates on the Canadian Prairies are not much different from those in neighbouring American states, and in some cases they are higher. For instance, from 1976 to 1980 the murder rate averaged 3.7 per 100,000 people in Manitoba, but only 2.4 in Minnesota and 1.2 in North Dakota.[2] Nor is there any clear connection between either tax rates or welfare rates and murder rates within Canada. New Brunswick, a province with low welfare benefits, had a murder rate of 2.9 per 100,000, higher than more generous Ontario (2.1), but lower than another generous province, British Columbia (3.6). It also had a

The Unimportance of Being Different 133

higher rate than the neighbouring states of Maine (2.7), New Hampshire (2.6), and Vermont (2.8) (Kopel 1992: 159 fn).

Of course, Canadians who attribute the greater rate of violence in the United States to its lighter-handed approach to government may also have in mind the official deference paid to Americans accused of crime, beginning with the famous *Miranda* decision in 1966. Our own police's approach to criminal suspects often seems less gentle. In recent years, a surprising number of young, black residents of our major cities have fallen victim, during police apprehension, to the accidental discharge of state-owned revolvers, while in Montreal in 1993 a recalcitrant (white) taxi driver subdued by the police fell into a coma from which he eventually died, a misadventure for which the police officer in charge was sentenced to forty-five weekends in jail. Evidently, our greater use of government in the interest of preserving peace, order, and good government may sometimes take turns that are neither so kind nor gentle as we are accustomed to think. Perhaps the lack of a sufficiently aggressive government *is* the Americans' problem.[3]

The mayor of Baltimore, among others, has argued, in contrast, that much of American urban violence is caused by too much government – in particular, by the prohibition of various kinds of recreational drugs, which drives the drug trade underground, increasing both its risk and its return and thereby creating an irresistible financial incentive for young urban males, many of them black, to become involved in it. Stop the war on drugs, he argues, and you will stop most urban violence. He may be right. The financial return to drug trafficking may now be so great that even a very generous, Canadian-style welfare system, one with our 'Don't ask, Don't tell' approach to catching cheaters, would not greatly alter the incentives that such huge financial temptations create. When children can earn hundreds of dollars a week serving as lookouts, an increase in welfare payments of even $50 or $75 a week may not cause all that many to alter their occupational choice. Put American ghettoes on 'pogy,' and the infusion of cash might simply increase the demand for drugs, thereby raising the return to trafficking still further.

Overregulation of big-city housing markets, in the form of

aggressive rent controls, may also have played a part in the demise of many American inner cities. Rent controls reduce the incentive for landlords to put up new buildings or maintain old ones. The mere fact that a nation's housing stock is ageing needn't lead to urban violence, of course. Many Europeans live in literally ancient dwellings, and yet the murder rate is lower in Rome, Athens, and Paris than in Detroit, Chicago, and New York. But when even non-ancient buildings are not maintained, those who live in them may become increasingly demoralized. When the landlord is of a different race, such neglect can result in racial hatred. When the landlord is the government, it can result in anarchy. Best remember that 'the projects,' the generic urban tenements of cinematic, literary, and folkloric fame, were invariably public housing projects.

The racial make-up of American inner cities is also quite different from Canada's, or at least from what Canada's has been, so it may be that violence in these areas has less to do with government than with the sociology of whatever it is that causes racial differences in social data. 'The overall death rate for non-Hispanic white Americans from all types of shootings (murder, suicide, accident, etc.) is the same as the rate for Canadians,' while if, whatever their race, Americans born in the south are excluded, the American crime rate is comparable to Canada's (Kopel 1992: 159). In many ways, history and even geography (despite our harsher weather) have been kinder to us than to the Americans. If 12 per cent of our population were the descendants of slaves, and another several million had entered our country illegally, we might be a much less peaceful place than we are. But history largely spared us the legacy of slavery – for reasons having very little to do with our greater love of government or, for that matter, black people – while geography decreed that the southern neighbour with whom we share such a long and lightly garrisoned border was richer than ourselves, not several-fold poorer, as is the case with the United States's southern neighbour.

But even if the white United States *is* a more racial or racist society than white Canada – a premise that would be difficult to establish with certainty until we had lived with the U.S. demo-

The Unimportance of Being Different 135

graphic make-up for a time – is it really Americans' lesser use of government that has caused the higher level of racial tension in their society? In fact, the problem may result from *overgovernment*. Until the middle of the last century, American courts generally sanctioned private property rights in the ownership of human beings, while, for the purposes of calculating intergovernmental grants and congressional representation, its constitution notoriously counted slaves as equal to three-fifths of a white person. One of the most famous U.S. Supreme Court decisions of the pre–Civil War era – the case of fugitive slave Dred Scott – ruled that property rights in slaves had to be enforced throughout the United States, even in non-slave states. No doubt slavery would have been much less successful an institution had it not been so effectively policed by government.[4]

In fact, economic analysis argues that discrimination usually cannot succeed without enforcement by government. The reason is that in a market system any firm that can pay a worker less than his or her productivity will become very profitable. Moreover, such success will be emulated. Other firms will wish to employ members of the underpaid group, and the consequent rush to employ them will raise their wages, thus eliminating the exploitation. If workers are to continue to be underpaid, some way must be found to enforce sanctions against employers who bid wages up to acquire more of the cheap labour. Vigilante terrorism, such as that practised by the Ku Klux Klan, may do the job, but compared to rigorously enforced laws against various racially homogenizing practices terrorism is an unreliable means of social control.

Many of the civil rights marches of the 1960s in the southern United States were aimed at government ordinances, particularly polling laws, that enforced discrimination. More recently it has become clear that even laws designed to end discrimination, if they are race-conscious, can contribute to racial tension. In the 1996 elections, Americans in several states struck down racial hiring mandates that in many voters' eyes perpetuate racial division, rather than eliminate it. In the usual Canadian way, we are beginning the wholesale adoption of such practices, just as, on the basis of their lengthier experience with them, Americans are deciding that they do more harm than good.[5]

In sum, if we wish to make our society better than the Americans', and are convinced that some of the improvements that we seek can be achieved only by using government more than they do, then we should go ahead. But before doing so we should be as sure as we can that the differences between our societies really are the result of public policy, and not other historical, geographical, or cultural differences or simply pure chance. And if we conclude that the Americans' policies are as good as policy can be – which obviously needn't mean perfect – we should feel no compunction about adopting the very same policies, including on more frequent occasions than has been our recent custom, the policy of having no policy at all.

Perhaps this way of conducting our affairs is so obviously sensible that no one would disagree with it. But if that were the case, statements such as 'we do things differently here' or 'collective action comes more naturally to us' or (with a sneer) 'that's the American way of doing things' would not be so common a refrain in our politics. Whether to use government in a given instance would be decided instead on the basis of a clear-headed judgment about whether such use could reasonably be expected to improve matters – that is, create more benefits than costs. If as a result we end up with policies that are greatly different from or exactly the same as the Americans' is of no real consequence. Policies are means. What count are ends. The important thing is that *we* decide our policies and decide them so as to attain the ends we want. Whether our ends are best achieved by means similar to or different from what the Americans do may be of interest to sociologists but should not worry the rest of us.

All this may sound very much like the Liberal pragmatism ridiculed above: every case will be examined on its merits and no pre-judgments will be made. All problems will be treated as unique, a way of looking at the world that leads, in Kundera's phrase, to the unbearable lightness of being: because every case is different, no learning can take place from experience. In fact, experience can teach, even in social science. As chapters 17 and 18

The Unimportance of Being Different 137

relate, decisions to intervene should be informed by reasonable estimates of the costs of future interventions, based partly on knowledge of the often-substantial costs of past interventions.

THE LEFT: SELECTIVE OSMOSIS

The idea that we needn't differ from the Americans in our choice of policy, if that is what will provide us with the best outcomes, often rankles. Many Canadians seem to see it as a national obligation to be as different as possible in as many ways as possible from the Americans. This is particularly true of the left, which is generally contemptuous of American society, no more so than when busy pilfering policy ideas from it. (Always scornful of branch-plant industry, they have never much minded branch-plant ideas.) Richard Gwyn recently charged Canadian neoconservatism with the same crime: 'For the first time in Canadian history a clutch of distinctively American political ideas are being injected into the Canadian bloodstream' (Gwyn 1995: 60). The idea is, of course, preposterous. Most of the causes the Canadian left has injected into the Canadian bloodstream in recent decades – from participatory democracy, to affirmative action, to pay equity, and charter rights – were straight steals from the American left, albeit with the usual five-year lag.[6]

Canadian intellectual osmosis is ideologically selective, however. The ideas of American conservatives – or, even worse, the despised 'neoconservatives' – are always resisted, invariably on the grounds that we Canadians must maintain our distinctiveness. Should anyone think of imitating the Gingrich Republicans or introducing term limits or parliamentary recall or cutting arts subsidies, well, 'that's not the way we do things here.' But when we rip off the Peace Corps with the Company of Young Canadians or, on a larger scale, the Great Society with the Just Society, for some reason national distinctiveness is no longer an issue. We and the Americans may join arms and march off together singing the *Internationale*.

Maybe the Canadian left really does make its choices on the basis of ends. Thus it copies the Americans when the means they have adopted are good ones for achieving left ends and ridicules them when the left, or at least the non-right, no longer controls the White House or Congress and American means therefore are no longer appropriate to left ends. The ends sought are unchanging – bigger and bigger government, greater and greater social control – and the left will use whatever arguments work. If appeals to nationalism do, fine. But if the Americans actually are doing the sorts of things the Canadian left would like to see done here, appeals to nationalism are put on hold. In effect, the maple leaf is strategically useful only when the right is running the United States. Thus the Canadian version of 'my country, right or wrong' is 'my country, whenever left.'

A foolish consistency may be the hobgoblin of small minds, but consistency in fundamental arguments is not foolish. If the maple leaf really is just a flag of convenience, run up the pole if whichever policy being pushed is deemed sufficiently distinctive from related American policies, but kept in its canister when the Americans already have regulated or legislated in the areas where action is desired, it would be more seemly to banish from our political discussions any and all reference to how such-and-such a policy is needed so we can 'establish our distinctiveness.'

THE NON-LEFT

Of course, even Canadians who aren't social democrats – and there are some – also seem to value distinctiveness from the Americans. Perhaps there is an innate human desire to want to be different, even if humans also crave conformity. The wish to accentuate national differences is in fact a strange mix of these desires, for we must conform enough among ourselves to establish a recognizably Canadian way of doing things, yet be different enough collectively to diverge sufficiently from the American example. Or perhaps our wish to be distinctive is really a craving for attention. How do we make ourselves noticed, living cheek by jowl with the crass menagerie that is the modern United States? But if so, our reason for struggling as we do to distinguish ourselves is mere exhibitionism, to attract the attention of foreigners, which hardly seems worthy of us – and certainly doesn't accord with our official version of ourselves, which is that we are rather becomingly modest, at least when compared with the rampant egoists living south of us.

We may overestimate our modesty, of course. Unlike the truly modest (Mother Teresa almost never told people how modest she was), we often proclaim it ourselves, and it has rarely prevented us from expounding at great length on the important question of by exactly how much our society is superior to the Americans.' The historians Thompson and Randall (1994) refer to 'two centuries of feeling morally superior to the United States' (196). At times, oxymoronically – or just plain moronically – we even seem proud of our modesty.

A better life might be regarded as its own reward, but we want both the better life and to be famous for it. If our sometimes more interventionist public policies do get us this better life than the Americans, then perhaps people will notice us. However, while good men die unknown, crazed gunmen become famous. There are much easier ways of being noticed than running a good society. The route we are on now, to be known as the North Americans who love paying taxes, is one. Being the North Americans whose governments have Third World–sized debts is another.

CANADIANISM AND DARWINIAN CULTURAL SELECTION

Another possible reason for consciously striving to be not just better than the Americans, but also different, possibly even at the expense of better, has to do with an essentially horticultural view of societies. As is well known, monoculture can be bad for forests. Grow only one species of tree and your forest is much more vulnerable to disease and destruction. The greatest such disaster was U.S. shipping tycoon Daniel Ludwig's failure to transplant the hardwood gmelina tree to a tract of Brazil half the size of Belgium, a misadventure that cost his company $1 billion (Foster 1995). In horticulture, as in the stock market, diversity is much the sounder strategy. In this view, the world should quite self-consciously resist the overwhelming thrall of American culture and society and deliberately cultivate alternatives. If instead the alternatives, such as Canada, become extinct, human cultural and societal evolution will be deprived of species that – we will never know – may have been better adapted to the different stresses and strains to which societies will be subject in future decades. Northrop Frye may have had something like this in mind when he wrote: 'It is of immense importance to the United States itself that there should be other views of the human occupation of this continent, rooted in different ideologies and different historical traditions' (Frye 1982: 70).

But argument by analogy is always dangerous. The world is not a forest, and the societies that make it up are not species of tree. Unlike the pine or chestnut, they can adapt, often rather quickly, to changes in their environment. Before there was Darwin there was Jean-Baptiste Lamarck (1744–1829), whose theory of evolution was that animals adjust their characteristics to changes in their material circumstances and then pass these new characteristics on to their progeny. Thus short-necked giraffes can grow long necks in a few generations if that is what changing tree heights require. Darwin and his successors have shown that the biological world is not Larmarckian. But the societal world may well be. Even if the American style of society were to become universally dominant in the next fifty years, this does not mean that it could not adapt to whatever challenges arose in the decades after that. In fact, there is every evidence that modern, American-style societies both crave change and are very good at it. From Kitty Hawk to Tranquility Base took only sixty-six years and transformed the industrialized world utterly. To be sure, contemporary humans suffer all sorts of change-related neuroses; still those who live in the industrialized countries, including Canadians, regularly tell their pollsters, however, that they are quite happy – and there is no question that they live longer and more comfortably than their forebears.

Survivability isn't everything, of course. A single, dominant culture might not be subject to the perils of biological monoculture, but its dominance probably would involve a reduction in cultural diversity (even if there is great diversity within the

United States), and that probably would be a bad thing. Diversity is not necessarily good, however. If everyone spoke a different language, diversity's main effect would be Babel – universal incomprehension. If we all spoke the same language, however, there would be no chance for cross-fertilization of languages. Between these extremes of complete diversity and no diversity at all there presumably is some optimal level of diversity: enough to allow differences to persist but not so much as to prevent cultures from rubbing against each other in creative ways. But how do we find the optimum? Cultures have to interact enough so as to leaven each other, but not so much that one devours the others. Thus when Japan had not yet been 'discovered' it was of no cultural use to the West, but neither is it any use if the Japanese become Americans. Somewhere between complete integration and complete isolation is the optimal amount of cultural interaction. Managing diversity is obviously a very tricky task. An economist predisposed by training to mistrust grand plans is bound to think that first calculating and then achieving this optimum is an impossibly difficult piece of social engineering.

An obvious counterargument is that even though the optimal degree of cultural intermingling is hard to calculate, it is unlikely to be zero, as it would be if all non-American cultures were allowed to die. So perhaps it is true that deliberate attempts to preserve Canadian distinctiveness should be made – with government's help, if necessary. 'If necessary' should be emphasized, however. If Canadians really do benefit from having a separate culture, they may be willing to support it in other ways than paying higher taxes, the first resort of most cultural nationalists.

Maybe, however, we needn't struggle against our fate but instead should face up to the no-doubt-depressing possibility that even if the world does need cultural diversity, it may not need us. We may be the OECD-equivalent of one of the sixty Native Canadian languages said to be on the verge of extinction: the world may little note our passing nor long remember us after we are gone. On a planet that also includes fundamentalist Islam, Chinese communism, and the tribal dictatorships of Africa, we offer precious little social variation from the Americans. Like it or not, as societies go, we just aren't that different. Foreigners lump us in with the Americans not simply out of ignorance but for the very good reason that if we were that much different, they would have heard more about us. Even Seymour Martin Lipset, perhaps the leading American Canadophile, says that the two countries 'probably resemble each other, more than any two nations on earth' (quoted in Kopel 1992: 136). If we really do wish to do our bit for the diversity of the world's cultures, we might be better off sending foreign aid to other, more different societies. As for getting our own place on the Ark, any of a dozen European countries – Belgium, Holland, Norway, perhaps – should be ahead of us in line: each is even more different from the Americans than we are, and each has its own language, to boot.

15
Distinct Society?

For all the emotional and legislative effort we have put into creating our own distinctiveness, just how different are we from the Americans? By world standards, not very different at all. And what differences there are don't always run in the direction we normally think. A quiz may help. In which of the two countries are people more educated? The OECD says that Canadians spend a larger share of their GDP on education than any other industrialized country, and everyone knows how expensive U.S. university tuition is. So presumably we are more educated. In fact, in 1980, 'the average native-born American male in the adult labour force had 12.7 years of education, whereas the comparable Canadian had 11.3 years' (Reitz and Breton 1994: 99). University education? Almost one-quarter of Americans (24 per cent) have university degrees, compared to only 15 per cent of Canadians (Bishop 1996: Table 6).

How about economic data? In Table 15.1, which country is Canada and which is the United States? Maybe that's too easy. Everyone knows that the United States has a less equal distribution of income than we do. Which means that, yes, 'country A' is the United States and 'country B' is Canada. But the underwhelming size of the difference may be surprising. The poorest fifth of our population makes more than the poorest fifth of theirs, but it still makes less than 5 per cent of total income. And our bottom 40 per cent make only 15.6 per cent of the total. Granted, that's more than in the United States, where the bottom 40 per

144 The Meaning of Canadian Life

TABLE 15.1
Before-government income distributions, 1987

Share of pre-tax, non-transfer income (in per cent) earned by:	Country A	Country B
Poorest fifth of population	3.5	4.8
Next poorest fifth	9.6	10.8
Middle fifth	16.7	17.4
Second highest fifth	26.0	25.5
Highest fifth	44.2	41.5

SOURCE: Blackburn and Bloom (1993), Table 7.4.

cent make only 13.1 per cent of all income, but it's not that much more.

It's also not very much, period. However, statistics on income distribution are notoriously tricky. The bottom fifth probably includes most pre-med students, whose annual income is very low now but who will do quite well financially once they graduate. It may also include people who have a good deal of wealth. If you own a million-dollar house in West Vancouver, live in it rather than rent it out, and get by on the interest on $300,000 worth of bonds, you're very likely still to be in the bottom 40 per cent of the income distribution. Nipissing University economist Christopher Sarlo reports that in 1990 42 per cent of the 150,000 Canadian households and individuals who reported having no or negative income were employed, while 26 per cent were homeowners, most mortgage-free (Sarlo 1996b: 165).

Table 15.2 involves a slightly more difficult pick. It shows how people in the two countries do after the government has both taxed them and redistributed the resulting revenues in the form of cash transfers to old-age pensioners, the unemployed, scholarship students, and so on. After taxes and transfers, country A has 1.7 per cent more of its population classified as 'poor' than country B does (using the American poverty line for both countries). That is, 1.7 more out of every 100 of country A's citizens falls below the poverty line than is the case in country B. Country B, however, has 1.5 per cent more 'near poor' than country A, and it

TABLE 15.2
Income needs, 1986

	Country A	Country B
Poor (below poverty line)	13.5	11.8
Near-poor (1 to 2 times poverty line)	16.7	18.2
Upper income (more than 2 times poverty line)	69.8	70.0

SOURCE: Blank and Hanratty (1993), Table 6.4.

has slightly more upper-income citizens, with 'upper income' defined as more than twice the income at the poverty line. Which country is which? Not to end the suspense prematurely, but Country A is the United States, and Country B, Canada. That more Americans are poor presumably doesn't surprise most Canadians. That Canada has both more near-poor and more upper-income citizens than the United States probably does.[1]

Still, most Canadians probably would have thought that the difference was more than 1.7 fewer poor citizens per 100, especially since that number includes the effect of our more redistributive tax and cash-transfer programs. There's little doubt, incidentally, that government redistribution of income does work. We actually start out with 17.5 per cent of our population in poverty (compared with only 15.4 per cent in the United States). Taxes and government cash transfers reduce that to the 11.8 per cent shown in Table 15.1. That's a 5.7–point drop in the poverty level resulting from our higher taxes and more generous transfers. In effect, out of every hundred Canadians, almost six fewer people end up poor than started out poor before taxes and government kick in. By contrast, only two Americans get moved above the poverty line as a result of taxes and transfers. So we do get something for all the extra taxes we pay.[2]

But given all that we do spend through our public sector – almost half of GDP – you might think that we would get even more of a reduction in poverty. We do manage to narrow the 'poverty gap' – the difference between the poverty line and what people classified as poor make on average. To be precise, we narrow it by U.S.$2,297 (in 1986 dollars). But the Americans, who tax and spend much less than we do, nevertheless manage to close it by $1,553. So we're doing only $744 per poor person better than they are at closing the poverty gap. That's U.S.$744, but it may not be as much as we'd like to think. Multiplying $744 times the number of poor Canadians[3] gives $2.38 billion. Translating from U.S. dollars to Canadian dollars gives $3.3 billion. So in total we did about $3.3 billion better than the Americans at closing the poverty gap.

But in 1986, the year studied in the research from which all this is drawn, Canadian governments spent a total of $233 billion, of which our $3.3 billion better-than-the-Americans anti-poverty performance represented 1.4 per cent. In 1986, however, our public sector wasn't 1.4 per cent larger than the Americans'; it was 36.5 per cent larger. The extra 35.1 per cent – almost $82 billion – apparently isn't going into poverty reduction.[4] If we made our public spending less 'universal,' and instead targeted it more directly at poor people, we could have both a smaller public sector, which would mean lower taxes, and a 'bigger bang' for our poverty-reduction buck.

One reason our social welfare system gives more money to the poor than the Americans' does, as all Canadians know, is that we provide much more generous social assistance than they do. If you compare welfare payments across states and provinces, how many of each end up in the list of the top ten most generous North American jurisdictions? In 1995, as many Canadians no doubt would have expected, the result was 10–0. Except that it was 10–0 for the Americans. Not one Canadian province made the top ten, though Ontario did come in at number 11.[5] Beating it out were Hawaii, Alaska, Connecticut, Massachusetts, the District of Columbia, Rhode Island, New York, New Jersey, California, and New Hampshire – 'Live free or die,' rock-hard Republican New Hampshire! Ontario offered a single parent with two children $22,087 a year. New Hampshire provided $22,352, New York $24,804, Rhode Island $24,954, Connecticut $27,868 (with all figures in Canadian dollars, converted at an exchange rate of 73.8 cents per U.S. dollar). Where did the other provinces end up?

British Colmbia was 16th, PEI 30th, Nova Scotia 31st, Quebec 38th, Alberta 39th, Manitoba 44th, Newfoundland 51st, Saskatchewan 53rd, and New Brunswick 56th. Only five states – Louisiana, Arkansas, Tennessee, Alabama, and Mississippi – paid less than New Brunswick's $15,714 (Walker and Emes 1996: Table 1). We clearly have to start rethinking our traditional view of the United States.

Which country has the higher wages? Canadian opponents of the Canada-United States Free Trade Agreement (FTA) argued that opening our markets would force our wages down to U.S. levels. In 1994, however, U.S. manufacturing wages averaged US$17.10 an hour, while Canadian manufacturing workers received only $15.68 (Gordon 1996: 27). Of course, 1994 was five years into the FTA, so perhaps our lower wages are proof of the damage the deal has done. However, while he was still busy denouncing free trade in 1990, David Peterson's government in Ontario was running ads in *Fortune* magazine that showed potential industrial investors how Ontario's wages were lower than those in neighbouring states (Watson 1990). So perhaps it's not free trade's fault, after all.

Though they may be lower than the Americans', at least our wages are not so unequally distributed, right? Only partly right. According to a Harvard University labour economist, 'the United States leads the industrialized world in earnings inequality' (Freeman 1996: 158). The top 10 per cent of full-time American workers make 5.65 times what the bottom 10 per cent earn. In a sample of fifteen OECD countries, who's second? We are. Our top 10 per cent of workers make 4.00 times what our bottom 10 per cent do. In Sweden, by contrast, the ratio is 1.96. Our similarity to the United States is even starker when you examine how the bottom compares to the middle. In the same fifteen OECD countries, the bottom 10 per cent of full-time workers made between 37 and 76 per cent of what the median worker in each country made. The United States was at 37 per cent. We were at 42 per cent. The next closest countries were Japan and Austria, at 61 per cent. Eleven other countries were grouped between 62 and 76 per cent (Freeman 1996: Figure 1). Graham Spry's famous phrase was that in

148 The Meaning of Canadian Life

Canada it's 'the State or the United States.' In many of these comparisons it's 'us and the U.S.' and then the rest of the world.
Which three advanced industrial countries have the 'most conflictual' system of labour–management relations? The United States, the United Kingdom, and, yes, Canada, according to American economist David Gordon, who in a recent book argues that bad industrial relations have caused American corporations to become top-heavy with supervisory personnel, whose job in effect is to police their firms' labour forces. Any idea which country has the rich world's second most top-heavy administrative structure? You guessed it, and the difference is infinitessimal. According to Gordon's data, 13.0 per cent of the American non-farm workforce and 12.9 per cent of ours consist of 'managerial and administrative employees.' In seven other rich countries the share ranges between 2.6 per cent (Sweden) and 6.8 per cent (Norway).

In which of the two countries do unions get higher approval ratings in public opinion surveys? This question obviously wouldn't be worth asking unless the surprise answer were 'the United States,' which it is. When the Gallup organization asks people in both countries whether, in general, they approve or disapprove of labour (or labor) unions, unions invariably get a higher favourable rating in the United States. In 1984, for instance, only 51 per cent of Canadians approved of them, while in 1985 58 per cent of Americans did, a pattern that held from 1949 to 1985, a period during which unions' approval rating fell more or less steadily in both countries (Riddell 1993: Table 4.10). In a recent review of the data, Queen's University political scientist George Perlin (1997) notes that throughout the 1980s 'the number of Canadians who said they had almost no confidence in unions exceeded the number who said they had a great deal of confidence in them, by from 30 to 40 per cent' (92). Poll results such as these cause University of British Columbia labour economist Craig Riddell (1993) to conclude flatly: 'There is no empirical support for the view that the Canada–U.S. unionization differential can be attributed to fundamental differences in social attitudes toward unions and collective bargaining ... Canadians and

TABLE 15.3
Attitudes towards economic systems

Respondents agreeing with	Canada	United States
'In a fair economic system, people with more ability should earn more'	71	78
'Competitiveness leads to better performance'	73	81
'It's very important to be the best at what you do'	74	55
'The profit system teaches the value of hard work'	61	54

SOURCE: Fletcher (1992), cited in Reitz and Breton (1994), 20.

Americans evidently have very similar attitudes toward unions. Changes in these attitudes during the past four decades have also been remarkably similar in the two countries' (140–1).[6]

If Canadians aren't that fond of unions, how do they feel about capitalism and capitalists? On the basis of the information provided in Table 15.3, which country do you suppose is the most achievement-oriented? Americans more frequently provide classically 'capitalist' answers to the first two questions, though Canadians aren't that far behind: 71 per cent of us think that people with more ability should earn more. But Canadians outdo Americans in believing that being the best is important and that the profit system teaches the value of hard work – yes, the profit system, that hallmark of Americanism!.

George Perlin reports similar results. Eighty-one per cent of Americans and 83 per cent of Canadians, both English- and French-speaking, agreed that 'big corporations have far too much power in society today.' However, asked 'Who do you feel best serves your personal economic interests – business, government, or unions?,' Canadians were more likely to say 'business.' In Quebec, business beat out government 67–21, but even English Canadians (52–20) gave higher marks to business than did Americans, who split 48–22 in favour of business. In the late 1980s, however, only 48 per cent of Canadians, compared to 54 per cent of Americans, said that they felt that they could 'count on business to act in the public interest most of the time' (Perlin 1997: Table 3.A7).

Turning from economics to symbols, what about guns? Most Canadian intellectuals regard guns as American males' phallic substitutes, a crutch, as it were, not needed by us kinder, gentler but also more naturally virile Canadians. About 70 per cent of Americans tell pollsters that retail-store owners are at least sometimes justified in using a firearm in self-defence. How many Canadians do? Well, actually, about 70 per cent. Moreover, 58 per cent would allow store owners to have licensed handguns (Kopel 1992: 161). But at least actual gun ownership is a lot lower here, right? Not exactly. 'While Japan and Great Britain have been relatively unarmed for centuries, Canada has one of the highest rates of gun ownership in the world' (Kopel 1992: 136).[7] The estimates are that between one-quarter and one-third of Canadian households own a firearm, while half of American households do. Roughly the same percentage of Canadian and American households owns a rifle, however. The rate of firearm ownership varies from 67 per cent in Yukon and the Northwest Territories to 39 per cent in Alberta, 32 per cent in the Maritimes, and only 15 per cent in Ontario, which helps explain the strongly regional reaction to recent changes in our gun laws (Kopel 1992: 160).

The biggest difference in patterns of gun ownership across the two countries is that while 15 per cent of American women tell pollsters that they own firearms, only 1 per cent of Canadian women do, which casts a whole new light on the phallic-substitute argument (Kopel 1992: 161). University graduates are more likely to own firearms than people with only a high school education, though perhaps that's not really surprising: because of their higher average incomes university graduates are more likely to own everything than are people with only a high school education (Kopel 1992: 161). One Canadian student of public opinion on gun control concludes: 'Nationwide surveys in both Canada and the United States show remarkable similarity in the public's attitudes towards firearms and gun control ... [A] strong majority of British Columbians believe that they, as Canadians, also have a right to

Distinct Society? 151

own firearms ... Despite the greater strength of British traditions and Canadian institutions and mythology, the Canadian public apparently shares much of the American culture, including its mythology about firearms' (Mauser 1990: 586, 587). Canadian traditions count for something, however. Mauser argues that one reason we don't have as strong an anti-gun control lobby is that 'key interest groups are subsidized by the federal government and hestitate to put their grant support at risk by lobbying the government' (Mauser 1990: 587). Money may not buy love; but it can buy silence.

How about crime and incarceration? We think of ourselves as a much safer society than the United States, and we do have a lower murder rate. However, that rate, while only one-third the Americans', is more than three times Japan's, almost two-and-a-half times Switzerland's or England and Wales's, almost two-thirds greater than Scotland's or New Zealand's, and almost 10 per cent higher than Australia's (Kopel 1992: 407). How about crimes against property? Which four industrial countries had the highest rates of property crime? Australia, Canada, the Netherlands, and New Zealand did, in that order. For once, the United States didn't make the top four (Gordon 1996: 143). As everyone knows, the United States has the highest incarceration rate in the industrialized world. Care to guess who's second? Hungary. But we're third, with 129 per 100,000 of our citizens in jail. The United States was way out front with 330, while Hungary had 146. Other countries do as follows: the United Kingdom (92.1), France (83.5), Australia (79.9), Belgium (60.5), Italy (56.0), Sweden (55.0), and Turkey (44.0) (Correctional Service of Canada 1994: 4). George Perlin (1997) finds that views on the handling of crime are 'remarkably alike in both countries. Majorities in both, on the order of 70 per cent, favour tougher sentencing by the courts, the use of capital punishment, and tougher regulation of parole. And on subjects for which there are extended time-series data, these opinons have shown no significant variation for twenty years' (88).

Finally, how about one of the best-known features of our collective self-image – our view of ourselves as a less racist, more tolerant society than the United States? The historians John Thompson and Stephen Randall (1994) put it this way: '[The] melting pot/mosaic metaphor accurately describes Canada's historically greater degree of ethnic diversity, but there is no evidence that this diversity resulted from a greater Canadian appreciation of, or tolerance for, cultural minorities' (173) and they quote another Canadian historian, Allan Smith, as saying that 'circumstances have imposed the pluralist idea' on Canada, and many Canadians have 'bitterly resented these circumstances' (173).

Still, our greater-than-American tolerance remains a crucial part of our image of ourselves. How has it held up lately? Between 1971 and 1981 which nation got more of its immigrants from the (mainly white) countries of Europe? We naturally think of the United States as the more racist society, but in fact we were the ones with the stronger preference for Europeans. More than one-third of our immigrants in that period came from the United Kingdom or other parts of Europe. In the United States only 17 per cent did (Borjas 1993: Table 1.1).

Which country uses a points system for immigrants that 'biases the admission of immigrants toward national-origin groups that originate in high-income, high-skill countries' (Borjas 1993: 36)? Right again. Canada does. As of 1993, a visa applicant was given one point per year of education and only fifty points were needed to gain admission. People from countries such as Belgium, whose emigrants to Canada between 1975 and 1980 averaged 16.6 years of education, were therefore more likely to be admitted than Greeks, for example, who averaged only 8.2 years. Applicants from many Third World countries were at an even greater disadvantage – which presumably was what was intended.

Anti-immigrant bias is nothing new, of course. There were strong anti-Irish feelings in the 1840s and 1850s, while in the 1920s 'large population inflows led to xenophobia.' Immigrants from the Russian and the Austro-Hungarian empires, large numbers of whom settled the Prairies in the first quarter of this century, were new peoples for Canada, 'with different languages, religions, and customs. The result was controversy and consider-

Distinct Society? 153

able anti-immigrant feeling' (Owram 1994: 103) We are the country, recall, that imposed a head tax on the Chinese labourers brought over to build the railways. During the First World War, Richard Gwyn reminds us, we 'interned Austrians, Germans, Ukrainians, and stripped naturalized Canadians of their vote.' Our 'attitude towards Jews in their years of horror was "None is Too Many." In Halifax, Africville was as desperate a ghetto as Davis Inlet is today' (Gwyn 1995: 187).

Even though at times in our history we actively sought immigrants from the United States, we usually took care to exclude those who were dark-skinned. When in the first decade of this century the American civil rights activist W.E.B. Du Bois inquired about this, our officials responded: 'There is nothing in the Canadian immigration law which disbars any person on the ground of color, but since colored people are not considered as a class likely to do well in this country all other regulations respecting health, money etc., are strictly enforced, and it is quite possible that a number of your fellow countrymen may be rejected on such grounds' (quoted in Thompson and Randall 1994: 81). In case what today would be called systemic racism failed, however, the dominion government in 1911 prepared, though it never enacted, an order barring black immigrants (Thompson and Randall 1994: 81).

One advantage of forgetting so much of our history is, of course, that we can be so much easier on ourselves. Today Saskatchewan is regarded as such a progressive place, yet in the mid-1920s the Ku Klux Klan swept through the province like a brushfire, igniting a 'nativist Protestant revolt feeding on the fears of displacement by alien immigrants and Catholics.' In the 1929 provincial election the Klan was instrumental in helping end a quarter-century of Liberal rule (Robin 1992: 83). Similarly, there is a general consensus among historians that Japanese Americans were better treated than Japanese Canadians both during and after the Second World War. The Canadian ban on the Niseis' returning to the Pacific Coast remained in force until 1949, four years after Hiroshima.

The sociologists Raymond Breton and Jeffrey Reitz of the University of Toronto investigated other aspects of tolerance in a 1994 book whose title, *The Illusion of Difference*, suggests the iconoclastic nature of their findings. In the United States, they found, 47 per cent of those asked about immigrants' habits, while in Canada only 34 per cent, favoured 'the maintenance of "distinct cultures and ways"' (Reitz and Breton 1994: 28). So much for the mosaic over the melting pot.[8] In Canada 90 per cent of respondents and in the United States 86 per cent agreed that 'all races are created equal' – a difference, Reitz and Breton note, that is 'insubstantial' (Reitz and Breton 1994: 67).

Which country's respondents were more likely to say that they never told racial jokes? In fact, 46 per cent of Americans claimed this, compared to only 38 per cent of Canadians (Reitz and Breton 1994: 70). In 1987, 34 per cent of Canadians agreed that Jews were 'pushy.' By contrast, in a 1981 poll, only 16 per cent of Americans agreed that it was 'probably true' that 'Jews today are trying to push in where they are not wanted' – which admittedly is not quite the same thing (Reitz and Breton: 72).

In which country did 63 per cent of respondents agree that 'while equal opportunity to succeed is important for all [citizens of this country], it's not really the government's job to guarantee it'? In fact, the country was Canada. Reitz and Breton judge that, 'in the context of race, Americans have been more likely than Canadians to favour government action' (Reitz and Breton 1994: 85), which obviously runs counter to Canadians' preconceptions of their views of both race and government.

Among the other conclusions of Reitz and Breton (1994) are that: 'The level of ethnic identification appears to be much the same in the two countries.' In terms of racial and ethnic intermarriage, which is fairly common in both countries and increases from generation to generation at about the same rate in both, the United States is not more assimilating. '[There is] the same pattern in both countries of language loss over time: by the third generation, knowledge and use of the ethnic language is very low (61). Canadians and Americans are more or less alike in 'tending to prefer individualistic explanations of minority disadvantage to explanations that cite discrimination' (70). These explanations may be wrong, however, since the results of racial discrimination 'field trials,' in which job applicants identical in all attributes except race apply for the same job, suggest that 'discriminatory practices are not widely different in the two countries' (85).[9] There is also little difference between Canada and the United States in 'net earnings differentials [between non-white immigrant groups] after adjustment for education and other human capital variables ... In particular, black immigrants in both countries seem to earn between 70 and 80 percent of what the benchmark group earns' (113). Though 'analysis ... has not eliminated discrimination as a possible cause of the lower earnings of racial minority immigrants in either country,' the situations of these minorities are 'not consistent with what one would expect if there were more racial discrimination in employment in the United States than there is in Canada' (124).

After their exhaustive examination of the available data – their 133-page book refers to 230 different studies – Reitz and Breton arrive at the following conclusion: 'Our comparison of the Canadian mosaic and the American melting pot reveals that the differences between them are not overwhelming. At any rate, they do not appear to be large enough to justify the distinction implied by the choice of metaphors ... Where there are differences, they are much more likely to characterize the attitudes of the majority group toward minorities rather than either their behaviour or the experiences of the minorities themselves' (Reitz and Breton 1994: 125). In other words, we Canadians think we're more tolerant than we actually are.

The point of all this is not to suggest that either Canada and the United States or Canadians and Americans are identical. They obviously aren't.[10] But while differences between the countries do and presumably will remain, they are almost certainly not as great as many Canadians would like to think, especially on questions where, with characteristic smugness, we have traditionally believed ourselves morally superior to the Americans. Many of the differences between our two countries are small. They may be, to quote the title of a recent book, *Small Differences that Matter*. But they are small nevertheless.

156 The Meaning of Canadian Life

THE DOOMSDAY QUESTION

If, as the previous chapter argued, it really isn't crucial that we be different from the United States, and if in fact we express many of the same views as Americans do and display the same sorts of behaviour, why not simply join the United States? 'Without our ethic of egalitarianism and our sense of collectivism,' writes Richard Gwyn (1995), 'we will become simply a poorer version of the United States. Once akin to them, we would have no reason not to become them' (258).[11] To those who pose it, the question seems obvious. In fact, it is bizarre.

Not all people who live in essentially the same way form families. For that matter, not all families live together. As Bruce Hutchison put it 1943: it is 'a very simple fact long known ... that relatives can often live best and most amicably apart, in separate houses, shaped to fit their different tastes, sizes, and temperaments' (175). My own family recently moved into a neighbourhood in which, as we drove through it, many of the inhabitants seemed culturally and professionally similar to us. No doubt we and our neighbours-to-be will conduct our households in similar – perhaps to the outside observer, identical – ways. But that doesn't mean that we want to merge with them. We are happy with our separate household. And so, evidently, are Canadians as a nation.

To be sure, one reason we might not wish to join the United States, even assuming that it would have us, is to retain the choice of behaving differently from the Americans whenever that makes sense to us. In the elementary-school history classes of the early 1960s, much store was set by the difference between August 1914 and September 1939. When in August 1914 the British declared war on Germany, the British dominion Canada was also automatically at war. In 1939, however, the British declaration came on 3 September, but Canada, the nation, did not follow suit until 9 September. The six days between were symbolically crucial.[12] Given our history and the state of Canadian public opinion, it was inevitable that we would also declare war. But in fact as well as in theory, the decision was ours to make. We ended up fighting

Distinct Society? 157

because, having debated the issue, we felt that it was the right thing to do.

All our policy should be made this way. If, having debated things, we decide that what the United States – or any other jurisdiction – is doing in one or another area of policy is correct, we should not fear to imitate it. But even if a long time passed in which our policies were exactly the same as theirs, it still would not make sense to abandon the possibility of one day behaving differently. By contrast, forcing ourselves always to do something a little differently from the Americans is as true a form of servitude as always doing exactly what they do. A policy that must be different from American policy is just as surely determined in Washington as a policy that is always the same. There is also the fact that creating differences for difference's sake is a demeaning way for grown people to behave. How would the advocates of Canadian uniqueness have reacted if Bill and Hillary Clinton had succeeded in giving Americans Canadian-style medicare? By proposing that we reinstitute private health care, so as to restore the necessary measure of difference between our two societies?

The true measure of our independence is our confidence, when it makes sense to us, to do exactly what the Americans are doing. It is confidence that until recently we have not possessed – though 'Brian Mulroney's free trade deal,' as its critics invariably called it, may finally have set us free from our self-consciousness about the Americans.

16
Cement for a Nation?

The previous two chapters argued that, even if the world does need different cultures in case the dominant American culture should prove unsuited to the future social environment, the fact that at bottom we aren't very different from the Americans puts us quite far back in the queue for a place on the Ark. One way to move up, of course, would be to make ourselves more different.

The most famous proponent of this course, though also a fatalist about its likelihood – by the mid-1960s he thought it an option already foreclosed – was George Grant, philosopher, professor, Platonist, Christian, conservative, anti-abortionist, and author of the brilliant if prophetically flawed 1965 polemic *Lament for a Nation*.[1] Grant, who was born two days after the end of the Great War that marked Canada's coming of age, and who died in 1988, two months before the election that approved the Canada–United States Free Trade Agreement, was a lucid and powerful writer, a 'well-loved' broadcaster (Cayley 1995: vii), a far-reaching thinker, and, by all accounts, wonderful company. He favoured a separate path for Canada, not simply for the sake of being different, of course, but because he thought that the United States, 'the spearhead of progress,' was perpetuating a liberal, modernist, Western experiment that had itself already largely failed.

Liberalism, by which Grant meant a view of the world that places prime importance on individual freedom – '*liberal* just means free, doesn't it?' (Cayley 1995: 47) – was at its zenith in Canada at the end of the last century and, as we have seen, lived on in

Cement for a Nation? 159

our politics for several decades after that. As the present century closes, however, some professional economists are among the last remaining proponents of the traditional liberal view. Though we economists consider many possible human motivations and study a presumptuously broad range of subjects, at the centre of our intellectual training is a model in which people – 'individuals' we call them – are free, subject to constraints normally imposed only by 'the market,' to decide most things in the way that best suits their 'preferences.' The declining popularity of this kind of thinking, even as, paradoxically, individual freedom and market economics spread throughout the world, is a main reason for believing that *Lament for a Nation* was prophetically flawed. Grant's anti-technological view, far from from being extinct, is now typical of how educated people think all across the Western world. Hardly anyone believes in progress any more – or at least will admit to it.[2] Anti-technological environmentalism has become a quasi-official religion: as U.S. presidential candidate Pat Buchanan complained in 1996, California schoolchildren now celebrate Earth Day but not Easter. As for spiritual transcendence, there apparently is widespread yearning for transformation of the sort that Grant first experienced in his famous opening of a country gate in Buckinghamshire in December 1941 – '... all I can say is I got off the bike, opened the gate, went through it, shut the gate and it just came to me that I thought "God is"' (Christian 1994: 85–6, n. 62).

What can an economist say about about Grant's ideas that people and societies should pursue order, not freedom; virtue, not comfort; transcendence, not progress? What can a moneychanger say to a prelate, one whose flock is large and growing, at that? Because this economist, in particular, is used to shallower waters than Grant favoured,[3] this chapter makes only three small points: that comfort is not unimportant in the overall scheme of things; that it may not be inconsistent with virtue or, for that matter, transcendence; and that much comfort might have had to be sacrificed had Canada decided to follow the path that Grant wished for us. That he was well aware of these criticisms is no reason not to repeat them. Each generation of Canadians must choose whether to follow Grant through his gate, and those who decide

160 The Meaning of Canadian Life

not to should not spend their lives feeling ashamed of their choice.

BACKWARD TO VIRTUE?

Those who even today invoke Grant's name in the cause of larger-than-American government may not understand the truly radical nature of the distinctiveness that he proposed for Canada. He did not simply favour free, universal health care or a modest protective tariff, though favour them he did. It wasn't sufficient for Canadians to be left-wing Americans, as are so many of those Canadian 'progressives' who in fact take their lead from the Henry Wallace–George McGovern–Jesse Jackson wing of the Democratic party. From Grant's perspective, both Lyndon Johnson and his 1964 presidential opponent, Barry Goldwater – yes, Barry Goldwater, Senator Strangelove – were merely 'different species' of liberal, for '"freedom" was the slogan of both' (Grant 1965: 65). In fact, American liberalism and Marxism were 'utterly at one' in their belief that 'their proper end is the building of the society of free and equal men here on earth' (Cayley 1995: 117). Political philosophy, it seems, makes even stranger bedfellows than politics.

Grant's own politics emerged from his philosophy, which sided with the ancients against the innovations of Enlightenment philosophers such as John Locke, Adam Smith, David Hume, Jean-Jacques Rousseau, and Immanuel Kant. In the classical tradition, the purpose of life – and it does very much have a purpose – is to pursue virtue, not mainly as the individual sees it but as it has been defined through the centuries by those, such as Plato and Christ, who have established a higher code of behaviour, 'an eternal order by which human actions are measured and defined' (Grant 1965: 73). Liberal thought proposes instead that human happiness be achieved through personal freedom – that is, the absence of external constraints on people's behaviour – and that adults generally should be free to pursue their own desires, virtually as far as they wish to take them. Indeed, 'it is the very signature of modern man to deny reality to any conception of good that imposes limits on human freedom' (Grant 1965: 56).[4]

Cement for a Nation? 161

At first blush, all this sounds very attractive to Canadians. After all, our constitution seeks 'peace, order, and good government,' while the Americans' exalts 'life, liberty, and the pursuit of happiness.' If the former is 'conservative' and the latter 'liberal,' then perhaps Canadians *are* natural conservatives, made for 'sterner civic necessities than [merely] the liberal pursuit of happiness, namely the necessity to respond to the demands of the good' (Cooper 1992: 153). As Grant himself concedes, however, his conservatism goes much deeper than most Canadians – in fact, most Westerners – would be likely to accept. The liberal emphasis on freedom leads to the idea that nature exists for humanity's benefit, 'that everything and everyone ... [is] raw material to be made over according to the unstable requirements of the will' (Cooper 1992: 153). The expansion of man's control over nature is achieved by means of technology, the elaboration of which, because it makes possible an easier life for the mass of people, is commonly regarded as progress. For Grant, however, progress is utterly unimportant; indeed, it may actually be harmful, since it offers people less opportunity to experience the redemptive value of suffering. A truly conservative society, one that did not place the will of the individual foremost, would have to part ways with progress. True conservatives do not merely advocate 'a sufficient amount of order so the demands of technology will not carry society into chaos'; they are rather 'custodians of something that is not subject to change' (Grant 1965: 67).

'Something that is not subject to change' is a proposition worth pondering. It obviously would be wrong to compare what Grant proposed – or rather, idealized – for Canada with the isolation that Albania imposed on itself for forty years following the Second World War. The society that existed behind the walls he would have wished for us would not have been totalitarian, though it probably would have been less democratic, the Canadian tory[5] tradition in which he was writing having usually counted the excessively democratic nature of the United States as a fault. But democratic or not, the Canada that Grant wanted us to become would have been, like Albania, backward by choice.

WHAT MONEY CAN BUY

It is a platitude, even to the point of being the subject of pop songs, that all our wealth has brought us neither happiness nor meaning – even if, when asked, the great majority of Canadians tell pollsters that they are satisfied with their lives. Technology has at least, however, brought immense convenience and unprecedented comfort. Grant's biographer notes several occasions on which Grant himself conceded, in the sexist 1960s way, that washing machines and other household gadgetry made life much easier for his wife.[6] Moroever, he was always at pains to preface any statement of his concerns about technology with an appreciation of its achievements. For one thing, it made the contemplative life that he enjoyed available to a much greater proportion of humankind than has ever been true before. In 1920 there were just 423 graduate students in Canada; by 1990 there were 104,045. In 1920, no degrees at all were given in fine and applied arts; in 1990, 4,053 were. In 1920 the country produced a grand total of 24 PhDs. In 1990, for better or for worse, it produced more than one hundred times more, including 43 in philosophy and 58 in religious studies, Grant's two fields (Urquhart and Buckley 1983: Series W344, W444, W512; Statistics Canada 1995: Tables 1, 10, 21). For Grant, 'anybody who has time to think has been given a great privilege by society' (Cayley 1995: 170). Thanks to this century's unprecedented economic growth – yes, its 'progress' – many more people have time today to think, even if not all of them take advantage of it.

Nor are worldly goods necessarily incompatible with transcendence. In fact, they may make it easier. Though Grant loved Mozart above all, he was also devoted to Bach. On his deathbed he told a visitor 'The greatest height of western music is the words "And he took the cup" in Bach's St Matthew Passion' (Christian 1993: 369). Yet, as the poet Frederick Turner has written, 'The combination of recording and musical scholarship has brought about the paradox that we are probably more in Bach's musical presence now than any eighteenth-century German would have been' (Turner 1995: 62). 'Technology [has] revolutionized the arts ...' says Eric Hobsbawm, 'by making them omni-

Cement for a Nation? 163

present' (Hobsbawm 1994: 501). Because of technology, the experience of great art, a traditional aid to transcendence, is now available to the millions. Without Sony and several other of those corporations whose baleful influence on man's spirit and sense of community Grant decried, this almost certainly would not have been possible.

Grant was not a simpleton. He obviously understood very well that modern technology brought tremendous convenience. 'In the pre-industrial age,' he told the Halifax Community Chest in 1953, 'the mass of people were so tied to back breaking labour that only the very few had the possibility of any freedom from the continual task for twelve or fourteen hours a day of earning just enough to stay alive' (quoted in Christian 1993: 166). In thoughtlessly dismissing technology, he told David Cayley in 1986, 'one talks nonsense, and therefore one talks offensive nonsense. It's a question that must be discussed with the very greatest care' (Cayley 1995: 136). Or, finally, as he put it in *Lament* (p. 94), 'Those who criticize our age must at the same time contemplate pain, infant mortality, crop failures in isolated areas, and the sixteen-hour day.' But this nod to physical well-being is immediately followed by: 'As soon as that is said, facts about our age must also be remembered: the increasing outbreaks of impersonal ferocity, the banality of existence in technological societies, the pursuit of expansion as an end in itself.' The passage continues: 'The powers of manipulation now available may portend the most complete tyranny imaginable.'[7]

What the future holds is obviously hard to say. We do know, however, that past eras, which may also have been banal in their own way, certainly involved widespread suffering, suffering from which, as we await the advent of global tyranny, many of us have for the moment been relieved. As a Christian, Grant believed in the expiation of spiritual care through suffering – even as he understood his own aversion to it: at one stage he thought of abandoning the professorial life and buying a farm, but wrote to a friend that 'it would be hell of course – the hard physical work I would loathe' (Christian 1993: 141–2). Suffering may well have its virtues and is certainly admired – which presumably is why in the 1996 U.S. presidential election campaign Bob Dole repeatedly referred to his convalescence following the Second World War. But given the choice, most of us, like Grant, probably prefer to appreciate it at second hand.

Being ourselves unprecedently comfortable, we middle-class North Americans are apt to forget the true extent of human suffering in less technologically advanced times. In Canada in 1921 the median age of death – the age by which half of the people had died – was 41.3 years for males and 43.5 years for females. In 1981 the comparable numbers were 69.7 and 75.8 (Nagnur 1986: Table 1). The life expectancy of a male baby born in 1920–22 was 58.8 years, and of a female baby, 60.6 years. In 1980–82 this had increased to 71.9 and 79.0 years, respectively (Nagnur 1986: Table C1). If modern life really is only half as meaningful as that in earlier centuries, perhaps this is at least partly made up for by its being twice as long.[8]

A main reason for the increase in longevity is a dramatic decline in child mortality. At the turn of the century in Montreal one-quarter of children died before they lived a year, 'a percentage ... double that of New York and, among large cities of the world, exceeded only by Calcutta' (Bothwell, Drummond, and English 1987: 16). In Quebec in 1921, 128.3 of 1,000 children born died in infancy, ten more per year than in modern-day Bangladesh (United Nations 1993: Table A16). By contrast, in 1981 only 8.5 of 1,000 infants died.[9] Much of the improvement results from better medical care: in 1871 there were 1,249 Canadians per registered physician; in 1975, 585. In 1871 there where 10,928 Canadians per dentist; in 1975, 2,563. In 1926, 77 Canadians per 100,000 suffered an attack of diphtheria; in 1975, only 1 in 200,000. In 1926, 85.1 Canadians per 100,000 were hit by typhus; in 1975, only 1 in 120,000 (Urquhart and Buckley 1983: series B518, B525). More lives, mere numbers of people, may not mean anything, of course. Grant's philosophical hero, Plato, said that the unexamined life is not worth living – though on such an important point it may be prudent to consult those actually living the life in question.

The agricultural revolution of the last hundred years has also played a crucial role in making us all richer. In the United States in the nineteenth century, half the population was engaged in

Cement for a Nation? 165

growing food; today fewer than four people in 100 farm (Baumol, Blackman, and Wolff 1989: 30). Eric Hobsbawm (1994) has observed that 'the average Briton [is] far more likely in the course of everyday life to encounter a person who ... once farmed in India or Bangladesh than one who actually [farms] in the United Kingdom' (289). The 'untold quantitites of food' with which this 'tiny fraction of the labour force [can] flood ... the world' have brought revolutionary changes in food costs (290). A survey of urban Massachusetts in 1874-5 found that an average family of five spent 91 per cent of its income on food, clothing, and shelter (Baumol, Blackman, and Wolff 1989: 32-3). In Canada, forty years later, an average family spent 71.9 per cent of its income on food and shelter, never mind clothing (Board of Inquiry ... 1915: 1016). By contrast, in the 1990s in Canada a family is considered poor if it spends more than 54.7 per cent of its income on these necessities, and in 1993 only 13.2 per cent of Canadians did (Sarlo 1996b: Table U1-1). Why 54.7 per cent for Statistics Canada's 'low-income cut-off'? Because this is 20 points higher than 34.7 per cent, which is what the average Canadian family spent on necessities in 1992. Thirty-six point two per cent is, of course, almost precisely half what the average family spent on food and shelter alone in 1913.[10]

Three American economists have recently written that, even in the United States, as late as the nineteenth century, 'the reality of life for the great majority of the population was unrelieved drudgery and deprivation' (Baumol, Blackman, and Wolff 1989: 30). In the mid-nineteenth century United States – one of the world's richest countries at the time – the average diet was 'minimal and nutritionally inferior ...: potatoes, lard, cornmeal, and salt pork were consumed in large quantities, particularly outside the population centres' (35). Living conditions were primitive: 'In New York City in the 1860s an average of six persons living in a single 10-by-12 room was common' (41). Most homes in the mid-century rural United States were 'small houses of logs or loosely boarded frame construction, usually without glass windows' (41, quoting Frederick Olmstead). In 1855, New York City, population 630,000, had only 1,400 baths and 10,000 'water closets': 'outdoor privies were the norm and baths, for the great majority, a luxury' (42).[11]

In 1850 paid labourers typically worked 11 hours a day, 6 days a week (48). For most people, there were no vacations, retirement was rare; and there was little time for recreation. In 1860, by one estimate, 'each person in the United States received during his or her lifetime, on average, only 434 days of schooling (or 21 school months plus 14 days)' (51). In 1870, 20 per cent of the population was illiterate, and only 2 per cent of seventeen-year-olds graduated from high school (51). In 1879 there were only 149 hospitals 'and allied institutions' in the country, one-third of them for the mentally ill (55). 'Everywhere, ordinary sanitary precautions were neglected, and mosquitoes, flies, and other germ-harboring pests were regarded with equanimity' (56). And, of course, the United States was one of the best places in the world to live, as evidenced by the flood of migrants to it.

The three economists conclude as follows: 'Among the items that have reached mass markets during the lifetimes of many of us are video recorders, personal computers, microwave ovens, and jet airplanes. Yet few people regard any of these with the wonderment that early in this century greeted the advent of electric lighting, the radio, and the automobile. Change has become so commonplace that we have all become blasé about it. That is a striking departure from virtually anything that humanity has experienced before' (57).[12]

It is hard to escape the conclusion that, despite his protestations, like most twentieth-century anti-technologists Grant was also fundamentally blasé about achievements made by progress. He does do his best not to sound blasé. At one point, for instance, he illustrates the harshness of pioneer life by referring to the eating of human flesh by Loyalist settlers of New Brunswick: 'They'd been thrown out of the U.S., they were thrown into a very pioneering place without much support from the British government, they nearly starved to death; therefore, when people died, they had to do it' (Cayley 1995: 139).

A society in which the end of humanity has become technologically possible obviously is far from ideal, but so is one in which

Cement for a Nation? 167

most people's material conditions are miserable. How to choose between past and present misery is, of course, the classic dilemma of the preservationist. At what point in history should progress be stopped? Which era exactly does a conservative conserve? If technological evolution had ceased in 1965, a comfortable time for many people – even if real incomes in Canada were only half[13] what they are in the mid-1990s – well, why not in 1930, or 1400, or 700, or, for that matter, 500 BC? As Grant himself conceded, 'To talk as if interference with chance [technology's role in respect to nature] is not necessary is obvious nonsense. But the question of how far it should go is another matter.'

But if we do not wish all progress to stop, how do we take those parts we like and leave the rest? Such decisions *are* made, of course. The United States chose in the 1970s not to build a supersonic jet transport, and as a result the British-French Concorde is the only option for travellers wishing to cross the Atlantic in three hours. In our own country, British Columbia's Clayoquot Sound will not be developed in the manner desired by Macmillan Bloedel. Off Newfoundland baby harp seals now grow to maturity without being clubbed to death, while around the world countries are deciding how to deal with the moral problems posed by genetic engineering of humans.

But these examples are essentially peripheral: any invention that is cheap and provides great convenience seems very likely to become available sooner or later. Like Innis, McLuhan, Heidegger, and many others before him, Grant was perfectly right that technology is not neutral. Each new generation of machines changes how we live and does so in ways that we neither imagine beforehand nor, once they have had their way with us, remember afterward. (In fact, we often need social historians to help us recall the way we were.) But how, short of the tyranny Grant fears, could we possibly stop this process?[14]

A CANADIAN GAULLISM?

By 1965 Grant thought it too late for an independent Canada. For this reason, *Lament* does not actually recommend policies for its own era. It does suggest, however, that things might have turned out all right for Canada if in the early 1940s we had closed the country to foreign investors and instituted a form of Gaullism – national capitalism, as it were, in the sense that the state would have closely controlled Canadian capitalists. But after the influx of American capital following the war, it was too late. By 1965, the year of *Lament*, Grant could write that 'nearly all Canadians think modernity is good, so nothing essential distinguishes Americans from Canadians' (Grant 1965: 54).

It is hard to imagine how Canadian Gaullism could have been put in place, even if the politicians and public opinion of the day had permitted it. Even late twentieth-century bureaucracy might not be up to the job, but the bureaucracy that existed in the 1930s was tiny by modern standards. As late as 1939, for instance, Canada's entire Department of Finance employed only 330 people, including 125 who ran the Royal Canadian Mint and another fifteen, half of them stenographers, who administered the Treasury Board (Bryce 1986: 222–4). The government was much larger by the end of the war, of course, and perhaps Grant's idea really was that the wartime control of industry could have been carried over into peacetime, though that presumably would have involved at least a mild form of tyranny.

There is also the problem of whether it would have been sufficient for Grant's purposes merely to establish Canadian control over corporate capitalism operating on Canadian soil. Or was corporate capitalism itself not the problem? Grant's *Lament* includes several choruses on the spiritually demoralizing effects of the corporate form of enterprise. Diefenbaker's populist democracy, he argued, 'belonged to the Saskatchewan or Wisconsin of [his] youth, not to those who work for Simpson-Sears or General Motors' (14). But the modern corporation, especially the large corporation, was the linchpin of an organizational revolution that made possible most of the impressive technological innovations of this century (see Chandler 1977).

Even today, though small may be beautiful, big is often efficient, and much of the world's business, including two-thirds of its international trade, is done by very large corporations.[15]

Cement for a Nation? 169

Would postwar Canada simply have outlawed this form of organization and, if so, with what effect on economic life? Grant is wonderfully sardonic in citing official Liberal arguments about the excessive costs of a 'Gaullist' policy. But he makes no attempt to refute them, conceding: 'If the terms for American investment had been tougher, there would have been less investment. Canada would have developed more slowly and with a substantially lower standard of living than the United States' (40). But this is just the cost of limiting investment by foreign capitalists. If the real problem is the corporate form of organization itself, what cost would Canadians have paid by banning *that* and in effect standing aside from the organizational revolution? Canada has never had a peasant society, so presumably we would have achieved a higher living standard than the Albanians. But just how much higher?

It is commonly argued and apparently widely believed, as John Turner told Brian Mulroney in their 1988 television debate, that there is a price to pay for being Canadian. The thesis of this book is that this argument is wrong: there surely is a price to pay for the excessive use of government, but since overgovernment of ourselves is not essential to our Canadianness the only price for being Canadian is that we must endure both the weather, which some of us actually like, and the endless nattering of Canadian nationalists. This is not yet a majority view, however.

Suppose the more common view *is* correct, and, as Grant suggests, an economic price does have to be paid. If being Canadian means paying higher taxes than Americans, many Canadians have declared themselves ready to pay such a price, while the rest of us, by our submission, have shown that we regard the overall package as worthwhile, even as we begrudge what we consider its unnecessary 'downside.' But how many of us would be willing to incur the downside that Grant had in mind, which seemingly included not only the cost of denying ourselves American investment, plus the cost of any retaliation from Washington, but also the economic cost of forgoing the benefits of even our own rather torpid, branch-plant version of dynamic capitalism? The answer, obviously, is 'not many.' And who could blame them? Grant himself admitted: 'I'm not especially good at paying prices' (Cayley 1995: 58). Or as his biographer puts it: 'George could not unequivocally condemn those who succumbed to the beguiling allure of modernity' (Christian 1993: 250) – a nice piece of condescension from someone who drove a maroon Volvo, periodically rhapsodized over 'wonderful American machines' such as the vacuum cleaner, and in retirement enjoyed floating in his above-ground pool and watching *Coronation Street* on television with his wife (Christian 1993: 367, 168, 262, 352). As Grant understood perfectly well,[16] though a professor of philosophy and religious studies might trade all the good that progress had brought, including the possibility of being a professor, in exchange for freedom from nuclear terror, impending universal tyranny, and rampant individualism, this might not be a trade-off that most non-professors would accept.

Should other Canadians feel guilty because they have chosen 'comfortable self-preservation' rather than the purpose of life as the ancients defined it: 'openness to the whole ... to know the highest good, which is God' (Cayley 1995: 74)? Perhaps they should. Maybe in the end, however, physical comfort is not incompatible with the highest good. Grant himself had a reasonable standard of living yet devoted his life both to worrying about such questions and, so far as can be learned, pursuing virtue. Perhaps even a man who owns an American vacuum cleaner may pass through the eye of the needle.

THOSE THINGS WE CHERISH

But if English Canada was not essentially different from the United States, what was there to lament in its passing?[17] In a word, tradition. 'Those who loved the older traditions of Canada may be allowed to lament what was lost, even though they do not know whether that loss will lead to some greater political good' (Grant 1965: 96). Grant did not provide a single list of these traditions, but at different places in *Lament* he suggests they were: first, the British connection; second, greater state interventionism – 'Until recently,' he wrote, 'Canadians have been much more will-

Cement for a Nation? 171

ing than Americans to use government control over economic life to protect the public good against private freedom' (Grant 1965: 71); and, third, the vestigial hope, or at least the memory of that hope, that a truly conservative society could be built in this country – that is, one in which the community had the right to 'restrain freedom in the name of the common good' (Grant 1965: 64). A late-century reader, by contrast, is not so certain that these things have gone.

On the British connection, Grant was surely right that by 1965 it was fast disappearing. The most obvious symbol of its demise was the adoption of the maple leaf flag in February of that year, forty-one days before *Lament for a Nation* was published. That put paid to part of the symbolic connection, but much of the literal connection already had ended, and at British, not Canadian institgation. As even Grant writes, by the late 1950s 'the English ruling class had come to think of its Commonwealth relations as a tiresome burden' (Grant 1965: 32). The Canadian economic historian Bruce Muirhead has shown that the dramatic postwar redirection of Canadian trade away from Britain and towards the United States – exports to the United Kingdom were 40 per cent of our total exports in 1937 but only 15 per cent in 1957 (Muirhead 1992: Figure 1) – occurred not mainly because our Massachusetts-born industry minister, C.D. Howe, favoured it (in fact he didn't),[18] but because the British, whose hard currency reserves had been exhausted by their war effort, did not have the means with which to buy Canada's exports, which nevertheless had to be sold. Since all other industrial economies except the United States, Australia, and New Zealand were in essentially the same condition as Britain, trade had only one way to go: south. We were not so much pulled into their orbit by the Americans as pushed by the British. As Muirhead writes: 'Canadian policy was multilateral by preference, bilateral by necessity, and manifestly continental by default' (Muirhead 1992: 15). Mackenzie King's postwar government did its best to prop up the British trade connection, even to the extent, in 1946, of lending the mother country equivalent to ten per cent of our GDP, twenty times what our foreign aid budgets provide today, but to no avail.

On our second tradition, interventionism, it is hard not to be jarred by Grant's use of 'until recently' in: 'Until recently, Canadians have been much more willing than Americans to use government control over economic life to protect the public good against private freedom.' In the first place, as we have seen, this greatly overestimates both the Americans' historic devotion to *laissez-faire* and our own reliance on the state. But as *Lament* was being written, Lester Pearson, Grant's villain, was instituting medicare and bilingualism, now widely regarded as the twin hallmarks of Canadian distinctiveness. And as chapter 5's charts demonstrated, it was in the 1960s, beginning under Diefenbaker and continuing with Pearson and Trudeau, that Canada's fiscal distinctiveness from the Americans truly began. Of course, these were innovations, not traditions. Before the middle of this century, as we have seen, the Canadian governmental tradition was neither greatly interventionist nor even greatly different from the American. Someone who, like Grant, favoured tradition above all else could just as easily have hearkened back to the Canadian social traditions of the first three decades of this century, those that extolled self-reliance and opposed the intrusion of the state into new areas of economic, social, and personal life, even on such an innocuous matter as family allowances.

The final phrase of Grant's sentence on interventionism, in which he says that we have used the state to 'protect the public good over private freedom,' also begs comment. No doubt we, like the Americans, have at least occasionally used the state to do just that. But it is simply naïve to assume that every time the state is used public good is promoted and private freedom restricted. And even when government does further the public good, it also frequently serves private interests. The building of the CPR probably did keep the Prairies Canadian, which was a good thing for Canadians, Aboriginal Canadians perhaps excepted. But it also enriched the owners of the CPR and set the social and economic structure of the west for decades to come. In 1995, the federal cabinet's granting of a licence to a second Canadian satellite broadcaster may or may not have improved life for Canadian television viewers, but it certainly increased the profitability of a firm

Cement for a Nation? 173

headed by the then prime minister's son-in-law. There are many other cases, of course, in which the power of the state has been appropriated by private interests and used without any redeeming social purpose. As the next chapter argues at greater length, someone who regards frequent and aggressive use of such power as a defining part of a country's way of life is asking for this kind of trouble. That more and more people have come to realize this is one reason Grant's 'until recently' may be appropriate to the 1990s, though it clearly wasn't in the 1960s.

And then again, those who would reduce the size of the state must topple the third pillar of Grant's version of Canadian distinctiveness, the very durable idea that this should be a more virtuous society than the United States and that to achieve virtue individual freedom must be restrained. Eric Hobsbawm (1994) has written that in the new, technological age in which we live 'the old moral vocabulary of rights and duties, mutual obligations, sin and virtue, sacrifice, conscience, rewards and penalties, [can] no longer be translated into the new language of desired gratification' (338). Each will have his or her own impression of modern public life, but to some of us it seems that, far from being forgotten, the vocabulary of obligation is ubiquitous. In English Canada, certainly, the pursuit of public virtue verges on obsession. As the generation raised in the 1960s has aged, its streak of libertarian 'do what you like as long as you don't hurt anyone' has been replaced by more intrusive doctrines and all manner of restraints on behaviour, with more coming every day. Guns must be registered and encased. Cigarettes must be smoked outdoors, even in winter. Any form of speech that can possibly be construed as promoting hatred is rigorously circumscribed. Political correctness has captured the universities and is spreading quickly to other institutions. (The phrase itself may be universally ridiculed, but the doctrine is methodically enforced.) Employers no longer may hire and fire whom they please, nor pay what wages they like. Human rights commissions, pay equity commissions, and the like all have their say about what may and may not happen in the labour market. That it is not possible to legislate morality apparently has escaped the attention of our legislators, who spend much of their time trying to do just that.

Grant would respond, of course, that even our moral intrusiveness is liberal, in the sense that our tastes in virtue are of our own invention. Thus in enforcing public morality we seem to consider ourselves free to 'experiment in shaping society unhindered by any preconceived notions of good' (Grant 1965: 57–8). We do take collective action to enforce virtuous behaviour, a Tory notion, but we do so in the liberal manner, making the morality up as we go along, figuring it out for ourselves, ignoring the lessons of most past thinkers on the problem of virtue. For Grant, the current concern with 'values' would be proof of this. Values that are consciously chosen are merely another manifestation of freedom: 'The language of value is above all the language of Nietzsche. It is what is left once you have eliminated the idea that there are purposes that intrinsically belong to being, like breathing' (Cayley 1995: 121).

As for the personal seeking after virtue, while it is true that the state has become increasingly a-religious, and is likely only to become more so as official holidays such as Easter and Christmas come under attack from non-Christians, in their private lives many millions of people, including scores of millions in the United States, are as preoccupied by the search for transcendence as Grant was, while even the secular humanists at the Canadian Radio-television and Telecommunications Commission have seen fit to authorize not one but two religious television channels. No doubt partly because of the decay to which moral relativism has led, there is a yearning, even among the not especially religious, for a return to notions of good that prevailed in an earlier age. In this sense, the American 'moral majority' may be moving in a direction that Grant would have approved. One of its best-known spokesmen, Republican notable William Bennett, recently sold several million copies of *The Book of Virtues*, an anthology of moral writings.[19] In this country, the Reform party's concern with what are called 'social issues' is thought by the liberal – that is, in Grant's usage, freedom-seeking – elites in the national media to be misguided antiquarianism, but despite that, it seems to sell. For all his pessimism, it's hard not to conclude that in many ways Grant's way of thinking has won. Environmentalism, transcendence, 'ought' – these are the concerns of the 1990s. They are,

Cement for a Nation? 175

however, concerns throughout the Western world and therefore cannot serve as the basis for Canadian uniqueness.

The current ascendancy of many of Grant's ideas is not without irony. In *Lament*, he complained of a complete absence of pluralism of tastes in the public sphere: 'The conquest of human and non-human nature becomes the only public value' (Grant 1965: 57). This was obviously an exaggeration, even then. But accepting his broad-brushed metric for a moment, there is still an absence of pluralism in such matters, except that now the monolith is Grant's own style of thinking. It is today exceedingly unfashionable to believe in progress. Those who argue that we do not have the right to dominate nature – taking nature to be other living things and the places they inhabit – are clearly in the ascendant, at least in the industrialized world. Even to hint at the appropriateness of human dominion over the environment and its inhabitants would today be widely regarded as blasphemous, something only economists and other misfits would do.

Not everything has gone the way Grant would have wished, of course. Science, which he regarded as the effort to dominate nature by unlocking and exploiting its secrets, remains largely revered. Spending in support of scientific research and development (R&D), especially R&D that (a double insult to Grant) might conceivably result in an economic payoff, typically is spared the deepest cuts when governments tidy their budgets. And medical research is almost universally approved, especially medical research designed to cure AIDS, the ultimate moral relativist disease.

In other areas, what Grant would have regarded as licence reigns. Despairing of morality he complained in 1965 – 1965! – 'No one minds very much if we prefer women or dogs or boys, as long as we cause no public inconvenience' (Grant 1965: 57). In fact, these days people who prefer dogs would run into great difficulty with animal rights' groups, while boys are also strictly off-limits, even if there is some debate about precisely what age should, as it were, separate men from boys. Those who prefer women are generally still free to do so, though at risk of displaying outmoded tastes.

A final way in which Canada seems to be moving away from Grant's conception of the virtuous society is in what is currently regarded as a democratic revolt against its governing elites (see Newman 1995), though the main symptoms of this revolt may result from unique historical circumstances – consecutive constitutional crises, the second involving a national referendum – which seem unlikely to be repeated. The virtuous society, by contrast, places no great premium on democracy: what virtue consists in is not decided by ballot. It most certainly is not a place in which anything that can command a majority goes. Its time-tested rules have to be taught and ingrained. Unlike an increasing number of Canadians, Grant likely would have had little trouble with the idea that, if need be, elites should play a disproportionate role in society. His quarrel would be with our more recent choice of elites, in particular our deference to business elites. As he told David Cayley in 1986: 'Up to about 1940, Canada was overwelmingly an agricultural society, with small groups of lawyers, doctors, teachers in the towns who thought of themselves as really running Canada. Now, I was part of that class of lawyers and teachers, and it was extraordinarily astonishing for me to see, after 1945, that my class was disappearing in Canada. The place of these older-fashioned teachers and doctors and lawyers was now taken by the E.P. Taylors and C.D. Howes of the world' (Cayley 1995: 55).

Still, as a piece of prophecy, *Lament for a Nation* has largely failed. Despite slippage on the major fronts just mentioned, many of the ideas and beliefs whose more or less inevitable passing it mourned have in fact taken on new life late in the century. The idea of progress – that 'society always moves forward to better things' (Grant 1965: 2) – is almost universally sniffed at. Personal transcendence is widely sought. Nature worship has become almost a religion, a development of which Grant, who believed Christianity quite an acceptable religion, would not wholly have approved. The earning of profits, even historically modest profits, is widely denounced. 'The corporate ethic' is universally regarded as an oxymoron, despite the proliferation of ethics chairs in business schools, furniture as incongruous as confessionaries in bawdy-houses.

Cement for a Nation? 177

As prescription, rather than prophecy, *Lament for a Nation* is also flawed, for it venerates the in fact relatively recent Canadian tradition that more government is both better for us and more Canadian. As the next two chapters try to show, this is a good recipe for mischief.

17
The Rising Cost of Civilization

Even supposing it has secured our longed-for sense of separateness from the Americans, our national belief that our government must be more interventionist than theirs often blinds us to the costs of intervention. If what is at stake really is national survival, then almost no cost is too high – a theory of budgeting certain to please the beneficiaries of government activity. But if the nation is not at risk, then the effects of excessive government need to be scrutinized. The costs of overgovernment come in several forms, ranging from obvious out-of-pocket expenses, through the 'excess burden' of taxation and regulation and the surreptitious redistribution of power and privilege in society, to the morally corrosive effect of perpetual bickering over spoils. The first two costs are dealt with in this chapter, the remaining two in the chapter that follows.

OUT-OF-POCKET EXPENSE

The most obvious cost of government is taxes, the out-of-pocket expense of paying for it. Oliver Wendell Holmes, Jr, wrote that taxes were the price we pay for civilized society – though he wrote it in 1904, before the United States had an income tax. If Holmes was right, we Canadians must be extremely civilized, and much more civilized than we once were, since as the charts in chapter 5 showed, taxes used to be less than one-quarter of our national income and now are approaching 40 per cent.

The Rising Cost of Civilization 179

Because Canadian governments also borrow lots of money, what we pay in taxes doesn't fully reflect the resources commandeered by the public sector. In 1995 our three levels of government borrowed almost 4.3 per cent of our GDP. When combined with the taxes and other revenues they raised, this enabled them to spend 47.6 per cent of GDP, including debt interest (Perry 1996: Tables 6 and 7). Because borrowing today means that taxes must be higher tomorrow our twenty-year habit of deficit spending may not be healthy over the long haul – which means that it may not be healthy over the short haul, either. When people realize that tax rates will be higher in future, they may decide not to make investments that would pay off in future, which is why many economists now believe that when governments spend borrowed money economic output may be boosted very little if at all: higher government borrowing simply means lower private investment, with no net gain in economic activity.

Potential investors who aren't discouraged by worries about higher future taxes may be even more forcibly 'crowded out' by the higher current interest rates that result when governments gobble up so much of national saving. In 1994, individual Canadians saved a grand total of $39 billion dollars, which sounds like a lot but was actually $423 million *less* than their governments borrowed: in effect, everything that Canadians saved in 1994 was lent to their governments (Statistics Canada 1995: Tables 2 and 3). In the heyday of Keynesian economics, economists believed debt-financed government spending meant more national income. Nowadays, most economists believe that, except in the deepest depressions, it simply means that government projects displace private projects. We buy more things collectively but fewer privately. If you think that society needs fewer factories, homes, and apartment buildings and more town halls, bocce courts, and swimming pools – the sorts of things bought with the mid-1990s federal Infrastructure Programme – you'll be pleased by the switch from private to collective use. Others may think that the money would have been put to better purposes if left in private hands.[1]

That taxes average roughly 40 per cent of national income

doesn't mean that all Canadians pay 40 per cent of their income in taxes, of course. Just about everyone does pay some tax. With virtually everything being taxed, the only way not to pay is to assume a new identity and not reveal it to Revenue Canada. And even then you pay sales taxes.[2] Most Canadians don't live underground, however, so they do pay income taxes. How much varies with their incomes, since income taxes are 'progressive': people who earn more usually pay a higher share of their income. For example, Montreal economist France St-Hilaire found that in 1991 the bottom 20 per cent of tax filers – 3.8 million Canadians – had incomes below $6,000. On average, out of every $100 they earned they paid one dime in federal income tax. One dime. At the other end of the taxpayer line, in 'Freedom-55 Land,' 58,190 Canadians made more than $200,000. Though they represented only 0.3 per cent of all filers, they made 5 per cent of all income and paid $5.4 billion in tax – 9 per cent of all federal income tax paid. Their tax rate averaged 23.2 per cent – $23.20 for every hundred dollars earned, 232 times the rate faced by the bottom three million (St-Hilaire 1996: Tables 4, 5). Add sales taxes, excise taxes, import duties, and so on and so on, and at the top end tax rates get very high.

In 1995, a typical upper-middle-class Quebecer – your author – paid more than half his income in taxes: 38.3 per cent in federal and provincial income tax; 1.7 per cent in payroll taxes; 5 per cent in property taxes; plus 15 per cent in GST and Quebec Sales Tax on the roughly 40 per cent of income not spent on taxes, saving, charity, or groceries. In total, his 'average' or 'effective' tax rate, total taxes divided by income, was 51.5 per cent. Counting sales taxes on what was spent after income taxes have been paid, his marginal tax rate – the rate paid on the last dollar of income earned – was over 60 per cent.[3]

Table 17.1, adapted from a paper by University of Alberta economist Bev Dahlby (1994), provides a more systematic estimate of just how much – or little – Canadian workers got to keep out of any labour income they earned in 1993. The calculations underlying it take into account personal income taxes, including surtaxes, flat taxes, and selective tax reductions; sales taxes,

The Rising Cost of Civilization 181

TABLE 17.1
What taxpayers kept per dollar of labour income, 1993

Province	Cents kept out of *last* dollar earned	Decline from 1986	Cents kept out of *all* dollars earned	Decline from 1986
British Columbia	45.2	5.3	53.7	5.1
Alberta	52.8	3.0	60.7	3.7
Saskatchewan	44.4	5.4	55.0	5.3
Manitoba	43.2	5.0	53.8	5.2
Ontario	40.1	6.8	49.3	5.4
Quebec	35.1	4.2	45.1	5.4
New Brunswick	43.2	4.9	53.6	4.8
Nova Scotia	45.8	4.7	56.1	4.8
Prince Edward Island	45.3	6.0	55.1	7.3
Newfoundland	41.0	4.5	51.1	5.7

SOURCE: Adapted from Dahlby 1994, Table 1.

including sales tax rebates; and the payroll taxes that finance unemployment insurance, the Canada and Quebec Pension plans, workers' compensation, and (where applicable) medicare. The table shows how much workers got to keep both out of the last dollar they earned and out of all the dollars they earned.[4]

What does it show? If you earned an extra dollar of labour income in Quebec in 1993, then, taking all taxes into account, on average you got to keep 35.1 cents; in Ontario you kept 41.1 cents; in British Columbia, 45.2 cents. The best you could have done was in Alberta, where, on average, you actually were allowed to keep more than half of what you earned – 52.8 per cent, to be exact – the only province in Canada where this was true. Of course, because these are *average* retention rates for the population as a whole, some people paid even more tax and therefore got to keep even less of their labour income. They weren't just people on the top rungs of the earnings ladder, either.

The highest marginal tax rates, and therefore the lowest marginal retention rates, occurred at lower levels of income. For instance, in a detailed examination of Alberta's tax rates, Dahlby found that the highest marginal tax rates – over 60 per cent – were paid at $12,031 and $29,591 a year of income. At below $12,031, taxpayers didn't have to pay Alberta Health Care premiums. Above $12,031 they did, so their marginal tax rates jumped by the per-dollar assessment. But Alberta's health care premiums, like most payroll taxes, have a ceiling, so after a certain level of income they no longer impose a tax burden on new dollars of income earned, which means that once the full premium has been paid the taxpayer's marginal tax rate falls. So rates can be lower at the top end of the distribution even though top income-earners have paid full premiums for these programs.[5]

Nor are tax spikes at low levels of income a strictly Alberta phenomenon: they occur any time people reach an income level that makes them either eligible or ineligible for a new tax. The combined effect of both regular income taxes and phase-ins and phase-outs of other taxes and benefits is shocking. According to Dahlby, 'In Alberta in 1993, more than 96 percent of labour income was subject to a marginal tax rate of 40 per cent or more, 35.5 per cent to a marginal rate of 50 per cent or more, and 5.9 per cent to a marginal rate of 60 per cent or more.' And that's in Alberta, which has the highest last-dollar retention rate in the country.

The news wasn't quite as bad for retention rates on workers' overall income. They were actually a little higher than the retention rate on the last dollar of income.[6] Even so, they were pretty low. In Quebec and Manitoba they were less than 50 per cent, which means that taxes took over half of all the labour income that people earned on average. (Your author wasn't alone.) In five more provinces, retention rates were below 55 cents on the dollar. Only in Alberta did the rate reach 60 cents on the dollar, and then just barely, at 60.7 cents, which means that taxes took just less than 40 per cent of Albertans' overall labour income. Again, these are averages: some people paid more than the average amount of overall tax, some less.

Taxes are only half the public-sector equation, of course. Canadians get a wide range of public services in return for the taxes they pay, and many of these public services are very valuable. But

The Rising Cost of Civilization 183

whether at the margin public services are still worth the extra taxes is something that Canadians seem more doubtful about in the 1990s, and naturally so, as their tax bill has risen. Between 1986 and 1993, the table shows, the tax bill on labour income rose a nickel on the dollar on average. There is good reason to suppose that over the same period the value of what people got from government went down.

LESS FOR MORE (I)

In at least a couple of senses, Canadians' growing suspicion that taxes don't buy as many public services as they used to are extremely well founded. For one thing, a good part of today's taxes do *not* buy public services; they pay for yesterday's public services. In the early 1980s, the federal government ran 'operating deficits': it spent $1.10 on public services, not counting debt interest, for every dollar that it raised in taxes (Statistics Canada 1995: Table 3). It could do this only by borrowing, and it continued borrowing to pay for public services until 1986. Since then, in most years, it has borrowed only to pay debt interest. Thus in five of the first six years of the 1990s Ottawa ran 'operating surpluses' – took in more in taxes than it spent on public services – a fiscal stance that may have worsened the recession of those years but was needed in order to rein in a runaway national debt. By 1994 the federal government was collecting $1.10 in taxes for every dollar spent on public services – exactly the reverse of what it did in 1984.[7]

The effect of such a policy is that most Canadians pay more in taxes than they receive in services, which naturally does little to improve their mood. It may be ungrateful of us to forget that ten years earlier we received more services than we paid for, but forget we usually do. The bad news is that if we are to get rid of the federal deficit, it's only going to get worse. In the fiscal year 1997/ 98 the federal government was scheduled to pay $46.0 billion in interest (Martin 1997: Table 3.1), which means that if we were to cover all federal spending with taxes, we'd have to raise $46.0 billion more than we spent on public services. That's almost 6 per cent of GDP. Collective self-denial this great obviously will hurt, though if it's not done, the problem will only get worse: eventually we'd spend $50 billion a year on interest and then $60 billion – assuming that people would still lend to such a profligate borrower as the Canadian federal government – and to get to balance we'd then have to tax ourselves $60 billion more than we were spending on public services. Self-denial is therefore unavoidable. But there is no question it hurts.[8]

LESS FOR MORE (II)

A second reason why higher taxes seem to be buying less in the way of public services is that such services are becoming more expensive. It's not just that people who work in the public sector are paid more than private-sector workers – though they are: one estimate put the public-sector premium at between 20 and 40 per cent in the early 1990s. With the compressions of the early 1990s, that may have declined somewhat, though times were tough in the private sector, as well, and the estimate did not put a value on the greater job security most public-sector workers still have (Brown 1994: Figure 5).

And it's not just that wages have grown more quickly in the public sector than in the private – though they did all through the 1980s boom (Brown 1994: Table 3). There's the additional problem that by all indications productivity doesn't grow as quickly in the public sector as in the private sector. 'By all indications' because public-sector productivity can be hard to measure: a brewer's output can be counted in litres per hour, even if there are problems in controlling for differences in the quality of beer. But how do you measure a doctor's output, or a university professor's? In wellness provided or wisdom imparted, presumably, but what are the units for counting these 'products'?

Of course, if public-sector productivity is hard to measure, maybe it's growing *more* quickly than private-sector productivity, not less. But there are two good reasons for supposing that that's not the case. The first is that in much of what it does the public sector is a monopoly. Anyone who has dealt with a monopoly or

The Rising Cost of Civilization 185

listened to Lily Tomlin's comedic rendition of a telephone operator understands that monopolies are exempt from the competitive pressure that often forces improvements in productivity, which admittedly can be painful. The second reason is that many public services are very labour-intensive, so that efficiency-enhancing machines can't easily be substituted for the labour that produces them. If doing good social work means talking to people one on one, then even though computers may help a bit with the paperwork, a half-hour's consultation with a difficult client is still going to take a trying half-hour no matter how advanced technology gets.

But if productivity does grow more slowly in the public sector, then as wages rise throughout the economy public-sector costs outpace private-sector costs. In the private sector, rising wages are offset by rising productivity, so the price of the product doesn't increase as much as the price of the labour that makes it. In fact, in some cases – computers, clearly – the price of the product may actually fall. But in the public sector there may be no productivity offset, or if there is one it may not be as great. So over time the price of public services rises just as quickly as the price of public-sector labour. This means that even if public- and private-sector wages rise at exactly the same rate, public-sector output becomes more expensive more quickly than private-sector output. To get the same level of service as before, you therefore have to pay more. To get more you have to pay even more than that, while if you're only willing to pay what you had been paying you get less. This is very much the way many Canadians currently feel about their public sector – that they have been paying more to get the same amount of service, or even less.

MORE IS LESS

Of course, in many areas of government, Canadians have been paying more to get ... more, vastly more. They're just not sure that they want what governments have bought on their behalf. For example, in the early 1950s, unemployment insurance (UI) was true insurance. What people paid in was related to a reasonable expectation of how much they would take out. But since then, UI privileges have been granted to lots of workers who were not originally covered. Seasonal workers, fishermen, foresters, and construction workers are the prime examples. Work ten weeks and you are entitled to three or four times that in benefits, year after year after year. Because unemployment is *always* high in these industries, there's simply no chance that people employed in them will ever pay into the system what they take out.

As a result the same pattern of payments and benefits repeats itself over the decades. On average between 1986 and 1990 – years of low unemployment for the economy as a whole – forestry workers got $6.17 in UI benefits for every $1 they paid in premiums. Fishermen and trappers got $4.70; agricultural workers, $3.58; and construction workers, $2.90. Who pays for these subsidies to our seasonal industries? Workers in non-seasonal industries do. In the financial sector, workers got back only 51 cents per dollar paid in premiums; in transportation and public administration, only 59 cents; in 'community, business, and personal services,' only 81 cents (Corak and Pyper 1994).[9]

Was this just a case of the recipient industries experiencing bad times even though the economy as a whole was doing well? No, it's the same pattern of benefits and subsidies that an earlier study found for the years 1975–82. Seasonal industries are always net beneficiaries; non-seasonal industries are always net payers. In a real insurance system, of course, if your house burns down year after year after year, either your premiums go up or you can't get insurance at all. Lloyd Axworthy's much-heralded reform of the UI system in 1996 was supposed to end this permanent subsidy to our natural-resource industries. As it turned out, intense lobbying by the Liberals' Atlantic caucus limited reform to a five per cent phased-in penalty for repeat users of the system.

In addition to departing from the strict insurance principles on which it was founded, over the years the UI program has also become more diversified in what it spends money on. Once a simple system of income replacement, it now provides maternity leave, paternity leave, and extensive retraining assistance. It even helps unemployed workers start their own businesses. For UI the

The Rising Cost of Civilization 187

usual saw that 'we can't afford it any more' simply isn't true. What we bought in 1950 we could easily afford. What we can't afford are the many frills that we have added since then, many of them during the supposedly miserly 1980s.

A quick thumb-through of the section of the Public Accounts that describes federal grants to persons, corporations, or associations suggests that the same is true in many other areas of government. In the 1995–96 edition of the Public Accounts this section ran to seventy-seven pages and listed roughly 150 grants per page. To start with the very first page (Canada 1996: 3), the Department of Agriculture and Agri-Food spent $1.78 billion. First grant: for 'agricultural research in universities and other scientific organizations,' $995,650. This sounds like a good cause, though perhaps it could get by with less. Second grant: 'Grants under the Specialized Counselling Assistance Grant Program,' $17,064. Maybe farmers could get by without counselling. Have farmers always had counselling? Besides, this program probably costs more than $17,064 to administer. Third grant: 'Grants under the Canadian Rural Transition Plan,' $750,465. Does rural transition really need grants? How much rural transition is left to take place? Fourth grant: 'Grants to Canadian Farm Women's Organizations,' $50,000. Farm women are good, deserving people, no doubt, but shouldn't such groups do their own fund-raising? Fifth grant: 'Grants for the Northwestern Ontario Grain Transportation Payments Program,' $75,200. We have a comparative advantage in producing grain. Should we really be subsidizing it? Sixth grant: 'Grants for the Feed Freight Adjustment Program': $20,000,000. Same question. If feed has to be subsidized, should we be focusing our agriculture on livestock? The grants so far described get the reader one and a quarter inches down the first column of the first page of transfers, which includes another 101 entries, the biggest of which is $207,499,144 for dairy subsidies, which presumably are intended to offset the higher prices brought about by dairy marketing boards. Would it not be simpler just to do away with the marketing boards?

The prevailing view in Canada is that because we are poorer than we used to be we no longer can afford all the public services

188 The Meaning of Canadian Life

to which we have grown accustomed. This is wrong on both counts. We are *not* poorer than we used to be. To be sure, GDP per Canadian did not grow as quickly in the 1970s and 1980s as it did in the 1960s, but it did grow, and in 1994 it was almost twice as high in real terms as it was in 1965. If all we did in the public sector was buy what we bought in earlier decades, we would manage quite easily. The problem is that, in part because we have founded our identity on a large government, there is now almost no area of public or private life in which government intrusion or assistance is not accepted. What is not sustainable, what we cannot afford, is the continuing growth of government, our preference for more and more and more of it.

It is widely believed that neoconservatives wish to abolish government entirely. They do not. Without government there would be very little in the way of civilization. David Frum, perhaps Canada's best-known neoconservative, has said that he cannot conceive of how a modern government could spend less than 30 per cent of GNP and still perform all the functions that it rightly should perform, form policing to defence to financing education to providing income safety nets, and so on. His estimate obviously could be disputed. Perhaps the number is 35 per cent, perhaps 25 per cent. But it almost certainly is not 50 per cent. What is quite certain is that the larger government gets, the less the benefit produced by each additional dollar spent. More is not actually less – except in pathological cases, there *are* benefits from the extra spending – but with each passing dollar the benefit is less and less. The cost, in contrast, is more and more, as we are about to see.

THE 'EXCESS BURDEN' OF TAXATION

The out-of-pocket costs of taxation are high enough. Money is taken from you and sent to Ottawa or your provincial capital or city hall, where it either buys something – something useful, preferably – or is transferred to a (you hope) more deserving fellow citizen. But the cost of this transaction isn't limited to the dollar value of the money taken. Economists have also identified an 'excess burden' from taxation, and the latest estimates are that it's

The Rising Cost of Civilization 189

very high, in some cases as high as several dollars per dollar of tax paid.

Taxation's excess burden arises because taxes cause people to change their behaviour. Tax work, and they may work less. Tax a good that they enjoy consuming, and they'll probably consume less of it. Tax the return to their savings or investments, and they'll probably save or invest less. In each case, the direct cost of taxation is the money handed over to governments. But in addition, taxpayers are now doing less of something they formerly did more of, presumably because doing more of it benefited them.

In most market transactions you don't actually 'get what you pay for,' you get *more* than you pay for. For example, the first video you rent in a month is probably worth more in terms of enjoyment than the $3 (say) that you have to pay for it; the second, too, and maybe the third, depending on your fondness for videos. Eventually, however, you reach a stage, five or ten or twenty videos later, at which the thought of watching another is more than you can abide. The pleasure that you anticipate from an extra video now is less than $3, so you don't rent one. Suppose you rented five videos in all, for which you paid $15 in total. You presumably got more than $15 of viewing pleasure from them. Until the very last video you rented, each video gave you more than $3 of anticipated enjoyment, in some cases a lot more, and yet each cost you only $3.

Now suppose that the government puts a $2 tax on video rentals, which puts the rental price up to $5. What happens? You probably still rent some videos, and on each video you pay $2 in taxes, which goes to the government. But suppose that the higher 'tax-in' price dissuades you from viewing two videos a month. Each was giving you more than $3 of anticipated viewing pleasure – if it hadn't been, you wouldn't have rented it. But that viewing pleasure is now snuffed out. The government doesn't make any money from your decision not to view the extra two videos: it makes money only when you do rent videos. In fact, *nobody's* better off from your decision to rent two fewer videos. The government doesn't get any tax revenue; the video store doesn't make any money; and you're worse off, because you don't get to see two videos that, all else being equal, you would have liked to see.[10]

By exactly how much are you worse off? We can't say precisely, but we can get some idea. You would have rented the two extra videos at a price of $3 each, so they must have given you more than $3 of anticipated pleasure. But you don't rent them at a price of $5, so you must expect less than $5 of pleasure out of them. So they would have given you more than $3 but less than $5 of pleasure. And you would have had to pay $3 each for them. So you're at most $2 worse off per video.

What happens as the tax rate rises? You presumably cut back more.[11] But as you do, you cut back on videos that would have brought you higher and higher anticipated enjoyment. The parched man arriving at the oasis appreciates the first litre of water much more than the twentieth. You looked forward to the first video per month more than the second, and the second more than the third, and so on and so on, so if you play the string backward and cut back from the fifth to the fourth to the third video, you're cutting back on videos that would have provided more and more enjoyment. In sum, the higher the tax rate, the greater the excess burden the tax imposes, since it eliminates higher- and higher-value activities.

If it were just a question of depressing the market for videos, perhaps the excess burden of taxation wouldn't be very high. Siskel and Ebert excepted, it surely wouldn't kill anyone not to be able to watch as many movies as they pleased. But there are taxes everywhere, and they all create excess burdens. The federal equalization formula, which compensates the poorer provinces for their deficient tax bases, includes thirty-three – thirty-three! – different types of tax imposed at the provincial and municipal levels alone. Every one of the thirty-three both raises revenue and imposes excess burdens. And many tax much more important activities than video-viewing. Employment, for instance. Businesses presumably hire workers until the dollar value added to output by the very last worker hired is virtually equal to what he or she is paid.[12] If so, all workers except perhaps the very last one hired make more money for the company than they cost, which is

The Rising Cost of Civilization 191

a good recipe for corporate profitability. If the government imposes a tax on labour – which is what payroll taxes are: tax is levied on any wages the firm pays – the last worker now costs *more* than he or she contributes to output and therefore, as far as the firm is concerned, becomes expendable. The higher the tax, the more workers become expendable. So long as the firm employs at least some people, it will pay taxes (equal to the tax per worker times the number of workers employed).

But the firm also loses the surplus that it would have made from all the workers whom it would have employed had there been no tax. What's the value of that surplus? Before the tax, the overall benefit from employing the worker must have been greater than the old cost of labour – for example, $8 an hour. But at the new cost of labour – let us say, $9.50 an hour – the worker isn't worth employing, since he or she can't add value equal to that new, tax-inclusive cost. So the overall surplus lost is at most $1.50 an hour, the difference between the old cost of labour and the new cost, times the number of workers let go. The higher this tax wedge between the pre-tax and post-tax price of labour, the higher the lost surplus. In 1993, payroll taxes averaged $2,209 per employee across Canada and were as high as $2,700 per employee in Quebec. In 1966, by contrast, they had been just $466 per employee, also measured in 1993 dollars (Picot, Zin, and Beach 1995: 3.4).

That's not the end of the story, however. There's an excess burden for the worker, as well, who also loses a sort of surplus. The first hour you work in a week presumably doesn't cost much in terms of boredom, fatigue, or effort, yet you appreciate the money. If you're like most people, the first hour is a great deal: you might even pay your employer for getting you out of the house. The thirtieth hour in a week may also be a good deal, though presumably not as good a deal as the first. You're more tired, possibly less interested in what you're doing, and increasingly aware that work is cutting into the other good things you could be doing with your time. That wasn't a concern when you were working only one hour a week and had the remaining 167 hours to yourself. But thirty hours begins to pinch. How about the fiftieth hour? By now you're probably wondering whether there's any surplus at all. Family, housework, hobbies, and leisure all beckon, assuming that you're not too exhausted for them. You've put in forty-nine hours already, and you may be fed up. The dollars that you earn from the extra hours of work just don't seem that appealing.

If that's the way most workers do feel, then taxes have exactly the same effect on workers as on video-viewers and job-creating firms. Any tax on labour income – an income tax, for instance – reduces the net wage received for any hour of work. That fiftieth hour of work in the week is decidedly unappealing now that the government is taking a share of your earnings. And it looks less and less appealing the bigger the share taken. So you may cut back on hours. But doing so means cutting back on hours that would have created successively greater surplus for you. So long as you don't give up work altogether or take your work underground, the government does get tax money out of you. But as the tax rate rises, so does the excess burden.

Estimates of the size of this excess burden naturally vary: this is economics, after all. The answer depends on just what is assumed about how quickly people's surplus falls as they consume more and more videos, or hire more and more workers, or work more and more hours. The estimates aren't based solely on assumptions, of course: the size of the surplus can be gauged by how people react to price increases. Activities without much of a surplus can be completely wiped out by price increases: people simply decide that at a higher price their surplus disappears and the activity no longer is worth it. If price increases have little effect, however, on whether or how much people engage in an activity, that's a good indication that it produces lots of surplus. People addicted to alcohol or tobacco or gambling don't cut back their consumption even when taxes on these goods are steep, which is why they are such prolific generators of revenue for any governments that feel no qualms about preying on the addicted – which, these days, means just about all governments.

Using data on the price responsiveness of various activities, economists can provide at least rough estimates of this excess

The Rising Cost of Civilization 193

TABLE 17.2
Cost of an extra dollar of tax revenue, 1993

Jurisdiction	Cost of dollar raised by an increase in personal tax rate ($)	Cost of dollar raised by an increase in personal tax surcharge ($)
British Columbia	1.46	64.80
Alberta	1.40	3.65
Saskatchewan	1.56	4.02
Manitoba	1.72	not defined*
Ontario	1.62	4.59
Quebec	1.99	70.43
New Brunswick	1.60	4.68
Nova Scotia	1.55	not defined
Prince Edward Island	1.54	not defined
Newfoundland	1.67	not applicable
Federal government	1.38	13.26

SOURCE: Dahlby 1994, Tables 2 and 4.
*Further increases in tax rates actually *reduce* tax revenues. All estimates assume that a 10 per cent change in wages causes a 1 per cent change in hours worked. The federal surtax referred to is the super surtax.

burden of taxation. Table 17.2 shows recent estimates, again by Bev Dahlby (1994), of the effects of increases in personal taxes. Raising an extra dollar of public revenues by increasing the basic rate of income tax costs between $1.40 in Alberta, where taxes are relatively low to begin with, and $1.99 in Quebec, where they are already high. Using income surtaxes – that is, extra income taxes paid on incomes starting as low as $30,001 in Manitoba and as high as $92,656 in Prince Edward Island – is even more expensive, ranging from a low of $3.65 per dollar of tax revenue raised to a high of $70.43 in Quebec. Yes, under reasonable assumptions about how people's effort varies with tax rates, it costs $70.43 in excess burden to raise just one extra dollar of income using Quebec's income surtax.

In fact, the cost goes even higher than that. Dahlby's estimates of taxation's excess burden assume that people's supply of their labour is relatively unresponsive to changes in its price. A 10 per cent increase in the wage paid induces only a 1 per cent increase in the hours of labour they're willing to supply. If a response of 2 per cent is assumed, the cost of taxation is even higher. Raising an extra dollar by hiking the basic rate of income now costs between a low of $1.80 in Alberta and a high of $4.88 – almost five bucks – in Quebec.[13]

What it costs to generate public revenues has obvious implications for government spending. It's a truism in economics, if not yet in politics, that governments should spend money only if the benefit from doing so exceeds the cost. If the cost of public funds is just the one dollar taken from the taxpayer and turned over to public use, then public projects can be justified so long as they produce at least a dollar's benefit. But if the true cost of raising the last dollar of public funds isn't one dollar, but three or four, then projects should go forward only if they bring benefits three or four times greater than their cash costs. Though lots of Canadians may believe that most public programs are worth the tax dollars they cost, many fewer believe that they're worth three or four times that.

Thus the Canadian public sector finds itself ground between millstones. As tax rates rise ever higher, they bring in less and less extra revenue but cause greater and greater excess burden. With the economic cost of raising the extra dollar of revenue rising, public programs must be *increasingly* valued if they are to justify the taxes that finance them. But as it has grown larger, the public sector has often seemed to devote tax dollars to more and more marginal undertakings. The taxpayer fatigue that has resulted has caused widespread speculation about why the baby boomers are more mean-spirited and less generous than their parents were in the 1960s, when governments began expanding rapidly. In fact, people probably *haven't* changed. Circumstances have. The marginal cost of public funds is higher, and the marginal benefit of public spending lower than in previous decades. Confronted with today's tax rates and public programs, the boomers' parents might well have reacted with the same ill-humoured consternation many of their children now exhibit.

18
The Psychic Costs of Government

Government also involves costs that don't show up on T-4 slips or in the Public Accounts. If the Canadian Radio-television and Telecommunications Commission (CRTC) imposes Canadian content requirements on broadcasters or restricts competition in cable television, that raises cable rates. This cost doesn't show up in anybody's books as a tax, but that's exactly what it is: 'Can-con' providers and cable companies profit, and cable subscribers lose. A tax by any other name would redistribute as much. When the Canadian Dairy Commission restricts the supply of milk, or the Canadian Chicken Marketing Agency the supply of chickens – as they do – the prices of milk, cheese, and chicken rise. These price increases don't show up on any government's books as a tax, but producers are better off, consumers suffer, and the entire exchange is beautifully invisible – in short, the perfect crime. As a result of an extensive advertising effort, the marketing boards even have many poor souls believing that it's good, not bad, to pay higher prices for basic foodstuffs.

Examples of redistribution by regulation abound. Entrance to the taxi industry is strictly regulated in many Canadian cities. As a result, consumers pay higher prices and cab companies make more money than they would with free entry. Cab drivers may or may not be better off, depending on whether they can restrict their supply, too. If they can't, their wages remain low and the entire benefit of supply restriction goes to cab companies. If they can, they may share the proceeds from higher prices. Decent, well-meaning Canadians might regard this as a good thing, since most cab drivers presumably are not rich. But why fight poverty only among cab drivers or with a mechanism that may not reach them? Why not fight it instead with systematic anti-poverty programs for all Canadians, using the taxation and income-transfer system? That way cab prices will reflect the true cost of providing cab services, while only poor Canadians – and *all* poor Canadians – will get the financial help they need.

The common denominator in these three cases, and in the literally hundreds of other such regulations that Canadian governments at all levels have introduced, is that they create monopoly power. In 1973 OPEC demonstrated for all the world to see that if you can restrict your product's supply, you can raise its price and make yourself richer. Try as they might, fondly as they may wish it, cab drivers, cable companies, broadcasters, and dairy and chicken farmers couldn't possibly imitate OPEC and form successful cartels all on their own. A cartel would be too hard to organize and police: there are simply too many actual or potential competitors. Moreover, it would be illegal.[1] And even if they did succeed temporarily, with such large numbers of competitors – there are more than ten thousand dairy farmers – there would be an overwhelming incentive to cheat, that is, to shade prices so as to win market share, as has happened time after time in OPEC, though it has only thirteen members.

The only way these groups and dozens like them can hope to acquire monopoly power is if governments enforce it for them, which is exactly what obliging Canadian governments have done. Thus it is against the law to produce and sell more milk, eggs, or chicken than quota allotment from the relevant agricultural commission allows. If producers do exceed their quota, they can be fined or put in jail. It is similarly illegal to contest a broadcast market that the CRTC says is closed, or in many Canadian cities to enter the cab business without municipal permission. In 1995 the government of Quebec even made it illegal to enter the daycare business, at least for the year in which a provincial task force was going to take to plan the industry's evolution. People needed daycare for their children and were willing to pay for it.

The Psychic Costs of Government 197

Other people needed work and were willing to provide daycare. But the government simply declared the delivery of new daycare services illegal, as if daycare were prostitution or drug-peddling. Government interference in normal economic activities is now so commonplace that towards the end of his life a frustrated Jonathan Hughes asked anguishedly: 'What major line of economic activity ... is completely free today of federal regulation? Is the answer none?' (Hughes 1991: 225). And he was referring to the United States!

How much does all this regulation cost? An estimate for the United States by Thomas Hopkins of the Rochester Institute of Technology is that in 1995 regulations imposed costs equal to $668 billion, compared with federal spending of $1.5 trillion. The cost per household was $7,000, one thousand dollars more than the average American income tax bill. And this seems certain to be an underestimate, since it includes only the burden of complying with regulations for which cost studies have been done: in many industries regulation has not yet been studied closely (*Economist* 1996b: 19). No similar calculation has been done for Canada, but most Canadians believe that we are at least as regulated a society as the United States – as would befit a country that has lodged its identity in its greater-than-American use of government – so presumably the cost would be even higher here.

Not all regulation is bad, of course. Maybe many of the industries mentioned simply can't go unregulated. Consumers want to know that milk and chicken have been inspected for cleanliness, that cab drivers are acquainted with the rules of the road, and that broadcasters won't show smut over the air, or at least not more smut than local standards allow. Even in these cases, however, the need for government action should not be overstated. If dairies and chicken ranchers want to stay in business, they have every interest in demonstrating on their own, without government help, that their product is safe. Similarly, taxi companies that want repeat business will ensure that their drivers drive safely, while broadcasters who don't want to be boycotted will voluntarily conform with community standards. But even if governments do regulate quality standards, nothing requires them also to regu-

198 The Meaning of Canadian Life

late the number of competitors in an industry or the price at which competitors can sell their wares. If suppliers demonstrate that they can meet hygiene or safety standards, why should they not be permitted to compete? If some people want to set up daycare and other people want to send their children to it, what possible interest can the state have in forbidding this transaction? In the unlikely event that parents cannot be trusted to look out for the interests of their children, then by all means minimum standards should be enforced by the state. But anything more than that very likely is not regulation of service in consumers' interest but regulation of output in an attempt to raise producers' incomes.

Strange as it now seems, as recently as fifteen years ago, the government of Canada, through the Canadian Transportation Commission (CTC), regulated the price, time of departure, type of plane flown, and many other details of every single airplane route that the country's commercial airlines flew. And if the government didn't want them to fly at a certain time or price or to a given location using given equipment, they did not fly. In his memoirs, Jack Pickersgill (1994), former minister of transportation and first head of the CTC, was remarkably candid about why this was done. The reason was simple, to protect Air Canada. To be sure, Pickersgill's motivation was public-spirited: he didn't want a money-losing airline to drain the federal treasury, as money-losing railways had done in the first half of the century: 'CN had been created at the end of the First World War to rescue bankrupt railways and had been an almost incessant drain on the Canadian treasury and the taxpayers. Competition, I was determined, should not be allowed to develop to the point where Air Canada would be put in a similar position' (722).[2] Pickersgill writes that when in 1964 it became clear that rival CP Air was filling the one plane per day that it was allowed to fly between Montreal and Vancouver and was doing so in part because of lower fares, 'I told the presidents [of CP and Air Canada] that unless the airlines adopted equal fares voluntarily, I would ask the government to compel them to do so' (725). In describing how he divided Canada's international routes between the two airlines he refers to the 'division of the world outside Europe between Spain and Portugal by Pope Alexander VI,' a comparison disproportionate in terms of scale and historical importance but entirely reflective of the autocratic and arrogant nature of much Canadian regulation. The consumers who flew the airlines didn't know best. The airlines who operated the service didn't know best. The government of Canada knew best.

At bottom, of course, the problem was nationalism. The obvious remedy – selling off Air Canada, or in the 1920s, Canadian National – and letting it compete with whomever came along simply wasn't an option. Like those pitiable Third World countries whose rulers feel that they must have at least one 747 with their nation's name on it, we had to have a national airline, even if it cost consumers tens of millions of dollars a year in overpriced air travel. The custom in Canada has always been to ridicule Charles Wilson, the American secretary of defence and former General Motors executive who, in 1952 congressional testimony didn't actually quite say that what was good for General Motors was good for the United States but came close enough. Just why we laugh isn't clear, however, for in this country what is good for Air Canada and dozens of other organizations like it is deemed good for the country as a whole.

Who knows? Perhaps what was good for Air Canada *was* good for the country. We do still have Air Canada, if that makes people feel good. And we do not know whether, without Pickersgill and his imperial regulatory philosophy, we would still have it. However, Canadians do like to move about. They did even in the 1960s. Given the choice, they may even feel more comfortable flying in airplanes run by their compatriots. At the very least, an airline run by fellow citizens should have the distinct marketing advantage of knowing what pleases them. But whether or not regulation of this sort serves a public purpose, it clearly does alter the distribution of income. First and foremost it was good for Air Canada and its employees, who were able to appropriate a good chunk of the extra profits that protective regulation created, the best evidence of this being the passion with which they fought the deregulation that threatened their high wages. Nothing so arouses a Canadian's nationalist passion as an attack on his sinecure.

Evidence collected by economists over the last thirty years suggests that far from being a rare occurrence it is a commonplace that the people who benefit most from regulation are the very people being regulated. Regulatory commissions either come to identify with or in fact are simply co-opted by the industry. Canadian culture ministers, for instance, are routinely judged on their ability to plunder the public treasury and rig the tax, tariff, and employment regulations for the benefit of their constituents in the culture industries. What is most surprising is not that the culture industries themselves adopt this standard for judging ministers, but that the newspapers and television reinforce it – though of course television benefits from similar arrangements.

The capture of regulators by those being regulated is by no means a uniquely Canadian syndrome. In the United States it has been so common that, in the final chorus of his jeremiad on the sins of the modern congressional system of government, Jonathan Hughes wrote: 'As it stands, we have on the ground almost every kind of regulation that could be conceived of over time, and it was made mainly by those for whom the regulation pays, for whom money can be made by regulation the free market would never provide' (Hughes 1991: 230). The U.S. Federal Aviation Administration took the same approach to airline regulation as the CTC until desisting in the mid-1970s – ten years, in the usual lag, before we did. Both the persistent muckraking of economists and the much lower prices charged by airlines flying solely within the superstates of Texas and California and therefore free from federal rate-setting persuaded Congress, in the unlikely person of the liberal Democrat, Edward Kennedy, chairman of the relevant Senate committee, that consumers might benefit from a federal withdrawal from micro-regulation. Even stubbornly vested interests were unable to overcome such a powerful combination of forces (see Derthick and Quirk 1985; Noll and Owen 1983). The benefits of deregulation quickly became apparent. Fares fell in real terms, and many more people began flying. This created problems of its own, of course, as both airports and planes became more crowded. But in the travel business crowds are a symptom of success: more and more people could now afford to fly.

So we Canadians are by no means unique in giving ourselves over to regulations that operate in the interest of powerful groups or individuals. This is typical of democratic governments the world round: when people ask their legislatures for help, help is often forthcoming. Not surprisingly, few politicians like saying no to constituents. Moreover, the process is legitimized by what American economist Robert Higgs has called the 'now-dominant ideology of the mixed economy ... To take – indirectly if not directly – other people's property for one's own benefit is now considered morally impeccable, provided that the taking is effected through the medium of the government' (Higgs 1987: 195). But the appropriation of state power by private groups surely is even more likely in a society that sees its greater use of government – its 'pragmatic,' 'non-ideological' use of government – as its main claim to uniqueness. To be more egregiously manipulated by interest groups *is* a genuine form of distinctiveness, if not one to which most sensible people aspire.

A CONFEDERACY OF BEGGARS

The costs of running this type of society are greater than merely the shame that should result from repeatedly being had by sharp operators. The clearest lesson that it teaches is that success is achieved not by being inventive, innovative, or imaginative, but by successfully petitioning government. What counts is not what you know but whom you know, a principle that has governed life in the Atlantic provinces for several generations now. The career difficulty that the mid-1990s premier of Nova Scotia created for himself by not being sufficiently partisan in dispensing patronage appointments is but one sad incident in a long and inglorious history of sycophancy and supplication. The Atlantic provinces are an extreme case, of course. In 1946 the premier of Nova Scotia warned Ottawa about the effects of its plan to centralize the national economy: 'Provincial independence will vanish. Provincial dignity will disappear, provincial governments will become mere annuitants of Ottawa' (Creighton 1976: 114). Because Ontario resisted, the full flowering of the 1946 plans never came to pass. But the result warned of has. Government entirely dominates the Atlantic economy. Federal, provincial, and local government expenditure accounts for 77 per cent of all economic activity in Prince Edward Island, 71 per cent in Newfoundland, and 65 per cent in Nova Scotia (Damus 1992, Chart 36).

Matters are not yet so serious in the rest of the country. Still, it is not necessary to credit everything in Stevie Cameron's scandal-mongering *On the Take* to believe that good relations with the government help businessmen's fortunes. The chairman and chief executive officer of Teleglobe, Inc., speaking in the wake of a federal cabinet shuffle, said how 'delighted' he was to see the minister who oversees regulation of his firm continue on in his portfolio and how 'favourably impressed' he was 'by the careful and rigorous approach taken by the Government of Canada on telecommunications policy' (Sirois 1996: 65). It is possible that this is also his private opinion, but in a society in which displeasing the minister can be commercially catastrophic, there may be increasing divergence between the public and private beliefs of business people. 'Extensive government expenditure and intervention and large scale undertakings have raised the fundamental problems of morality,' wrote Harold Innis in 1945, in classic understatement (Innis 1945: xiii).

With their endearing habit of inventing secret names for everything, economists call this kind of behaviour 'rent-seeking' – 'rent,' as we have seen, being the economist's term for 'prize' or 'gift' or 'unearned income.' Government makes known, either by formal announcement or by its pattern of behaviour, that it stands ready to favour with largesse those who convince it that they should be favoured. In other words, it announces that 'rents' are available. Once this news is out, people get into the business of seeking rents. They hire lobbyists, cultivate bureaucrats, and contribute to political campaigns. They try to create a sympathetic public image for themselves. They consult public affairs specialists, set up government relations departments, and appoint vice-presidents for government affairs.

The Psychic Costs of Government   203

The politico-industrial complex that results provides careers, often very profitable ones, for large numbers of very bright people, most of whom could have made excellent social contributions doing truly useful things. But, of course, no public purpose is served by all this activity. The largesse does get distributed. Either company A or interest group B or public service association C gets the money, which obviously is important to the owners and employees of A, B, and C, but usually makes little difference as far as the greater society is concerned. What occurs is essentially a highly ritualized lottery. Wealth is transferred from one group to another without anything real being created. No invention takes place. No new skill is developed, except perhaps the skill of how to make a slicker presentation. No new knowledge results, save the self-knowledge of the participants and their greater familiarity with how the system can be worked to advantage. What results is a society of talented, well-heeled supplicants.

Such a conclusion may be regarded as extreme, but is there really any doubt that as more and more people in the society come to depend on the kindnesses of government, they take on many of the attributes of beggars? Because their grant or contract requires that they not give offence, they voluntarily curtail their freedom of speech, a phenomenon that explains the public timidity of most modern business people, for there are few entities more fearful of giving offence than the modern corporation. If share values would be damaged by speaking out, the modern business person can be depended on to clench down on his or her tongue. Thus when a newly elected separatist premier of Quebec openly threatened consequences for any brokerage firm whose economics department engaged in 'economic terrorism' – by which, of course, he meant speaking the obvious truth that Quebec's separation from Canada could be economically costly – this was widely denounced in the press as a tactic worthy of a banana republic. What was less remarked on was that in such republics intimidation invariably works, as it also seems to have done in Quebec, the economics departments of the country's financial institutions having been notably more reticent about the consequences of separation after the premier's edict than before. But perhaps it is not surprising that a man who allocates the brokerage fees on $6 billion of bond sales per year should wield such influence. It is yet one more reason why governments are not naturally averse to borrowing money.

Perhaps it is best that our children learn early that in the world as it really is privilege, power, and patronage, not inspiration, industry, and imagination, are the keys to success. Perhaps from an early age they should be taught to be flatterers, sycophants, and smooth presenters, since these are the attributes the society values most (apart, of course, from an ability to hit the curve ball). But if this does not seem a desirable way to run our society, an alternative course is to attack the source of the temptation. 'If you build it, they will come,' said the disembodied voice in W.P. Kinsella's *Field of Dreams*. The corollary is: 'If you don't build it, they will not come.' If government does not offer what the infomercials call 'free gifts' to those who seek them, then seekers after favours will have to find honest work instead. Lawyers will have to do real business, and lobbyists take up filmmaking or engineering or poetry for a living. Empty the honey-pots, and the ants will disperse.

If is, of course, naïve to suppose that governments will entirely abandon the truly ancient habit of handing out gifts. How else are they to ingratiate themselves to their constituents? Even so notorious a fiscal tartar as U.S. Senator Phil Gramm (Texas) appreciates the political virtue of good constituency work: 'Let's put it this way. If we should vote next week on whether to begin producing cheese in a factory on the moon, I almost certainly would oppose it. On the other hand, if the government decides to institute the policy, it would be my objective to see that a Texas contractor builds this celestial cheese plant, that the milk comes from Texas cows, and that the earth distribution centre is located in Texas' (quoted in Williams 1995: 168). So fragile a thing as a good intention will make little impression when flung against the stone wall of such resolute self-interest.

The only force in recent years that has caused any appreciable retrenchment in public expenditures has been the prospect of imminent public bankruptcy. Only the accumulation of govern-

The Psychic Costs of Government 205

ment interest payments, when pressed up against growing resistance to further taxation, has served to squeeze out public expenditures. Realizing this, fiscal conservatives are tempted to cheer secretly for those, such as journalist Linda McQuaig, who would have our governments pile their debts higher still, for experience shows that only a rising burden of interest payments will grind down the accumulated mass of programs and sinecures.

What happens, however, when and if the deficit finally is brought under control? The danger is that what used to be spent on interest charges will now be devoted to new programs. In 1995 Canada spent 37.8 per cent of GDP on government programs and 9.8 per cent on interest. Get the debt under control, and the awful possibility arises that we will spend all 47.6 per cent on programs (Perry 1996: Tables 5 and 9). If the governments of that (thankfully still distant) day make clear that money is available to those who ask for it, there certainly will be no lack of petitioners for extra spending. Ms. McQuaig herself favours denticare – free, comprehensive, universal dental care – but regrets that 'to argue ... for a national denticare program, in the face of the swelling movement for fiscal restraint, is to put oneself on the outer margins of serious national debate – even though such a program would probably improve our lives and save us all money in the long run' (McQuaig 1995: 13). Her faith that even in the face of a zero price for dental care Canadians nevertheless would ration their demands in such a way that the system would cost less on average than one in which they must pay for their own care is as touching as, after three decades of the welfare state, it is astonishing. And, of course, there is the ultimate question: if denticare, why not grocericare, or housicare or travelicare or computicare or even entertainicare? If interest payments eventually do fall to zero and there is another 9.8 per cent of GDP to spend in the public sector, why not indeed? Faced with this prospect, fiscal conservatives can only argue that if at the very least the benefit of the doubt could be reversed, if Canadians could be persuaded to take a harder look at proposed expenditures instead of foggily rhapsodizing about how yet another intervention will make us even more distinctive from the savage social Darwinists to the south of us, then some progress might be made in building a public sector that would pursue a limited number of worthy ends with a reasonable prospect of attaining them.

The alternative is to live in a society in which pleasing the minister becomes ever more important. Aversion to this kind of society should unite right and left alike, and in fact it has often been noted that what are called 'public-choice economists,' those who harvest the vineyard planted by 1986 Nobel laureate James Buchanan, are not much different from Marxists in their belief that public powers often are appropriated by private interests. Roger Douglas, leader of New Zealand's radical anti-statist reforms of the 1980s, was head of that country's Labour party. He has stressed that eliminating entrenched privilege from society should unite both free-marketeers and socialists.

We Canadians are perhaps more circumspect about entrenched privilege than we used to be. In the 1870s, the parliamentary committee that drafted the Bank Act sat together with MP's and senators who were bank presidents or directors and, in the words of one participant, were 'really a joint committee of Parliament and banks' (quoted in Naylor 1975: 75). We maintain more proper appearances these days. Nevertheless, from the time of the Family Compact and the Château Clique, privileged interests have used the power of the state to entrench themselves ever more deeply. John A. Macdonald supposedly invited the country's manufacturers to tell his ministers what the tariff rates should be. In more recent decades, George Grant argued that by the early 1960s what remained of the Canadian state had been commandeered by monied Toronto interests. In the same era, the sociologist John Porter attributed the vertical nature of our national mosaic to the same forces.

It doesn't do simply to replace one set of protected interests – the business class – by another, be it farmers, unions, social workers, or various minorities. If the goal truly is an open society and meritocracy, the remedy must be to eliminate privilege everywhere. The most obvious way of doing so is to make it impossible for people to clothe themselves with the powers of the state. But

The Psychic Costs of Government 207

that requires agreement, however un-Canadian it may seem, that we use the state's powers more sparingly.

CONSUMING JEALOUSIES

In 1990, in what turned out to be its last full-length review of the country now known as the 'former Soviet Union,' The *Economist* newspaper observed that each of the union's fifteen republics felt that it was being exploited by the others 'and that is the reason they do not want to stick together' (*Economist* 1990: 9). Everyone's being exploited has a distinctly Canadian ring. To put it another way: there is more than a little of the Russian in the sourness of our interregional relations. In 1967, by many accounts our greatest year, Blair Fraser wrote: 'Never in their history have Canadians demonstrated any warm affection for each other. Loyalties have always been parochial, mutual hostilities chronic' (B. Fraser 1967: 313).

Thus English Canada feels that it has long been subsidizing Quebec. Quebec feels that its economic growth has been crippled by political decisions – to build a St Lawrence Seaway, for instance – favouring Ontario. The Atlantic provinces have the good grace to concede that they currently receive more money from Ottawa than they pay in federal taxes but then argue that this is only fair, since for the last century federal economic policies have been dominated by central Canadian concerns. The west has always felt aggrieved, first by the CPR,[3] then by the National Energy Policy, and most recently by alleged federal neglect. Neglect at least isn't active abuse. Of late even fat, placid Ontario, for years the uncomplaining sugar daddy of Confederation, has taken to grumbling, alleging that under Brian Mulroney's Tories it was singled out for especially deep budget cuts.

There is more than anecdotal evidence of interregional jealousy, of course. In 1989, 70 per cent of Canadians told the Gallup organization that they thought that Quebec had benefited most from Confederation; 77 per cent of Quebecers who had an opinion thought that Ontario benefited most (Gallup Canada, Inc., 16 November 1989). Only 4 per cent of Atlantic Canadians believed that their region had done best; only 7 per cent of Quebecers thought that Quebec had; while only 3 per cent of Prairies residents and 9 per cent of British Columbians thought that 'the west' had done best. However, 34 per cent of Ontarians – but only 34 per cent – thought that their province had profited most from Confederation, though this was in 1989, before the special cuts in transfer payments to the three richest provinces.

None of this is new, of course. Fifty years ago the economist Harold Innis wrote: 'The hatreds between regions in Canada have become important vested interests. Montreal exploits the hatred of Toronto and Regina that of Winnipeg and so one might go through the list. A native of Ontario may appear restive at being charged with exploitation by those who systematically exploit him through their charges of exploitation, but even the right to complain is denied to him' (Innis 1945: xi). Innis naturally could not know that this right would be restored in the 1990s.[4]

The one and only cause of our transcontinental discontents is, of course, the excessively intrusive hand of government. What everyone complains of are government decisions: the tariff, the Seaway, the National Energy Policy, and so on. Despite a supposed contempt for market processes, nurtured assiduously over the last several decades by left-leaning 'pragmatists,' most Canadians are relatively content with market-based decisions, many of which – though they would never say this in so many words – they regard as essentially fair.

In 1986 the federal government awarded a $1-billion repair contract for the air force's CF-18 fighter planes to Canadair of Montreal rather than to Bristol Aerospace of Winnipeg, even though Bristol had submitted the lower bid and satisfactorily demonstrated that it could do the job. Ottawa's argument for contravening fundamental market principles and awarding the contract to the *higher* bidder was that, according to the latest incantations of its industrial-policy experts, the opportunity for beneficial spillovers would be greater in Montreal, where there was already a well-developed aerospace industry (mainly because of previous federal decisions, of course). Because such spillovers are notoriously hard to measure, many Manitobans

The Psychic Costs of Government 209

suspected that this techno-babble was actually a cover for political expediency, since Montreal had more cabinet ministers than Winnipeg. Their suspicions were confirmed during the 1995 Quebec referendum campaign when federalist participants in the decision conceded – indeed, boasted – that the real motivation had in fact been political succour for Quebec. Manitoba's resentment at being bilked, which repeated similarly seamy decisions both in 1949 to move Air Canada's headquarters from Winnipeg to Montreal and in 1964 to have its main repair base follow (see Pickersgill 1994: 652-8), is thought to have played a part in the province's rejection of the Meech Lake Accord and certainly did lead to the founding of the Reform party.

Resentment arose, of course, not because Winnipeg lost the contract, but because it lost it unfairly. Out in the market, people and firms lose contracts all the time and do not become bitter as a result. Even regions win or lose over the decades as economic growth either visits or passes them by. No one begrudges Silicon Valley its success: it earned it. By contrast, many Winnipeggers believe that Montreal earned its aerospace success mainly through political influence. Winnipeg was the lowest bidder for the CF-18 contract. It was capable of doing the job. But the political fix was in, and Montreal got the contract. Resentment being the Canadian condition, Montrealers were resentful in turn because of the accusation that they won only because the contest was rigged. If instead market rules had been followed and the lowest bidder had received the contract, neither city would have had cause for complaint. Winnipeggers would have felt that they lost fair and square. Montrealers, had they lost, would have been disappointed but, except perhaps for a normal human tendency to envy success, would have had no reason for bitterness.

'A man receiving charity practically always hates his benefactor,' wrote George Orwell, 'it is a fixed characteristic of human nature' (Orwell 1989: 186). And, of course, the giver is often resentful, too, especially if he or she thinks that the 'gift' has been extorted. Thus it is not surprising that two economists at the University of Calgary have been most diligent in tracking the path of expenditures and taxes from provinces, through Ottawa, and back to provinces. Nor that they find that Alberta has made by far the largest net fiscal contribution to Confederation since 1961 – $138 billion more in taxes paid than benefits received (Mansell and Schlenker 1995: Table 1).[5] Nor, given the conceptual complexity and political sensitivity of such calculations, that others have found quite a different pattern of interregional redistribution. The Parti Québécois, for instance, repeatedly calculates a net drain on Quebec as a result of Confederation. It is not wise to be wholly cynical about such calculations, however. Facts are stubborn things, and someone is right about the numbers, though it does seem unlikely, in the highly charged environment in which such sums normally are taken, that the true facts of the matter will ever command a consensus.

Orwell's remark offers an obvious lesson for Canadian policymakers. A philosopher-king put in charge of a loose confederation in which interregional jealousies were already pronounced might well decide to do as many things as possible according to market rules. It would be naïve, of course, to think that political considerations could be entirely removed from those allocations of large sums of money that do have to be accomplished through the public sector. But hope may not be entirely futile. The federal government apparently has learned from the CF-18 disaster. Now when it announces cutbacks in defence budgets it provides a careful breakdown of just how much is being lost province by province (see Martin 1994). The decision in 1995 to close the Collège militaire royale at Saint-Jean, Quebec, is said to have been motivated mainly by the need to show that Quebec was bearing its 'fair share' of military cuts, even if the decision itself may not have been wise, given the need in a bilingual country for a bilingual officer corps. Other expenditures also seem to be governed by similarly scrupulous egalitarianism – for better or for worse. When Ottawa set up a series of 'centres of research excellence' in the 1980s, the provincial distribution of such centres was suspiciously uniform. Though all areas of Canada may be equal in some fundamental moral sense, not all are equally excellent in research.[6]

Needless to say, perfect equality across provinces does not con-

The Psychic Costs of Government 211

stitute market rules. Maybe the Collège militaire should have stayed open. Maybe the Maritimes – because they are the Maritimes, and therefore more useful to a navy than Saskatchewan – really do deserve a higher share of military expenditures than other provinces. Maybe some provinces should not have received a centre of excellence. If Silicon Valley had been required to operate in all fifty American states in proportion to their population or poverty, the computer industry might still be at the Brainiac stage. But if scrupulous equality is inefficient, while favouritism will cause deep division, the only way to live by market rules is to have as many decisions as possible actually made by the market. If we are not good at deciding things collectively, if we are perpetually envious and petty, as we seem to be, then continuing to do so much through the public sector may end up literally consuming the country in jealousy.

There is considerable evidence that this is exactly what has been happening in recent decades. The University of Calgary's Mansell and Schlenker have calculated that 'the federal government has been generating a growing amount of redistribution across provinces over time.' Measured in 1994 dollars, the amounts paid to Newfoundland increased by $3,375 per capita between the 1960s and the early 1990s. PEI got $3,018 more, Nova Scotia $1,692, New Brunswick $4,409, Quebec $595, Manitoba $1,599, Saskatchewan $1,877, and the Northern Territories $8,879. At the same time, the net burden on Ontario rose by $1,056 per capita, on Alberta $1,058, and on British Columbia $641 (Mansell and Schlenker 1995: Table 3, p. 9).

These are not trivial amounts, especially when quadrupled to capture the effect on the proverbial family of four. New Brunswick, for instance, has gone from being a net contributor to interprovincial finance in the 1960s to receiving more than $20,000 a year per family of four. Is it mere coincidence that the thirty years during which Quebec separatism grew from almost nothing to majority status among French Quebecers was also the period in which the very visible hand of government came to dominate Canadian society?

In such a divided society as ours, as its most successful prime

212 The Meaning of Canadian Life

minister, William Lyon Mackenzie King, understood well, circumspection is a virtue. 'For King,' writes historian Jack Granatstein (1994), 'the time was never ripe for sweeping change' (125). It seems comical now to read of his worry in 1943 that, given French and English Canadians' differing birth rates, family allowances would set the two communities against each other. But for a time they did. Many of our most successful prime ministers have known the value of putting off decisions that do not have to be made. John A. Macdonald's nickname was 'Old Tomorrow.'[7] The historian P.B. Waite (1996) calls procrastination 'the first cousin of compromise' and says that Laurier was a master of it (17). King himself is famous for not having made decisions unless and until they could no longer be avoided. 'Conscription if necessary but not necessarily conscription' now is regarded as spineless temporizing, the stuff of farce, but it helped to get the country through the Second World War without the violent civil unrest experienced in the First. In contrast, by forcing decisions on a fractious society, our more emphatic politicians – Brian Mulroney being the latest and perhaps best example – have frayed the social fabric, perhaps irreparably.[8] The conclusion should be obvious: a Canada in which fewer decisions were made communally, by government, would be a Canada more at peace with itself.

AT WHAT BENEFIT?

The last two chapters have tried to suggest that the cost of our now-gargantuan government has become overbearing. At the margin, the economic cost alone may be three or four dollars per new dollar of public revenue raised. But there are other costs, in terms of arrogance nourished, privilege arrogated, timidity engendered, and resentment enflamed. What do we get in return? We get a wide range of programs, obviously. The Quebec government's phone book, thicker than that of all but the country's largest cities, lists 121 acronyms just for ministries, departments, and agencies, not every one of which has its own acronym. A 1993 compendium of programs offered in Quebec by both the federal and provincial governments runs to nine hundred pages (*Le*

The Psychic Costs of Government 213

Répertoire ... 1993). In this respect, if this alone, Quebec is not different from the other provinces.

Some of these hundreds of programs, both in Quebec and the other provinces, do achieve the ends set out for them. Medical care *is* universally available, even if waiting lists are longer and concerns about the quality of care are growing. University tuitions *are* low, though classrooms are crowded and becoming more so. Unemployed Canadians still do have ready access to cash, albeit not quite as much as formerly, and not for quite as long as formerly. Other programs either do or don't achieve ends that may or may not be as easy to justify. A public-service rationale for many of the things that government does is very hard to divine, though the political rationale for them is obvious.

But in addition to what they actually do or do not accomplish in a nuts-and-bolts way, the many hundreds of public programs whose cost is now so high are supposed to achieve another, more elusive end – that of helping us define ourselves, both to ourselves and to others. The question that remains is: do they? *Does our overgovernment of ourselves in fact create our national distinctiveness?* Or are we distinctive, even distinct, for other reasons? And what will become of this distinctiveness as people relate to one another with new technologies? What will it mean to be Canadian in a virtual world?

19
Virtually Canadian

The end of the nation-state is the most chronically foretold death of the 1990s. The predicted culprits are economic liberalism and the digital revolution. In the twenty-first century, it is argued, human beings will interact with one another in essentially two ways: locally and globally, either face to face, in the accustomed way of traditional reality, or screen to screen, in the wired way of virtual reality. Local government will be needed to regulate local relations among people – to keep them from smoking in the wrong places or running red lights, to collect their garbage, teach their children, and so on. And global government will be needed to oversee their global interactions: someone will have to be World Webmaster, for instance, to prevent the duplication of electronic addresses.

But there no longer will be a role for national governments in mediating among individuals who can now deal with one another directly. Between town hall and global assembly, who would need an Ottawa? Or, as Richard Gwyn (1995) says, 'today's operating slogan of "think global, act local" doesn't leave much for a national centre to do' (269). Already, at the dawn of the information age, national governments are said to be losing their powers both upward to global organizations and downward to local governments and citizens (Courchene 1994: 239). By the mid-1980s, just as globalization fever was catching on, there already were almost five thousand international organizations, of which 365 were intergovernmental (Hobsbawm 1994: 430).

Unfortunately, no one seems to have told the nation-states that they are not long for this world, for in most cases their parliaments, congresses, and assemblies meet almost year-round and legislate frenetically on all sorts of issues, while the species itself is proliferating at an almost unprecedented rate. This may simply be a final flame of energy before burn-out, of course. But just as the collapse of the Austro-Hungarian Empire splattered the map of Europe with a potful of new colours, so the collapse of the Soviet Empire has turned the map of Asia to abstract expressionism. To be sure, what leftists refer to as the American Empire is still intact and in fact now encompasses virtually the entire globe, with even China becoming more American, even to the point of hosting aerobics competitions. But because the empire now is unrivalled, the imperial grip has been relaxed and the emergence of tens of new nation-statelets, possibly even in northern North America, is contemplated with apparent indifference in Washington. So many poor and unheard-of places have achieved the nation-statehood futurists say is so soon to disappear that the International Olympic Committee has decided its Summer Games will no longer open with a march past of the athletes, this having proved insufficiently interesting to rich and heard-of countries' television audiences.

But suppose that, despite appearances, the futurists are right and the nation-state is doomed. The prospect is at once reassuring and depressing to Canadians. Reassuring because it suggests that our own pathology is not unique: dying from an epidemic that spares no one else is comforting in its way. All the world now has what used to be called 'the Canadian disease' – economic and cultural domination by the Americans. What open borders, high-gain TV aerials, and the coaxial cable did to us starting in the 1950s, satellite broadcasting and the World Trade Organization are doing to the rest of the world a half-century later. However, the end of the nation-state is also depressing because, as we have been told without respite for at least three decades now, if the Canadian state becomes impotent, a distinctly Canadian people will soon go the way of the dodo, another unglamourous, slow-learning, overly trusting species. Without a state to undergird it, our little nation cannot possibly stand – or so our betters have taught us. As so often, Richard Gwyn has put it briefest and best: 'Nous, c'est l'état.'

If we were to conduct a premortem for the nation-state in general and ours in particular, which of the two forces mentioned, economic liberalism or the digital revolution, would bear greater culpability? The first part of this book argued, in effect, that economic liberalism would be almost guiltless. Even accepting the premise that an assertively distinctive style of government is crucial to preserving the Canadian nation – a premise that the book's second part has challenged – economic liberalism does not impose debilitating restraints on nation-states. They obviously must dismantle barriers against foreign traders and investors, but beyond this, as we have seen, they remain free to have whatever social or other policies their citizens will agree to pay for. If Canadians really are kinder and gentler and remain willing to tax themselves more than other peoples so as to provide more generous public services, nothing in the liberalization of trade, capital flows, or even labour mobility prevents this.

Economic liberalism does not get off quite so easily, however. There are other ways in which commerce can alter a nation's sense of itself. The Canadian nationalist cry in the great Reciprocity election of 1911 was: 'No truck nor trade with the Yankee.' In fact, trucking and trading with foreigners probably do change a country. Removing tariff and regulatory barries brings people of different countries into contact, and contact alters them. Even so, the culturally homogenizing effects of commercial intercourse can be exaggerated. Canadians do buy lots of American products: the Americans' share of our import market is over 80 per cent, not counting smuggling. In most cases, however, we buy not directly from Americans but rather from Canadians working for companies whose purchasing agents do.[1] Canadians exposed to Americans on a daily basis, whether as buyers, sellers, owners, or employees, may take to talking loudly, wearing Hawaiian print shirts, and applying for gun licences, but these traits will infect the rest of us only indirectly. Moreover, the growth of the service economy, which now employs more than seven of ten Canadians,

Virtually Canadian 217

probably dampens the cultural effects of trucking and trading, for many services are not traded internationally. Canadian teachers, lawyers, doctors, bus drivers, plumbers, cable guys, hairdressers, and so on seldom sell directly to Americans.

Of course, even if most Canadians don't deal face to face or even ear to ear with Americans on a daily basis, we are all exposed to the United States by page, screen, and speaker. We watch American TV and movies, hum American music, and read American books and magazines – those of us who do still read – and now we visit American sites on the internet. Trucking and trading are minor influences compared to television, and it is the potentially Americanizing influence of TV and other mass media that is what most alarms those who fear for the survival of distinctively Canadian sensibilities and experience. As the broadcast universe expands, they worry, Canadians will spend less and less time interacting among themselves and more and more imbibing their neighbour's more intoxicating culture. Eventually, the fear is, what Canadians know, except perhaps for our greater familiarity with cold and snow, will be the same as what Americans know, and indeed what everyone in the world knows. In brief, the day is approaching when everyone will be American. The danger then is not that the nation-state will give away its powers in trade deals, but that the different nations, having become more or less identical, no longer will wish to exercise such powers.

There are a number of reasons, however, for supposing that this will not happen. But before listing them I should emphasize that the cultural homogenization about which people worry has almost nothing to do with economic liberalization. The problem, for those who regard it as such, is not the Autopact or the World Trade Organization or even 'the Mulroney trade deal.' It is the telecommunications satellite and the coaxial cable. To be sure, trade deals may prevent nations from legislating against the distribution of foreign signals by satellite or cable – though neither the FTA nor the NAFTA does – but the legalities are largely moot. In the long run, 'jamming' culture the way the Soviets used to 'jam' news cannot succeed. Yes, if we really wanted to, we could make possession of a satellite dish illegal and send the Royal

Canadian Mounted Police out to arrest anyone who would commit such a crime against our culture.[2] But Canadians rebelled against such a policy when it was tried in the late 1970s (there is at least some tradition of personal liberty in this country) and the dishes are a lot smaller now. Even if NAFTA did tolerate such infringements of free trade, in the long run Canadian consumers undoubtedly would not.

The idea that as a result of watching satellite television everyone in the world will become culturally American is but one possibility, of course. An obvious alternative is that, far from putting nation-states through a blender, thus leaving them all part of the same homogenized mush, the new technologies of the internet and the 500-channel universe will instead leave nations sliced and diced, as people forsake common national experiences in pursuit of their own special interests, possibly even to the extent of forming internet nations – worldwide communities of people interested in particular parts of knowledge. What then would become of old-fashioned nations and their identities, including – yes, that ancient obsession of ours – the Canadian identity?

IDENTITY TESTS

The way to an answer may be found in the work of Alan Turing, a brilliant British mathematician, cryptographer, and logician who killed himself in 1954 at the age of forty-two by eating an apple sprinkled with cyanide. He had helped decode the Nazis' Enigma machine, worked for a time at Princeton with John von Neumann, conceptual father of the computer, and was himself one of the world's first computer scientists. Though the dilemmas that Turing's homosexuality posed for him have been the subject of a successful British television drama (with Derek Jacobi in the lead), many of his theories about statistics and mathematics now are of interest to only a small number of specialists. He did leave at least one enduring intellectual legacy, however: the Turing test for detecting artifical intelligence, first proposed in his 1950 article 'Computing Machinery and Intelligence,' in which he considered the question 'Can a machine think?' (Hodges 1996; Turing 1950).

Virtually Canadian 219

The Turing test is quite simple. You engage the computer in conversation. You sit at a screen and type questions, answers, and comments, and the computer sends back questions, answers, and comments. How does a machine pass the test? You converse for as long as you want, and if, when you are done, you can't tell that you weren't dealing with a human, then the machine is deemed 'intelligent.' Thus the Turing test is a sort of duck test: if it quacks like a human, yaks like a human, cracks wise like a human, and so on, it must be – or might as well be – a human. Of course, to pass such a test the machine may have to be programmed to respond at something less than the speed of light and to pretend once in a while to forget things, seem confused, contradict itself, and need to eat or answer other calls of nature.[3]

Something very much like the Turing test could be used to investigate differences in national identity – to check, in particular, whether people are Canadian or American. Sit subjects down, and by conversing with them – through a voice filter or computer screen, if accents or lumberjack shirts would be giveaways – try to determine which nationality they are. What would be the result? It's virtually certain that a much larger proportion of Canadians could pass as Americans than the reverse. We know a great deal about them. They, notoriously, know almost nothing about us. To take but one example, according to a poll conducted in the spring of 1995, only 1 per cent of Americans knew that Jean Chrétien was the prime minister of Canada. Probably even educated Americans, those who daily read The *New York Times*, for instance, are no more familiar with Canadian culture generally than, for example, French and English Canadians are with each other's, which is to say, not very.

American ignorance of Canada is, of course, a staple, if base form, of Canadian humour. Any TV or radio show short of material can find a sure source of amusement in person-in-the-street interviews asking Americans tricky questions about Canada, such as how many provinces there are or the name of our capital city. Pity the poor Vancouver Grizzly who submitted to such an interrogation shortly after being drafted by western Canada's basketball team. He naturally did not know who the prime minister was.

220 The Meaning of Canadian Life

He thought that the country's capital was Montreal. He was similarly unaware that Canada was a federation. There were no states, he said, Canada was just, well, Canada. This was no ordinary American, of course, but, if not actually a college graduate, at least a college attendee for four years, albeit possibly with a major in free throws. *Due South*, the first Canadian-produced TV show to run in prime time on an American network, made frequent use of these secret Canadian facts. For instance, its hero, an RCMP agent on secondment in Chicago, went on dates with winsome women named 'Mackenzie King.' Americans presumably did not get this inside joke. Many Canadians did – for the time being, at least.

Besides being a source of amusement, what the Americans don't know about us provokes deep resentment in Canadians, though it is hard to know why. They are the largest and, even George Grant admitted, most 'progressive' country in the world. We are no more important in the global scheme of things than, for example, Belgium, even if we are much closer. Those Americans who live near us do generally know a good deal about us,[4] while the ignorance of those who don't merely adds to our distinctiveness: we are the North Americans who understand *two* societies. Canadian competitors on the American quiz show *Jeopardy* often do well despite the obvious American bias of many of the categories – 'U.S. Presidents,' for instance, or 'State Capitals.'

And yet, despite eighty years of radio and almost half a century of television, we Canadians also have hundreds of cultural references that mean more or less nothing even to very knowledgeable Americans. Consider the following list, compiled in 1987 as the free trade debate was heating up, and published under the title 'Things That Weren't on the Table' (Watson 1987). Yes, some came to us courtesy of bigger-than-American government, but by no means all, and even those that did might have shown up anyway:

Gretzky, the Grey Cup, Grey Cup parties, the Group of Seven, blizzards, sugaring-off, Front Page Challenge, eh?, block heaters, chinooks, the Musical Ride, black flies, the Premiers, the Krazy Kanucks, Jack Webster, kd lang, K.C. Irving, QCs, Conrad Black, Eaton's, question period,

Virtually Canadian 221

patronage, Canadair, the Governor-General, the Queen's Birthday, the Queen's Plate, the Queen, the Queen Mother, the Queen Charlotte Islands, tortière, Bill 101, Bonhomme Carnaval, the Calgary Stampede, Hudson's Bay Company blankets, the beaver, Pierre Berton, Bob White, Peggy's Cove, cod tongue, fiddleheads, pogy, muskeg, tundra, arctic char, the Montreal Forum, the CNE, the Yukon, the Klondike, Igloos, Inuit art, the ski-doo, the Riel rebellion, voyageurs, the Post Office, postal strikes, the Liquor Commission, liquor strikes, public transit, transit strikes, potholes, Mirabel, the Senate, Anne of Green Gables, Laura Secord, Joey Smallwood, the Blue Jays, two-fours, stubbies, Lake Superior, the northern lights, the Snowbirds, Anne Murray, Murray Westgate, potlatch, the Auditor-General, Stompin' Tom Connors, Sudbury Saturday nights, *Saturday Night, Sunday Morning*, the Laurentians, the canoe, the canoe trip, the summer cottage, Mordecai Richler, après-ski, the Brier, the in-turn, the out-turn, corn brooms, *As It Happens*, the Ontario Censor Board, coloured money, Canadian Tire money, native poverty, American indifference, Batoche, Paschendaele, the Plains of Abraham, Dieppe, the Dionne quints, Mario Lemieux, Celsius, the winter getaway, Knowlton Nash, the Bluenose, blue laws, Jean Drapeau, rubber-tired subway cars, the Canadarm, the retractable roof, rye and ginger, Moosehead, the notwithstanding clause, Alice Munro, Bryan Adams, deference to authority, reserve, the chill factor, frostbite, snow-blindness, the Rockies, no-yards, the twelfth man, Mel Hurtig, Tom Thomson trees, Arthur Erickson, Susanna Moodie, Mackenzie King's dog, Mackenzie King's mother, the Mackenzie Brothers, Wayne and Shuster, Radisson and Groseilliers, Brébeuf and Lalemant, Banting and Best, the B&B Commission, John Crosbie, the Friendly Giant, family allowances, Revenue Canada, Osgoode Hall, separate schools, Victoriaville hockey sticks, the British Preferential tariff, the Stratford Festival, the 36-cent letter, French immersion, Tommy Hunter, 6/49, the Vancouver Stock Exchange, the Candu, Eddy Match, branch banking, the budget speech, Thanksgiving in October, July 1st, mukluks, tire chains, battery warmers, first frost, the first robin, Robin Phillips, Prince Philip, Paul Henderson, Alfred Sung, Emily Carr, Peter Gzowski, vinegar on french fries, salt on the roads, poutine, maple syrup, the Argo bounce, United Empire Loyalists, the Anik satellite, the 401, Red Rose Tea, Red River boats, Ben Johnson, the National Research Council time signal, the

National Research Council, the Heritage Fund, Meech Lake, the Halifax Explosion, Hugh McLennan, Allan Eagleson, the Winnipeg General Strike, the Regina Riot, gun control, pemmican, portages, huskies, Newfoundland dogs, the seal hunt, the United Church, the St. Lawrence, Donald Creighton, equalization, Zena Cherry, Robert Service, Stephen Leacock, George Bain, the FLQ, western alienation, Paul Coffey, Dief, the Doukhabors, Greenpeace, the Acadians, calèches, screech, Farley Mowat, timber wolves, ptarmigans, the cry of the loon, economic nationalists, etc., etc., etc.[5]

The list could obviously be extended. Michael Ignatieff (1993) writes that 'to belong is to understand the tacit codes of the people you live with; it is to know that you will be understood without having to explain yourself' (10). Most of the cultural references just cited are understood without explanation by most English Canadians and probably could not be understood by other people no matter how long they were explained. And yet, English Canadians, the more culturally paranoid of our two peoples, have two cultures – or at least two experiences, 'culture' probably being too lofty a term. We have our own, but we also have the American. Very occasionally, the Americans share our experience: Bryan Adams, Alice Munro, and Karla Homolka are not unknown to them, while increasing numbers of Americans enjoy hockey, so much so that with each passing season more of their cities and fewer of ours have NHL franchises.

Much more often, of course, the cultural and experiential exchange goes the other way. We know about them but they don't know about us. Being Canadian is thus a little like stalking, albeit involuntary and harmless stalking. And we are very successful stalkers: most Americans have no idea that we are here. In a way, of course, this makes us superior to them (a conceit unlikely to displease us: in spite of our supposed penchant for self-deprecation, many of us will regard it as merely one more instance of our superiority). In many instances, of course, their ignorance of us is all to the good. What they don't know – for example, about the size of our trade surplus with them, which is much bigger than Japan's – presumably won't hurt us.

Virtually Canadian 223

THE PIE CHART OF KNOWLEDGE

The subject – evidently, unavoidably, unfortunately – is Canadian identity. Perhaps the solemnity traditional in Canadian discussions of it can be dissipated with a diagram. Apart from people's gender, colour, size, and shape, what makes them different is what they carry in their brains. Consider a pie chart, the pie chart of knowledge. Each wedge of the pie represents an area of knowledge. One wedge might stand for knowledge of one's own country, another for knowledge of one's neighbour's country. Still other wedges – and there are almost infinitely many – represent knowledge of literature, mathematics, baseball, accounting, or knitting. What each person knows could be represented by shading. A fully shaded wedge means that the person being charted knows all there is to know about whatever subject the wedge represents. Wayne Gretzky's hockey wedge might be completely full, though he presumably would be modest enough to say that it wasn't. Glenn Gould's musicology wedge was probably quite full, though, again, true wisdom is knowing how little one knows. A well-rounded intelligence would have a shaded area that was itself relatively round. Idiot-savants would reach almost to the boundary of a single wedge but would be mainly unshaded everywhere else. The average university professor would display a similar spike in his or her field of specialization but normally would have at least some shading in other areas, as well.

To put the preceding discussion of national experience into pictures: the average Canadian presumably has a fair amount of shading in the wedge called 'Knowledge of Canadian Life' (Figure 19.1).The average American doesn't. Except for vague impressions about igloos, cold fronts, beer, and, in recent years, Gretzky, Messier, and oddball movie comedy, most Americans' Canadian wedge may be all but entirely empty. By contrast, the average Canadian is nothing close to being shut out of the wedge called 'Knowledge of American Life,' even if the average American probably does know more about that subject.

So far, this is all about averages, of course. And national averages, like any averages, may not be as important as the dispersion

224   The Meaning of Canadian Life

The average Canadian

Knowledge of
American life

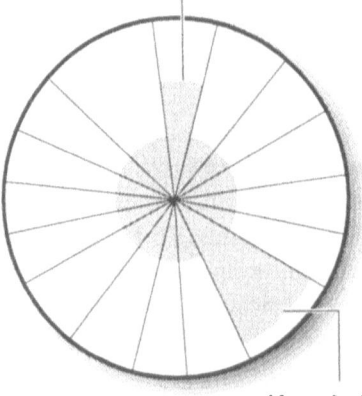

Knowledge of
Canadian life

The average American

Knowledge of
American life

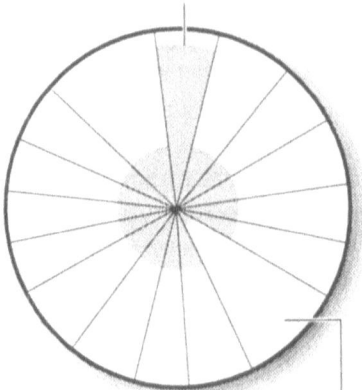

Knowledge of
Canadian life

Figure 19.1
Pie charts of knowledge

Virtually Canadian 225

that they summarize. Texas and New York are different, to say the least. Two-time presidential candidate Pat Buchanan went so far as to tell the 1992 Republican convention that the United States was at cultural war with itself – a stark way of saying that there is more than negligible dispersion of knowledge and preferences among the citizens of what is widely regarded as a melting pot. Thus individual Americans will have greatly different shading patterns in the pie charts of their knowledge, even if all but a very few – those who live near the border, have relatives here, or work for the State Department or the CIA – have essentially no shading in the wedge 'Knowledge of Canadian Life.'

The question of the decade, maybe even of the coming century, is what happens to the pie charts of people's knowledge as 'the information revolution' continues? And what happens to countries as their citzens' pie charts metamorphose? As both satellite broadcasting and the internet proliferate, will English Canadians still know two countries? We will know the Americans – presumably, everyone will – but will we still know ourselves? Will *we* still get the *Due South* joke about Mackenzie King? And if we don't, will we still wish to be our own country?

Though the gurus of the airport bookstores seldom emphasize this, the new technologies offer many possible results. Among them:

- Everybody in the world's – including Canadians' – 'Knowledge of the United States' wedge may become even more shaded, as sooner or later the Disney Channel reaches everyone on the planet. This may take a while yet; as late as 1996, 80 per cent of the world's population still was not able to make a phone call, let alone hook up to cable or the net (Wysocki 1997: A1).[6] But it does seem to be the way we are heading.
- As Disney goes more and more international, it may become less American, though what replaces the status quo may not be diversity but rather the unthreatening polyglot homogeneity – the gushing multicultural niceness – that, for example, characterizes all visitors to *Sesame Street*. In this scenario, we do all end up the same, though mainly because we all develop the

same shading in a new wedge in the pie chart, called 'International Commercial Culture.'
- Americans' 'Knowledge of Other Countries' wedges may become more shaded, too, as satellite TV and the Internet provide cheap on-line access to the world. In this scenario we all end up filling more and more of our 'Other Countries' wedge, as we all become more cosmopolitan. We become more alike in this respect, but better-rounded, as well.
- Or perhaps, like everyone else, Americans may simply consume more and more American software. And other countries' cultural software may become more American, so that Americans seeking escape from themselves will be increasingly unable to find it. Again, we all end up more alike, but this time by all becoming American.
- Canadians' own 'Knowledge of Canada' wedge may grow more shaded, as knowledge in general becomes cheaper. Other countries' nationals may find out more about us, too.
- Or it may become less shaded, as our knowledge of other countries, particularly the United States, comes to dominate.
- Or both wedges may become more shaded at the same time, as both Canadians and Americans come to know more about everything in general, including their two countries.
- Particularly in the set of wedges known as 'Current Events,' patterns of shading may become more similar from country to country, as, thanks to CNN and other satellite broadcasters, worldwide common knowledge increases, with the globe turning its attention now to the O.J. trial, now to the Bernardos, the Olympics, or the latest natural disaster or terrorist outrage, whichever country it befalls this week.
- Patterns of shading may become less similar *within* countries, as cheaper and more ready access to many different forms of information allows people to indulge their own particular curiosities or obsessions. A webbed world may become a series of overlain communities of enthusiasts, whether the enthusiasm be chess, astronomy, literature, film, finance, perversion, ornithology, ornithological perversion, or whatever.
- The pie chart of knowledge presumably will become larger, as

knowledge expands. There will be more history, certainly, as time passes, perhaps even too much to store.[7] So long as electronic languages do not change too frequently, thus rendering past knowledge inaccessible, there will also be readier and readier access to what already exists.
• There is also the possibility that, as the society becomes more oral and therefore less knowledgeable – in a blunter word, dumber – everyone's chart may become less shaded. In any case, whether the circle of knowledge expands or our shading of it contracts, most of us seem destined to know less and less of what there is to know. This is to say nothing of the pie chart of wisdom, which will not be discussed here, but which may or may not fill up as knowledge accumulates.

Beyond listing these possibilities, I have not much more to say about the future. Whoever ignores the past may be condemned to repeat it, but even those who steep themselves in history can still be surprised by what happens.[8] In retrospect, events take on the enamelly sheen of inevitability, but of course retrospect is a distorting lens. At the dawn of what people insist on calling 'the information age' – as if Watt, Gutenberg, and Columbus didn't deal in information – no one can really be sure what effects it will bring, either on people or on countries. So it seems, at the very least, premature to dance on the grave of the nation-state.

Quite apart from the question of what will happen, there's the at least equally important question of what ought to happen. The Irish conservative Edmund Burke wrote in 1790: 'It is with infinite caution that any man ought to venture upon pulling down an edifice which has answered in any tolerable degree for ages the common purposes of society' (Burke 1986: 152). The nation-state has caused much mischief over the last two centuries, but it has also been the mechanism for our government during the greatest accumulation of wealth and knowledge our species has seen. Correlation is not always causation, but it sometimes is.

Paul Samuelson, winner of the second Nobel Prize in Economics, is fond of saying that economists have successfully forecast seven of the last four recessions. Partly because our record of prediction is – infamously – less than stellar, most of us do not make forecasts.⁹ Quite the contrary, we spend our professional lives stressing the discipline's central theoretical result: that the world is complicated, that our ability to understand its complications is limited, and that it is therefore very likely to produce outcomes that we do not expect. As a profession, we think that 'foreseeable future' is an oxymoron, and we are especially suspicious of long-term forecasts on large subjects.¹⁰

As a *New Yorker* cartoon once put it, 'Honesty is one of the better policies.' To be honest, things simply may not turn out as we think. It bears repeating: No one can be certain what will happen. Still, economists' prejudice against forecasting is not universally shared. Far from it: futurology is rife. These days its message seems to be that the new information technologies will end up giving us all the same pie charts of knowledge, a convergence of data and personality that will doom the nation-state. George Grant's vision of the 'universal homogeneous state' – which he thought would lead to tyranny – evidently is about to be realized. But is it really? As a piece of logic, this forecast has two parts: first, that the new technologies *will* make us all more alike and, second, that this will mean the end of nation-states. In fact, on both counts there is ample room for doubt.

IS THE MEDIUM THE MESSAGE, OR IS THE MESSAGE THE MESSAGE?

Whether we will all end up being the same depends, of course, on how 'the same' is defined. In assessing how people are changed by computers, direct satellite broadcasting, and the internet, the important thing may be the medium itself, as was argued most famously by Marshall McLuhan, who got the idea, if not its precise formulation, from University of Toronto political economist Harold Innis. Thus a print society is a different – and more democratic – place than an oral society. How it differs from an electronic society – one that may be returning us to an essentially oral form of living – remains to be seen, though writers naturally tend to be gloomy on this subject. For the moment, of course, the illiterates are not yet at the gates: in fact, the internet, being a written medium, has given a great boost to the printed, or at least projected word, though with improvements in both audio and translation software that may be changing.

If the medium really is the message, there is little doubt that we will all be increasingly American. 'They really do change your life,' George Grant said of what he called 'American machines,' and he was right. If economic growth continues and its influence spreads, more and more of the world's citizens – and by definition all the developed world's citizens – will live like Americans, with their cars, shopping centres, computers, high-definition TVs, VCRs, and so on. Already as you walk through many Canadian neighbourhoods in the evening, the dancing electronic flame once cast on people's walls by the television set is being replaced by the cool blue glow of the computer screen. When incomes reach a level that permits it, these standard trappings of end-of-century American life do seem to be what almost everyone in the world wants. If how people lead their lives *is* what counts, many of us probably *will* end up leading increasingly similar lives, spending part of our time on the internet, part watching the satellite, part driving, part shopping, part travelling, and at least part (shall we say?) 'interfacing' with friends, family, and neighbours.

But how different would we really wish to be, even if it were possible? If, in this sense that George Grant meant, we all do become Americans, what of it? It may not be a bad way to live; it need not foreclose the possibility of personal fulfillment; and it does seem to be the way we are headed. Moreover, simply accepting these facts it is in many ways liberating. There is an obvious parallel in the way all Westerners – if not yet quite all earthlings – have accepted American political ideals. The collapse of Soviet Communism obviously did the greatest good for the several hundred million people who suffered under that noxious regime. But it did the next greatest good for Western intellectuals, and especially Canadian intellectuals, who were forced to concede, much as it might pain them, that in fact we had been on the winning side all along. If we really are all liberal, democratic, capitalists now – and outside China this is the only respectable political

230 The Meaning of Canadian Life

doctrine – then in a sense we *are* all Americans, since America, though by no means the sole author of liberal, democratic, capitalist ideals, has been their strongest and certainly their loudest champion.

During the Cold War we Canadians expressed our independence from Washington by affecting a calculated ideological ambiguity that led us, for instance, not to help with the Berlin airlift (Thompson and Randall 1994: 187), to sell wheat to those who authorized the organized terror of China's cultural revolution, and to cozy up to the likes of Fidel Castro, a habit we have not yet quite shaken. Unlike Barry Goldwater, we thought that extremism in the defence of liberty *was* a vice. But now we are obliged to concede that, however embarrassed we may have been with our neighbour's mawkish enthusiasm for these unsophisticated democratic ideals, they were right. Even Reagan – Reagan the simpleton, Reagan whom most Canadian intellectuals thought had Alzheimers' before he became president – even Reagan, it turns out, was right. The Soviet Empire *was* evil: those who actually lived under it have now told us so. As we are at last willing to admit, we were and are on the American side. It is ironic, but true, that the end of a Cold War that required an ideological conformity we and others found chafing has given way to a more relaxed but even greater ideological conformity into which we have entered freely. We and the Americans and everyone else in the respectable world now hold essentially the same truths to be self-evident. On becoming Czech president, Vaclav Havel spoke about how liberating it was finally to be able to live in a world of truth. Canadian intellectuals now can do the same.

Communism's end liberates Canadians in another way. For the longest time, we believed in 'one nation, one idea.' As a nation, the Americans clearly stood for certain ideals. In slavish imitation of their way of defining a nation, but also, ironically, in the interest of articulating our own independence from them, we believed that we must stand for a set of ideals, too. But because the purpose was to be different from the Americans, we had to stand for slightly different ideals. In a world of two hundred countries and counting, this is a silly road to self-definition: there simply aren't

Virtually Canadian 231

enough slightly different political philosophies to go around. The collapse of Communism therefore frees us to seek our identity in areas other than political philosophy. We are – and should be – liberals, democrats, and capitalists, and if the Americans are, too, and much more famously, well what of it? We don't dispute the laws of physics simply because they were discovered, in the main, by non-Canadians.

None of this means of course that capitalism and liberal democracy cannot develop in slightly different ways in different countries. The free legislatures that write countries' laws will come under the sway of slightly different circumstances, histories, and political coalitions and as a result will write at least slightly different code. So long as difference is not sought merely for difference's sake, there obviously is nothing wrong with this. With countries as with communicants: members of the same church will read its scriptures in different ways. Content does count.

The same very probably is true for the effects of technology on how we live. Even if the medium does have the greatest impact on our lives, even if we all do end up living mostly the same way, as once we were all mainly farmers, content surely must count for something. And there is at least the possibility that the content, though perhaps not the style, of people's lives will continue to differ even in a wired and dished world.

NARROWCASTING OR BROADCASTING?

Whether the pie charts of people's knowledge still will vary the world round depends largely on whether the new technologies end up being used for narrowcasting or for broadcasting. On this question wires and dishes probably lead in different directions. While the internet allows people to share their interests in relatively small groups, satellite broadcasting creates at least the possibility that everyone in the world – all those who are awake, at least – can watch the same thing at the same time. Thus two-thirds of humans are said to have seen the 1996 Olympics (though, of course, not everyone took the same meaning from them).[11] Whether we all do watch the same things depends very much on whether the internationalization of images follows a McDonald's or an MTV model.

A Big Mac is a Big Mac wherever you go in the world.[12] The language and location of its delivery obviously differ, but the product is almost exactly the same. Even now, France and Germany, not to mention French-speaking Canada, each has its own franchise of *Wheel of Fortune*. The foreign hosts even occasionally visit on the Hollywood set of the original version with the American hosts, Pat Sajak and Vanna White. A simple test of whether a country rates as a separate culture, at least as cultures will be defined in the twenty-first century, is whether it has its own version of U.S. game shows or merely pipes in the original. It's a test that English-speaking Canada usually fails, of course: we have only the American version of *Wheel of Fortune*.

By contrast, the European and Asian spin-offs of MTV, the American music video show, apparently respect local tastes, customs, and modes of expression and at least part of the time show music videos by local performers, presumably because MTV thinks that this is what is most profitable. MTV has also spawned even more distinctive homegrown competitors – 'V,' for instance, in Germany, which specializes, this being Germany, in particularly avant-garde forms of rock music. In a similar way, advertising agencies have for decades pushed the same products with entirely separate campaigns in different countries or regions. Ad campaigns for a given product are usually quite different in English Canada from what they are in Quebec. This is not because ad agencies are interested in preserving local cultures: they do it only because it is profitable, presumably because local populations still feel at home with local references. But if it *is* profitable, then local tastes, customs, or modes of expression may yet survive.

If content does count, the 500-channel universe may reduce the American influence as it increases the number of alternative sources of programming. For instance, this passage was drafted the day after the latest French elections, the celebration and analysis of which were available in Canada *en direct* via satellite from French television, only nano-seconds after the French themselves

Virtually Canadian 233

saw it. One of the great attractions of *CBC Newsworld* – which in a clear example of narrowcasting attracts fewer than 100,000 Canadians on a regular basis – is that it broadcasts the BBC World Service news, in many instances live. Eventually, it presumably will be possible to pick up the BBC's domestic service, as well. Granted, the British news-readers are as attractive and well-groomed as any CNN or NBC anchor and work in much the same style, introducing taped feeds from correspondents on the ground, most of which deal with the news concerns of a typical modern, American-style society. And yet somehow it all remains distinctively British. The same is even more true of much French programming, even the commercial variety, which, despite the appearance of *Wheel of Fortune*, persistently resists American norms of what constitutes good entertainment.

Apart from dramatically increasing the availability of foreign alternatives to U.S. programming, satellite broadcasting very probably will eliminate at least one incentive for homogenization by ending private Canadian broadcasters' thirty-five–year habit of importing American shows. As the argument goes, it has always been cheaper for the private network(s) to buy U.S. programming off the shelf than to produce their own. But Canadian broadcasters' focus on the one strategy that could make them the most money was an artefact of a few-channel system. If you are the only private alternative to a public broadcaster, then, you do choose the programming alternative that makes the most money. (If you don't, somebody who does buys your operation.) If five million Canadians want distinctive Canadian programming but six million favour simulcasts of American shows, the six million win out. But if there are dozens of channels competing for viewers' attention, eventually as many as 500 channels, they can't all show the same program at the same time. They have to diversify. When the mainstream audience is divided up into dozens of streamlets it becomes profitable to appeal to backwater tastes. What now shows up on the screen is not just the most profitable programming, but *any* programming that stands a chance of covering its costs – including original Canadian programming, if sufficient numbers of Canadians are willing to watch.

To be sure, if the Canadian viewing market is splintered by dozens of channels, the audience for original Canadian programming may be splintered, as well, and the profit-and-loss calculations may remain unfavourable. However, the advent of satellites dramatically increases the potential viewership for original Canadian programming. All the world's TV screens are now or soon will be available to any producer. If the relatively small domestic market has prevented Canadian producers from investing as much money as excellence requires, it needn't any longer, for their market is now the world. True, the tradition in exporting television programming has been that to get on a U.S. network all Canadian references have had to be expunged. Toronto has had to become Cincinnati.

But that isn't always true. There is a large audience, even in the United States, for distinctively British drama, the police series *Prime Suspect* being a prime example, and there are large English-speaking audiences even in countries where English is not most people's mother tongue. *Coronation Street*, the neverending soap opera of daily life in working-class England, which George Grant and his wife watched so faithfully, has always had a large and loyal audience in Canada. To aim for success in the export market no longer requires giving up any and all sense of Canadianness. French films are unmistakeably French, Australian films recognizably Australian, Swedish films often unbearably Swedish. For that matter, Avonlea is clearly in Prince Edward Island. The rule in successful filmmaking, the reverse of what is usually recommended to business, seems to be 'think locally, act globally.' This will only be more true as, increasingly, anyone anywhere in the world can watch what anyone anywhere else watches.

Two other factors favour a wider and wider menu of increasingly distinctive television programming. First, with the big increase in the demand for programming, the cost of purchasing other people's 'product' will rise, thus making it more profitable to produce your own. In effect, bidding for American blockbusters will get tight, thus making American blockbusters less desirable. The usual counterargument is that the Americans, who cover their costs in their huge home market and then dump product on the world market at bargain-basement prices, can always undercut their competitors. But as foreign sales come to constitute a larger and larger share of American producers' overall revenue, which has already happened in the film industry, films inevitably will be made that make money overall only if they make money in foreign markets. Any firm that follows this practice – and why would firms not, if the foreign revenues are there? – is no longer free to dump. The foreign revenues are no longer gravy, they are meat and potatoes.

The second reason to expect greater diversity is that, as more and more channels come on-line (or -beam), not all of them as slick as U.S. network programming, people will get used to the idea that what they see on TV needn't always consist of million-dollar hours, the standard cost of U.S. network drama (in U.S. dollars!). Cecil B. DeMille's cast of thousands has gone the way of the domestic servant, another occupation eliminated by rising labour costs. Million-dollar-an-hour television drama may suffer the same fate.

Whether satellite broadcasting leads to diversity or simply means that all the world's children will be raised on reruns of M*A*S*H obviously remains to be seen. The idea that the internet will create diversity and therefore radically different 'pie charts of knowledge' both within and across countries is much less controversial. In 1943, Winston Churchill said that the nations of the future are ideas. He was only partly right. They may also be hobbies, fetishes, professions, or religions. Aleksandr Solzhenitsyn's Gulag Archipelago referred to the class of political prisoners, spread like a system of islands throughout the Soviet Union, who nevertheless were 'fused into a continent' by their opposition to Stalin. Similar archipelagos have already formed, more openly and self-consciously, on the internet. Some people gather there to discuss chess, others politics, still others baseball, and so on and so on. Unlike Solzhenitsyn's, these internet archipelagos reach across countries. A current newsgroup on the economics and politics of regulation, run by a graduate student at Carleton University, brings together a Chinese student at the University of Chicago, bureaucrats from Tasmania, New Zealand, Washington,

Ottawa, and Toronto, and professors from Australia, California, Finland, North Carolina, Montreal, and many other places. In the not-distant future, presumably, the net will provide instantaneous translation by machine, so not even language will be a barrier to the formation of such groups. The same sort of splintering, though on a more modest scale, may happen in the 500-channel universe. In every country there will be fans of the chess channel, the semiotics channel, the garlic channel, the divorced parents' channel, and so on.

If the multiplication of international conversations does weaken national bonds, perhaps that is not a bad thing. However, the strength of the international linkages that will be created should not be overestimated. Various international brotherhoods formed over the years have not prevented nationalistic wars. Some of the most poignant of all war stories are of friendly competitors in the 1936 Olympics who later died on opposite sides in the Second World War. Nor have associations and societies of one kind or another always prevented civil wars. Methodists fought each other in the American Civil War, as did Catholics and Baptists and several other varieties of Christian. Lovers of literature died on both sides, as did enthusiasts of the new game, baseball. Few countries had deeper economic and other ties than Germany and the United Kingdom in the period before the First World War. Still, an increase in the number of such cross-national connections seems bound at least to lessen the likelihood of international strife, even if loyalty to chess, say, never really does replace loyalty to place of birth.

20
Do Countries Still Make Sense?

If it is hard to know exactly how the new technologies will change people, it is even harder to know what their effects will be on countries. The telephone presumably affected Canadians profoundly, which in turn must have changed Canada profoundly, though exactly how would have been as hard to predict in 1876 as it is to explain 120 years later. The beginning of wisdom on these questions may be to realize that for the most part there are no answers, even after the fact. *Does* nationhood require a minimum degree of common knowledge among citizens? Presumably it does, but can anyone say just how much? *Is* that common knowledge put in jeopardy by satellite broadcasting and the internet? Perhaps it is. What will the changes that are coming mean for countries? The internet pushes us towards having almost no experiences in common, as each web surfer catches his own wave. However, satellite broadcasting means that we can all see the same images at the same time. Will these effects cancel out, and will there be room for any experience at all between the purely private and the wholly global?

The contemporary Canadian nationalist view of what modern nationhood requires – that is, aggressive subsidy of common Canadian cultural experiences – relies very heavily on idealized recollections of the very untypical age that lasted a few fleeting years in the 1950s, after CBC television went on the air but before its monopoly was ended by antenna, cable, and, in 1961, CTV. For Canadian broadcasting, the 1950s were golden, not simply because of the quality of the programming – CBS and NBC showed live Shakespeare, too – but also because, during those years, Canadians who had televisions were a completely captive audience, the perfect vehicle for collective experiences.[1] In Montreal in those years, on Wednesday evenings 'ratings for the family saga of *Les Plouffes* were so high that one could conclude that there was nobody in French Quebec who wasn't watching' (Weintraub 1996: 232), while, local legend says, the streets were also quiet on Saturday nights, early on Saturday nights, at least – as almost everyone stayed home to watch the Montreal Canadiens. The rest of the country apparently had much the same relationship with Toronto's Maple Leafs and 'Our Pet,' Juliette.

If the goal of nationalist regulators was to have Canadians share uniquely Canadian experiences, monopoly broadcasting achieved that goal, even when the line-up offered by the broadcaster included *Doctor Kildare* (with Richard Chamberlain playing the telegenic young intern), and only *then*, with the game being joined halfway through the first period, *Hockey Night in Canada*. Even a diet including considerable American content, as this one did, provided ample grist for nation-building, Monday morning conversation, both at work and at school. We had all watched the American bits as outsiders – non-Americans – and we had a non-American reaction to it, as Canadians still do when, for instance, they see the American networks' inevitably jingoistic coverage of the Olympics.

Though no doubt there still will be events that from time to time command a large percentage of the Canadian viewing audience, the advent of both the internet and the multi-channel universe (which, of course, will constitute some couch potatoes' entire universe) ends any possibility of a captive Canadian audience and therefore any hope that Canadians could on a regular basis all be made to participate in the same electronic event at the same time. Since September 1972, not even international hockey tournaments have emptied the streets. If fewer common viewing or listening experiences do reduce the sense of community, then less community is what we are bound to have.

But the 1950s were, in this respect at least, a very strange era.

Do Countries Still Make Sense? 239

For most of history, human beings have *not* simultaneously experienced the same events. Eric Hobsbawm reminds us that it was only in the 1920s, with the coming of the radio, that 'for the first time ... people unknown to each other who met knew what each had in all probability heard ... the night before: the big game, the favourite comedy show, Winston Churchill's speech, the contents of the news bulletin' (Hobsbawm 1994: 196). And yet before the radio revolution of the 1920s and the television revolution of the 1950s they nevertheless had managed to form countries.

It is true that in nineteenth-century Canada, people who may have known very little about their fellow citizens in different provinces were intimately familiar with their way of life. More than half of Canadians lived on farms, while most of those who didn't lived by selling to farmers. But very few people experienced the same event at the same time. Last century's public speakers had stronger lungs than this century's do and an equivalently amplified gesturing style, but public gatherings were limited to the number of people who could stand within earshot of the speaker's voice.

The puzzle of our own era, of course, is that almost literally miraculous improvements in communication seem to be tearing countries apart. Many of the nations thus shredded were built in an age in which communications were much less sophisticated. In the mid-1850s, it took one month for the Hudson's Bay Company to get a letter to Montreal via Minnesota, five months by the overland Canadian route, at a cost estimated at £100 – in the days when a pound was really a pound (Bliss 1987: 205–6). In 1864, the trip from Quebec City to Charlottetown took the Canadian delegates three days. Fifteen years earlier, news of the burning of the Canadian legislature by a Montreal mob did not reach Halifax for one week, or St John's for two. And yet, in the middle of the last century, politicians from this gangly string of desperately isolated communities had begun planning for a transcontinental nation. Even earlier, city-pairs, or rather, town-pairs such as Toronto and Kingston, and Montreal and Quebec City, which were days apart by horse – in 1837 it cost the average labourer a month's wages to travel from Toronto to London, Ontario, by coach (Gentilcore

1993: Plate 25) – already had been linked in the same administrative units and had common British governors. In terms of travel time, Montreal and Quebec City were much further apart in the first half of the last century than Montreal and Vancouver are today, yet only now, with the distance between them reduced to only five hours, are some in Montreal contemplating a national life separate from Vancouver.

Common knowledge does not necessarily imply common understanding, of course, and from the beginning Canadians have been divided on quite fundamental questions – for instance, on whether we are one nation or two. At the time of Confederation a journalistic ally of George-Étienne Cartier's wrote: 'As a distinct and separate nationality we form a state within a state. We enjoy the full exercise of our rights and the formal recognition of our national independence' (Cook 1996: 18). Most English Canadians, it is probably fair to say, saw the Confederation pact otherwise. But this is a country whose history has always been differently interpreted by its different communities. For seventy years, Quebec's interpretation of what happened to Louis Riel shut the Conservative party out of that province's politics. Even during what in retrospect seems the period of our greatest unity as a nation, the Second World War, there were bitter disagreements (see Granatstein 1986; Morton 1983). The plebiscite of 1942 showed deep division between English and French on the question of compulsory service – Quebec voted 72.9 per cent against it, the rest of Canada 80 per cent for it, while the conscription crisis of November 1944 almost brought down Mackenzie King's government. This at least was better than anti-conscription riots, with troops brought in from Toronto shooting dead four Quebec City protestors, which is how the issue was dealt with in the First World War (Morton 1983: 175).

Richard Gwyn probably reflects many Canadians' views when he writes that we are 'far more fractured socially and culturally than we' used to be, yet he is almost certainly wrong. As we have seen, in 1945 the economist Harold Innis wrote about interregional hatreds – yes, hatreds – while more recently Michael Ignatieff, after describing the tolerant, bicultural Canada he had

Do Countries Still Make Sense? 241

always idealized, says he now thinks that 'English and French never did imagine [Canada] in the same way' (Gwyn 1995: 79; Ignatieff 1993: 145). The titles of a series of history textbooks produced for the schools provide an indication of just how turbulent our history has been: *Years of Conflict* for the decade 1911–21, which is perhaps not surprising, given the First World War; but *Decades of Discord*, the title for 1922–39, belies the notion of interwar tranquillity, while even the placid 1950s earn the rubric *The Years of Uncertainty and Innovation* (Morton 1983; Thompson 1985; and Granatstein 1986, respectively). Anyone who looks back on the 1960s as a period of national solidarity – the *Globe and Mail*, for instance, which is always hearkening back to the spirit of Expo 67 – should remember that Peter Newman's 1968 account of that era was called *The Distemper of Our Times*. The past is becalmed only from a distance.

The truth is that Canadians have never gotten along very well. In that very Expo year, which Pierre Berton has called Canada's last good year, Blair Fraser wrote: 'Never in their history have Canadians demonstrated any warm affection for each other. Loyalties have always been parochial, mutual hostilities chronic. No separatist of the 1960s spoke more bitterly than had Joseph Howe ... in his campaign of the 1860s against alliance with "three million frost-bound Canadians" in their alien fastness a thousand miles away. No French Canadian has used stronger languages against *les anglais* than was commonplace among western wheat farmers about the money barons of Bay Street and the tyrants of the CPR' (B. Fraser 1967: 313). Desmond Morton concludes his history of Canada by saying that we have 'mastered the self-restraint of democracy [and] learned to live in peace, *if without much affection for each other*' (Morton 1994: 331; emphasis supplied). For his part, in 1977 Northrop Frye wrote that 'everywhere in Canada we find solitudes touching other solitudes: every part of Canada has strong separatist feelings, because every part of it is in fact a separation' (Frye 1982: 59).

And yet, despite our differences, despite the stark differences in what various Canadians have possessed in the wedge of their knowledge called 'Canada,' the country has endured, even at times thrived. We certainly have given the world the impression that we are a country. Measured by international standards, we clearly have achieved the most important purpose of a country, which is to allow as large a number of its citizens as possible to enjoy a good life. Our repeated appearance atop the UN's human development index is a dubious achievement, given that index's severe methodological limitations, but there is no question that we are a successful country: our immigration rate proves it. So perhaps it is not necessary, if a country is to survive, that all its citizens share the same knowledge or beliefs.

Does familiarity breed contentment or contempt? Does deference require distance? Will Canada be better served if Canadians know less or more about each other? If less, then perhaps it is fortunate that history has become largely optional in many Canadian school systems. In Quebec's civics courses, Saskatchewan apparently is mentioned only once, while in Saskatchewan's recommended text, Quebec merits only two notices. But if a uniform curriculum *is* essential for nationhood, we have never been a very good nation. Textbooks have always caused trouble in Canada. In 1926 the history text written by George Grant's father was withdrawn from BC high schools 'because of its presumed pro-French and anti-British bias' (R.B. Howard, quoted in Christian 1993: 33).

'History is what Canadians have in common,' writes Desmond Morton (1994: 9). It is not the only thing we have in common – the space we inhabit is another, that we are stuck with each other a third, snow shovelling a fourth – but it is important. What makes people different, among other things, are their different memories. The same is true for countries. We are not as different from the United States as many Canadian nationalists argue, but we have been making our at least slightly separate way for four centuries now. The accumulated weight – or baggage – of this separate existence is now substantial. Or at least it should be, though it often appears that fewer and fewer people know anything about the last four centuries. The British historian Eric Hobsbawm tells of having been asked 'by an intelligent American student whether the phrase "Second World War" meant that there had been a "First World War"' (Hobsbawm 1994: 3). With more

Do Countries Still Make Sense? 243

and more young people seemingly unfamiliar with basic facts of the world's history, there is ample reason to worry that they may be losing touch with Canada's past, as well. If adolescents don't know who Winston Churchill was, and apparently many don't, they are even less likely to know about Mackenzie King – or, even more remotely, John Bracken or George Drew. In 1997 a poll of young Canadians conducted by the Dominion Institute showed a truly astounding lack of knowledge about Canada: only 54 per cent of 18-to-24-year-olds knew that John A. Macdonald was the first prime minister of Canada; only 36 per cent could identify 1867 as the date of Confederation; 42 per cent thought that Vimy Ridge was a battle in the Second World War; and only 11 per cent could say who won the Nobel Prize for the discovery of insulin (Dominion Institute 1997).

One remedy is obvious. Make history compulsory again, and provide lots of it, from the early grades on. Even someone who favours less government has no difficulty with paternalism towards children. (Paternalism for adults, which is what modern states increasingly provide, is something else.) Of course, education isn't available only in schools, which is probably a good thing, since people spend more years there than ever and seem less educated for it. There are also such things as books and CD-ROMs. Here Canada inevitably will suffer a comparative disadvantage. Educational material will always be cheaper in a larger market.

Consider the CD-ROM, a literally wonder-full technology. Medieval philosophers reportedly debated how many angels could dance on the head of a pin. Now thousands of literary works can be crammed onto a single silver wafer.[2] But CD-ROMs will always be cheaper in the United States. For example, though there are many more phone listings in the United States than in Canada, a CD-ROM containing all the phone numbers in the United States costs less than one containing all the phone numbers in Canada. The reason for the difference, of course, is that there are fixed costs in production and marketing. Acquiring the copyrights, designing the product and package, writing the advertising copy, and so on all cost the same whether you're selling thirty units of your product or thirty million. But if you *are* selling thirty million, you have many more sales over which to spread these fixed costs and can therefore sell for a lower price per unit and still make money. The same is true for history CD-ROMs. Writing a CD-ROM that covers four hundred years of history requires roughly the same number of historians, designers, and software specialists whether it's a history of Canada or the United States. But these identical fixed costs can be spread over a much larger market if the CD-ROM is about the United States.

For small countries, that's simply a fact of life. Information about a ten-times-larger next-door neighbour will always be less expensive. In this sense, there will always be 'a price to pay' to be Canadian. However, it may not be a very high price; it often falls as time passes; and it needn't always be paid by the taxpayer. In the summer of 1996, the U.S. phone-book CD-ROM cost $69, while the Canadian version went for $99, a difference of $30, not all that much. Less than $100 (plus GST) for all the phone numbers in Canada is hardly a high price to pay (for a business that uses the phones a lot, that is).[3]

Because many Canadians have a need for it, the Canadian phone-number CD-ROM probably won't be driven from the market even if it does cost more than the American phone numbers. But in exactly the same way, of course, Canadians have a need for CD-ROMs about Canada's history and may therefore buy them even if they *are* more expensive or less slick than CD-ROMs about American history. Canadian history books and CD-ROMs may not be as practical as a Canadian phone book or CD-ROM listings, but even contemporary Canadians presumably share the normal human craving to know what happened where they live before they themselves lived there. After the information revolution all history is going to be cheap. And if American history is slightly cheaper than Canadian, that may not make much difference. Apples may be cheaper than oranges – or for that matter, maple syrup – but people still buy all three.

At this point, of course, the nationalist custom is to propose that the difference in price between Canadian and American historical

Do Countries Still Make Sense? 245

materials be eliminated by means of a subsidy to Canadian producers, thus 'levelling the playing-field' and reducing 'the price of being Canadian.' But a subsidy does not actually lower the cost of producing anything; it merely redistributes it. Taxpayers in general pay; producers and consumers of, in this case, Canadian CD-ROMs benefit. If the subsidies aren't simply eaten up by higher salaries for people who work in the industry, as seems to be the case for at least some arts grants (see Watson 1988), then Canadian CD-ROM prices do fall, and if consumers are price-sensitive, more Canadian CD-ROMs get into circulation. That's clearly good for the people who consume them. But it benefits non-consumers – who can't avoid paying taxes even if they don't buy the CD-ROMs – only if somebody else's consumption of a CD-ROM somehow benefits them, too. Perhaps they'll hear and be entertained or enlightenened by a radio conversation between two CD-ROM users. But if not, they get no benefit from their taxes.

Industries that live off such subsidies naturally argue that if only people who consume their output pay for it, no one will consume it because it will be too expensive. They will go out of business, and ultimately, so, too, will Canada, because – on this we have the word of those subsidized – the subsidized activities are crucial for Canada's survival. The obvious flaw in all such arguments, of course, is that the goods we are asked to subsidize – Canadian books, art, music, dance, theatre, cinema, and so on – are supposed to be vital to large numbers of Canadians, crucial components of their sense of themselves. Yet large numbers of Canadians evidently will not pay a premium beyond what the market charges for the American versions of these cultural products. 'They tell us who we are,' 'they give meaning to our lives,' 'they inform our unique existence,' but we will consume them only if someone else pays for them. Thus does the Toronto aesthete justify having his or her cultural diet financed by the great unwashed. If people will not pay a premium to read or hear or view stories about themselves – a prospect that could hardly be more compelling, given humans' normal self-absorption – why should others pay on their behalf?

TV IS NOT LIFE

TV is not all there is to life, of course. Nor is the internet. In addition to people's relationship with the wider world, which may increasingly be brought to them by screen, they will continue to live in their own local space. They may travel more than people did in previous centuries, but they seem likely still to have home bases. Besides virtual reality, therefore, there will be reality itself. In some respects, this may involve *less* 'cocooning' and more sociability than it used to. Few doctors or milkmen do house calls anymore. In some regions of the country, the postman doesn't even ring once, let alone twice, while supermarkets are less willing to deliver groceries than corner stores once were. By contrast, before almost everyone owned a car[4] many forms of home delivery were available. As a result many homemakers experienced little interaction with the outside world; the household could be managed essentially by telephone. It may be that in future the modem will enable people to re-create pre-car cocooning and stay at home most of the time. Thus groceries will be ordered, children's illnesses diagnosed, mail read, banking done, and so on, all without leaving the comfort of the computer screen.

But despite the miracle of electronic networking, many jobs probably still will require real people to gather in a single, real place. For other activities people will *choose* to gather: in the end, real hockey is likely to be more satisfying to most six-year-olds than virtual hockey. Which means that their parents will continue to gather at the local rink at dawn or earlier. Moreover, one or two generations of technological changes, however astonishing, will not erase millions of years of genetics: we are bound by our DNA to remain a social species.[5]

If it really is true that future generations of Canadians will know two kinds of reality – what they experience in person, and what they see on their screens – the obvious question recurs: will there will be room for something between the here and now, on the one hand, and the whole world, on the other? Between town council and world government what happens to region or nation? The equally obvious answer is that people have always lived in

Do Countries Still Make Sense? 247

these two worlds: the one they experience directly – 'live and in colour' as it were – and the one they experience only indirectly. To begin with, this latter, largely imagined world was brought to life by travellers' tales, then by written accounts in letters and newspapers, and finally by telegraph and telephone. Its modern manifestation is more graphic, life-like, and immediate than its predecessors, but we are still *here* and they are still *there*. 'Beaming up' exists only in *Star Trek*. The surly bonds of place continue to bind. If nations, even large ones, had a role when life was almost irremediably local and most people died not far from where they were born, why should nations no longer have a role simply because people can move about more easily both within and among them?

ARE COUNTRIES COST-EFFECTIVE?

Hailing from a discipline that believes self-interest to be a crucial human motivator, an economist is bound to think that nations will survive so long as they continue to serve the interests of those who live in them. But will they?

Canadians who lived through the debates on the Charlottetown and Meech Lake accords will not be shocked to learn that Canadian economics has given the world an economic theory of – what else? – constitutions. According to that theory, developed by the University of Toronto's Albert Breton and the University of British Columbia's Anthony Scott, political jurisdictions come into being if they reduce the costs of governance – that is, of getting political decisions made (see Breton and Scott 1978). These costs come in four types: signalling, mobility, coordination, and administration. Signalling and mobility are incurred directly by citizens, who, when dissatisfied with what government is doing, either signal their discontent by petitioning, lobbying, or even running for office themselves, or, if they are truly upset, by picking up and moving to another jurisdiction, as English Quebecers have been doing for the last twenty years. By contrast, coordination and administration costs are incurred by governments, though, like all government costs, they ultimately are paid by taxpayers. Coordination costs arise from having to dovetail the activities of different jurisdictions, while administration costs are those that a government incurs running its own policies. As people decide how many provinces or states there should be in a country or how many countries there should be in the world, how these various costs would be affected should at least be in the back of their minds. If the nation-state were still, as economists might say, 'cost-effective,' doing away with it could be a big mistake.

What gives Breton and Scott's theory force is that these different costs of governance may vary by the size of the jurisdiction, thus producing the possibility that there is a best-sized jurisdiction, though that best size may vary through time as technology changes the four types of governance costs. An obviously crucial question for the twenty-first century is whether this best size is the city-state, which presumably is what's left if nation-states continue to fracture; the nation-state itself, thought by many to be on the verge of extinction; or One Big Government for the entire world, which presumably would be the end result if nation-states continued to cede powers to international organizations.

Though it requires futurology, thinking about Breton and Scott's four kinds of costs suggests that the nation-state may not be quite finished yet. Perhaps the best way to approach the problem of what changing information technology will do to governance costs is to ask how these costs vary as between micro-states and super-states. If super-states, or even a single world super-state, really are cheaper, and become cheaper every day, then that may be what we eventually end up with. But are they in fact cheaper?

If there are 'economies of scale' in government, then bigger probably is better, at least as far as administration costs are concerned. Setting up a tax system, for instance, involves large initial costs in establishing rules, designing tax forms, and arranging processing systems. But such costs are incurred whether there are a million taxpayers or a hundred million, so the cost per taxpayer will be lower the more taxpayers there are, which argues for bigger governments, other things being equal.

Signalling may be easier, however, with a smaller scale of gov-

Do Countries Still Make Sense? 249

ernment. A visit to the town hall, just down the road, is easier than a lobbying trip to the provincial or national capital. A phone call is much more likely to get through to the local mayor or alderman than to a member of the provincial or national parliament. Of course, the town council may have to listen to many views, and doing so may actually be more time-consuming than simply running a poll, which is how the provincial or national government might find out what citizens are thinking. Polls are thus a form of economy of scale in gathering information, which suggests that signalling may actually be easier in bigger units – for example, nation-states.

Mobility is clearly easier, however, the greater the number of jurisdictions. If you don't like life in one state, you move to another. With lots of states, you have lots of choice and not very far to move in order to exercise it. By contrast, if there were only One Big Government for the entire world, mobility would not be an option – unless it were to Mars. Because moving would be futile, much money would be saved in moving costs. But there would be many more disgruntled people about than if everyone could find a jurisdiction that suited his or her tastes in taxation, public spending, and regulation.

The fourth cost of governance, that of co-ordinating the actions of different governments, is also relatively straightforward. As the number of jurisdictions increases, so does the cost of making sure that they don't step on each other's toes. For instance, the more boundaries there are to cross, the more likely it is that pollution will spill across these boundaries, therefore necessitating more agreements between governments about how spillovers will be regulated. Negotiating such agreements will take time and money. Imagine United Nations or World Trade Organization (WTO) meetings if these bodies had two thousand members, not two hundred.

In this view of the world, national governments exist because they are cost-effective. They're big enough both to take advantage of any economies of scale in administration and to avoid the very high costs of coordinating a world of micro-states. But they're not so big that people can't signal within them, or move between them if they don't like what's going on. The president of the United States is now on the internet (at http://www.whitehouse.gov), but he presumably sees only a tiny percentage of his e-mail. Think how much smaller that percentage would be if (the Canadian Left's nightmare) he were president of the world.

Which way is technology taking us? Will economies of scale become even more important, thus pushing in the direction of larger national units? Will signalling within such units become easier as communication technologies continue to evolve, thus reinforcing the trend towards agglomeration? Will moving among states become easier or harder, thus raising or lowering the benefit of having more states? And will changes in communication and travel costs make it more or less expensive to coordinate a given number of states, thus making it more or less easy to have more states? It's obviously hard to say. On the one hand, computers presumably do reduce governments' administrative costs, since more things can be done with fewer people. But do they reduce administration costs more for larger administrative units such as countries or for smaller ones such as cities and towns? Cheque-writing machines make social transfer programs much easier to run on a large scale. As argued above, the same is true for the tax system. On the other hand – this being economics, there are many other hands – computers may make things easier for small political units, too. At the very least, the internet will give them lots of information about whether and how other small units have done things right or wrong. It may also give them useful administrative software at very low cost. In the information age, local governments themselves may be just one more form of software that can be mass produced.

Does the new technology alter signalling costs? Probably, though again in ways that may favour larger, not smaller political units. In the mid-1990s, all the talk in politics was about electronic town halls, where large numbers of people get on the same bulletin board or even vote by wire. Similarly, more and more political parties have dispensed with conventions, or at least redefined them to be telephone ballots of party members. So far the technology has been tried on a scale only of thousands of people, though

Do Countries Still Make Sense? 251

there appears to be no fundamental reason why it couldn't be made to work for much bigger groups – whole countries, for instance.[6]

In sum, it is not obvious the new technologies will so inflate the cost of running nation-states that their citizens decide to trade them in either for a World Assembly or for thousands of tiny statelets, which, freed by worldwide economic liberalization and linked by universal communication, will coexist in the political equivalent of molecular soup. As Richard Nixon might have put it, we may still have the nation-state to kick around for a while.

A MUTUAL FUND CALLED 'CANADA'

Another argument for larger as opposed to smaller political units – for nation-states as we have known them, rather than microstates, as many people anticipate them – is that they provide economic insurance. If all of a country's regions experience their economic highs and lows at the same time, then insurance is possible only through saving. But if their regional cycles are out of phase, so that some do well while others languish, with the pattern reversed every few years, then national taxation and redistribution programs, which not even neoconservatives would eliminate entirely, will act as a form of interregional insurance. Regions experiencing hard times will get help from other regions doing not quite so badly. In the early 1990s, British Columbia had less severe a recession than the rest of the country and so continued to pay unemployment insurance premiums that financed benefits elsewhere in the country, even in Ontario, which in that recession lost its accustomed fat-cat status. Of course, if future technological changes render the country's regions more or less identical in their economic cycles, this insurance effect will be minimized. For the time being, however, it seems to work.

Or at least it worked over the period 1962–91, as a 1994 study by two management professors at the University of British Columbia demonstrated (see Goldberg and Levi 1994). They found, in effect, that the whole Canadian economy was greater than the sum of its parts. Thus the aggregate economy experienced steadier growth with fewer fluctuations than did its component regions. Some regions, mainly in the west and in the north, had more rapid growth than the country as a whole. Alberta's economy, for instance, beat the national average by 1.2 percentage points over the three decades, but its economy fluctuated more than twice as much as the national economy. Canada therefore acted like a well-diversified mutual fund, offsetting lower-than-average growth in some regions with higher-than-average growth in others. Given the pattern of economic 'covariation' across provinces, an investor could have got a higher return with less risk by investing only in Alberta, Quebec, Nova Scotia, and, believe it or not, Newfoundland (Goldberg and Levi 1994: Table 3). Still, Canada as we know it was a good fund.[7]

An even more efficient economic insurance system would have all countries join in a world government that could redistribute resources across all the world's business cycles (though as economic integration proceeded there might eventually be only one large cycle). But for the time being, most people seem less willing to redistribute resources to other countries than in their own. For instance, the University of Calgary economists Robert Mansell and Ronald Schlenker estimate overall fiscal redistribution within Canada of roughly $30 billion a year in the years 1990–92, which was more than ten times what Ottawa was spending on foreign aid. Charity evidently does begin at home.[8]

There are still other reasons for hoping that nation-states endure and believing that they will. As we have seen, they generally constitute deeper pools of economic liberalism than even the regional free trade groupings that have become common since the 1980s. As demonstrated by the experience of the Canadian softwood lumber industry, which in 1996 was forced to agree to a regime of managed trade with the United States, the course of free trade agreements does not always run smooth. The world's various free trade areas and even the WTO may eventually provide economic movement between countries as free as it currently is within countries, but for the moment they do not. As noted above, in the European Union in 1992, trade between France and Germany was roughly the same in absolute terms as that between

Ontario and Quebec, which means that in proportionate terms it was only a third the size of Ontario–Quebec trade. Chapter 6 also described the now-famous study by Royal Bank economist John McCallum, which showed that trade within Canada is twenty times larger than it would be if, as might be expected in a borderless world, different jurisdictions' wealth and distance from each other were the only determinants of the trade between them. Integration continues, of course, most famously in Europe, but though the day may come when the European Union is a more seamless web than our own unfortunately still seam-ridden web, it hasn't arrived yet. Over the objections of the U.S. Congress, the WTO, too, may eventually provide smooth-running world government in trade matters and assure open access for all countries' products into all countries' markets, but that day is even farther off. For the moment, despite its flaws, our internal market is at least as open as Europe's and much more open than the international trading environment that the WTO provides.

JOBS FOR THE BOYS

The last few pages have argued in effect that nation-states will persist because they are efficient. What is efficient does not always happen, of course, and nation-states may endure even if technology does reduce the need for them, for the very simple reason that neither the people who run them nor the entrenched interests that benefit from them may find it expedient to give them up. At the very least, they can be counted on not to go down without a fight. History does not offer a long list of levels of government that have put themselves out of business. It is far easier to create new governments than to abolish old ones, not least because doing so means more jobs for politicians. Our own Confederation, in which many of the new dominion jobs were filled by former provincial politicians, is a good example. If the nation-state does expire, its death may therefore be a long, drawn-out affair, and, even if more and more powers eventually do pass to some sort of World Assembly, the administrative shells of the nation-states may never entirely disappear. Just as Canadian Confederation has member-provinces that are fossilized colonies, so may the World Confederation have member-states that are fossilized nations. There may even be a World Senate – though preferably not one appointed by the world prime minister. And, as in Canada, powers may flow back and forth among jurisdictions as technologies and fashions in such matters change.

THE VIRTUES OF INERTIA

Finally, whether they are efficient or not, nation-states may endure, our own included, simply because of our uncertainty about what would happen were we to do away with them. Preston Manning says that a Canadian optimist is someone who thinks: 'It could be worse.' Well, it usually *could* be worse. Yes, life might be better without the nation-state. But it might not be. Judging by their standard of living, citizens of the nation-state called Canada have been well served by the political organization that their forebears invented. Perhaps our income would have been higher with different constitutional arrangements. But perhaps not. Remembering Burke, we should think very carefully before 'pulling down an edifice which has answered in any tolerable degree for ages the common purposes of society' (Burke 1986: 152). Polls repeatedly show that Québécois like the idea of sovereignty but shrink back from it because of concern over what the negative consequences, the 'downside,' might be. Much as it may infuriate people in the rest of Canada, this is a perfectly reasonable way of approaching the world. Similarly, it might make some sense for Canada to join the United States, or fracture into two dozen micro-states, and for the United States to do the same, and so on, and for all the resulting micro-states everywhere to form a world federation. But we don't know – no one knows – what the 'downside' would be. Maybe if Canada did not exist it would not be necessary to invent it. But Canada does exist. The question is whether to do away with it. At the moment, neither trade liberalization nor the communications revolution provides any obvious reason to do so.

No doubt all this calculation sounds quite bloodless to non-

Do Countries Still Make Sense? 255

economists. In this bloodiest and most nationalist of all centuries, that may not be a bad thing. There is more to countries than accounting, including the not-unimportant fact that many of us have become very fond of our nation-states. In his first inaugural address, Lincoln spoke about the 'mystic chords of memory, stretching from every battle-field and patriot grave to every living heart and hearthstone all over this broad land.'[9] Canadians fought neither a revolutionary nor a civil war, but after four centuries of European presence, we, too, are a community based on memory, albeit sometimes imperfect and conflicting memory. An essentially utilitarian approach to the question of countries need not preclude emotional attachments of this sort. A ship is primarily a means of transportation, but this does not mean that those who sail her cannot be fond or proud of her or even love her, especially when she has served well through heavy seas. So it is with our own ship of state, even if the English-Canadian tradition, like the sailor's, is not to speak of such things too openly or often.

Notes

CHAPTER 1 Defining Moment

1 The first poll following the debate showed that 72 per cent of English Canadians thought Turner had won, compared to 17 per cent for Mulroney and 11 per cent for NDP leader Ed Broadbent. Even 47 per cent of Progressive Conservatives gave the nod to Turner, compared to only 50 per cent who thought that their candidate had won. Among Liberals the verdict was Turner, 95 per cent to 3 per cent (Gallup Canada, 27 October 1988). Among Tory insiders, however, no one pointed out the deficiencies of the prime minister's new clothes. Everyone to whom Mulroney talked by telephone later that night thought that he had done well. The last friend he talked to, at 1:30 a.m., told him 'Well, you can sleep easy tonight – you won' (Graham Fraser 1989: 293).
2 When Gallup asks about the actual impact of freer trade with the United States on Canada, mentioning that more U.S. goods enter this country without duties and more Canadian goods are sold in the United States, the results are more favourable, though they also indicate souring on the FTA after the fact. More Canadians said that they would be better off with free trade in polls taken in 1953, 1963, 1968, 1983, 1984, 1986, February 1987, and January, September, and October 1988, while more said that they would be worse off in November 1989. Strangely, the largest favourable margin (57–27) came in 1968, as Canadian nationalism swelled (Gallup Canada, 13 November 1989).

CHAPTER 2 The Globalization Hypothesis

1 I am grateful to Michael Bliss for this example.
2 World seaborne trade increased six-fold between 1950 and 1975 (Abrahamsson 1980: Table 1). The world's merchant fleet grew more than three-fold between 1960 and 1991 (McCalla 1994: Figure 3.1). In the fifteen years from 1975 to 1990 it almost doubled (Peters 1993: Figure 2). Even in Canada's not-very-competitive railway industry, labour productivity increased by a factor of four between 1956 and 1981 (Freeman et al., 1987: Exhibit 6.1), while the real cost of international air travel has fallen 15 per cent in the last decade. Already, according to the OECD, more than half the value of world trade takes place by air (quoted in Valaskakis 1995).
3 During the free trade debate, many long-time opponents of American domination of the Canadian economy nevertheless opposed the deal on the grounds that eliminating the tariff would remove any incentive for the theretofore-hated branch plants to stay. As left-wing economist Jim Stanford wrote: 'The consequences of the flight of foreign capital from Canada ... seem to be rather more severe than the consequences of allowing that foreign capital into Canada in the first place' (Stanford 1993: 152). Rather. The historians Thompson and Randall have referred to this style of argument as 'enchanting illogic' (1994: 253).

CHAPTER 3 Four Hundred Years of Globalization

1 In the Confederation debates themselves, A.T. Galt, soon to become Canada's first finance minister, said: 'It must be clear to every member of the House that the credit of each and all of the provinces will be greatly advanced by a union of their resources' (quoted in Naylor 1975: 32). A century and a quarter later the Canadian economist Douglas Purvis, contemplating the possible break-up of the country, coined the phrase 'the bonds that tie' – shorthand for the argument that with our large debts we could not possibly afford to become two or more countries. Many economists felt slightly shamefaced with so weak a rationale for continued Confederation. But if foreign debts

really were what brought us together, maybe it is only poetic justice that they should prevent our falling apart.
2 In 1994 U.S. foreign investment was $130.8 billion, 1.9 per cent of its GDP of $6.7 trillion (United States 1995).
3 This is not to argue that the Americans were slackers at international investment. In the sixteen years between 1950 and 1966 the number of foreign affiliates of American companies grew from about seven and a half thousand to over twenty-three thousand (Hobsbawm 1994: 278). This created such alarm in Europe, in particular, that a best-selling book of the 1960s was titled *Le défi américain* (The American Challenge). Even so, in 1993 foreign direct investment by all countries was less then 1 per cent of world GDP and accounted for only 4.1 per cent of world capital formation (United Nations 1995: Table 1.1).
4 Among other things, enabling twentieth-century Americans, for good or ill, to average seven-and-a-half hours of sleep a night, compared to the nine-and-a-half that their predecessors in the late nineteenth century are thought to have slept (Murphy 1996a: 22).

CHAPTER 4 Convergence?

1 The measure is the 'coefficient of variation,' which is the standard deviation for the sample of countries divided by its mean (or average). The standard deviation is calculated by taking the difference between each country's spending ratio and the mean spending ratio, squaring it, summing the squares for all the countries, and then taking their square root. The more closely grouped the countries are, the smaller this coefficient, while the more dissimilar they are, the larger it is.
2 Source: author's calculations from OECD 1996: Table 3, which is the source for all other data cited in this chapter, unless otherwise indicated. The nineteen countries are Australia, Austria, Belgium, Canada, Denmark, Finland, Germany, Ireland, Italy, Japan, the Netherlands, New Zealand, Norway, Portugal, Sweden, Switzerland, Turkey, the United Kingdom, and the United States.
3 Turkey was the lowest-taxing OECD state throughout the period.

Germany had the highest tax ratio in one year (1955), Italy in one year (1960), Denmark in two years (1970–1), Norway in four years (1972–5), and Sweden in five earlier years (1965–9) in addition to its most recent string.

4 It fell by four-tenths of one per cent of GDP from 1977 to 1979 – pre-Reagan/Thatcher years, of course. It held steady on two occasions in the early 1980s, at 36.3 per cent of GDP and again in the late 1980s, at 37.8 per cent. And it fell by three-tenths of one per cent of GDP between 1988 and 1989, as the Reagan/Thatcher years ended, and again by a further one-tenth of a per cent between 1992 and 1993. But it rose in every one of the other twenty-nine years shown in the table.

5 We are back to using the coefficient of variation, an abstract number, so the units, instead of being percentage points of GDP, are just percentage points.

6 So is another graph, not shown here, of the difference between the highest-tax and lowest-tax countries among the 'original six.' In 1965 the difference was 9 points of GDP (with Italy at 25.5 and France at 34.5). By 1978 it was 21.4 points (separating Italy at 27.4 points and Luxembourg at 48.8). Finally, in 1994 it was down to 7.3 points of GDP, with Germany as the low-taxer, at 39.3 per cent of GDP, and Belgium the high-taxer, at 46.6 per cent of GDP.

7 As, in our own debates on these matters, did the Canadian nationalists who simultaneously sneered and look down their noses at her, not an easy trick.

8 The statistical stew is even stranger if we look at these same six countries in the 1950s. In the four years 1955–9, the spread in tax ratios across the 'original six' was between 11 and 12 per cent. In other words, even though the six economies remained separated by a large number of barriers – the European Economic Community was not born until 1957, after all – the difference in their tax rates was no greater than at any time up to the late 1980s, and it was actually less than in many of these years (1973–81, for instance). Though not nearly as integrated economically or politically as they are now, the six founding members of what has become the European Union had tax rates every bit as similar as they are today. The same patterns hold in a larger sample of thirteen European countries, as well.

9 Since 1975, Luxembourg has had the highest tax ratio in nine years,

Notes to pages 38–44 261

with Belgium filling in for four and the Netherlands for five. In 1987 Belgium and the Netherlands were tied at 47.5 per cent of GDP. Before 1975 the Netherlands had the highest tax ratios for eight years in a row. Only in the first two years of this period, 1965 and 1966, did France lead the league. On the low side, Italy had the lowest tax ratios until 1990, when Germany took over.

CHAPTER 5 Home Truths

1 Source: OECD 1996, Table 3, which is the source for all data in this chapter, unless otherwise indicated.
2 For 1955 and 1960 the European data do not include France and Luxembourg, though other data sources show that around this time these two countries were above average taxers and spenders. Their absence would therefore tend to understate the European average.
3 Though only 42.5 per cent of their health care spending is done through the public sector, versus 72.2 per cent of ours, their total spending on health care is 13.2 per cent of GDP, compared to 9.9 per cent in Canada. In effect, their public sector's smaller share of a larger overall number almost equals our public sector's larger share of a smaller overall number (Tholl 1994: Tables 7 and 9).
4 The sources for these series are *Economic Review* (Ottawa: Department of Finance, various years) and *Facts and Figures on Government Finance* (Baltimore: Johns Hopkins University Press for the Tax Foundation, various years). Some care must be taken in interpreting differences across countries, since the two series are based on different definitions, but the overall pattern of change is the same as provided by other series.
5 Though we spent a lot on our military in the 1950s – 7.5 per cent of our GDP in 1953, almost six times what we spend now (Thompson and Randall 1994: 191)
6 In an important challenge to conventional Canadian wisdom, Muirhead (1992) argues that it was the cold shoulder from Britain, rather than C.D. Howe's pro-Americanism, that in the 1950s forced our opening to the United States.
7 As far as 'moulding a national character in his own image' is concerned, many of those close to Diefenbaker having testified that he

262 Notes to pages 48–55

was almost clinically paranoid, one interpretation of our present constitutional schism is that he succeeded.

CHAPTER 6 Are We There Yet?

1 Total immigration over the ten years was 1.856 million people, against an initial population of 25.9 million (Department of Finance 1995: Reference Table 2).
2 In 1995, just less than half of Canadian households had a home computer. Future readers of this book, if there are any, presumably will think so low a ratio quaint.
3 The exact increase was 39.7 per cent (Bank of Canada 1996: Table J4). This compares with a 23.8 per cent increase in trade in the previous five years, during which real economic growth was 11.9 per cent (Bank of Canada 1996: Table H2).
4 McCallum's results are confirmed by two American economists (Engel and Rogers 1995), who, using other data, looked at differences in prices between Canada and U.S. cities and calculated that to observe such differences within a single country the cities in question would have to be 1,760 miles apart. In effect, they concluded, the Canadian–U.S. border is 1,760 miles thick.
5 Given the relatively rather low volume of intra-European trade, this can be taken as evidence that the Europeans have not yet succeeded in integrating their economies, rather than evidence that as a result of liberalization they are now in a situation where only distance and size do determine trade flows.
6 We can also hope that it will force the removal of the trade, investment, and mobility barriers that remain between Quebec, Ontario, and the other provinces: after years of negotiation, Canadians *still* don't have full free trade in one of their culturally most important products, beer. Unfortunately, the 'Internal Trade Agreement' of 1994 between the provinces and the federal government grandfathers many existing restrictions on the movement of goods, services, businesses, and people across provincial borders. One obvious danger of McCallum's results about the enduring strength of east–west trade is that it will produce a sense of complacency about these remaining intra-Canadian trade barriers.

CHAPTER 7 Free to Choose

1 Tanzi's data show that in Canada in 1971 revenues from corporate income taxation were 3.1 per cent of GDP, and in 1990, 2.1 per cent of GDP. This wasn't because tax rates on corporations had fallen, however: they hadn't. Rather, corporate profits had continued their fifty-year slide as a share of GDP. Nevertheless, in the mid-1990s Canadians were treated to indignant newspaper and television reports about how companies were making 'record profits' and at the same time laying off workers. In fact, profits were at record levels only in absolute dollar terms. As a share of GDP they were near all-time lows. For example, in the 'record' fourth quarter of 1995, before-tax corporate profits were running at 8.3 per cent of GDP. Since 1926 there had been only ten years in which profits accounted for a lower share of GDP: 1930–3, 1982, and 1990–4 – in other words, the ten worst years of the century in terms of economic growth (Statistics Canada 1995: Table 1).
2 Slemrod's study produces another surprising result: the rate of tax on foreign corporations is twice that on domestic investment. That's true whether you measure total taxes paid by domestic investors of country X who invest in other countries or total taxes on foreigners investing in country X. On average, both groups pay taxes twice as high as investors of X investing in X. Slemrod's numbers can't take account, however, of the fact that transnational investors can 'shift taxes' by moving income out of high-tax countries and into low-tax countries, though whether they can cut their taxes in half by such means is another question. If they can't, and foreign investment really is taxed more than domestic investment, that's just the opposite of what globalization theory would predict, since foreign investors, who already have demonstrated a willingness to pick up and move, presumably are more mobile than domestic investors (Slemrod 1996: 296).
3 An obvious question: if firms can reduce the wages they pay in response to a tax increase, why wouldn't they reduce wages to an irreducible minimum all on their own? They would if they could, but they can't, not all on their own. If one firm tries to, workers *will* find employment at their old, higher wage elsewhere in the economy. If

all employers cooperate in the attempt to lower wages, they may succeed, but that, first, would be illegal and, second, would create big gains for any firm that cheated on such an agreement, since by cheating it could get all the labour it wanted at slightly above whatever price the cartel was offering. The only legal way to achieve a wage cartel would be with government-enforced wage controls. Tax increases also do the trick, but then firms don't actually gain from the lower wages that result; only the government does.

4 The nineteenth-century French economist Frédéric Bastiat wrote a famous satire in which the National Association of Candlestick Makers petitioned for a tariff to be imposed on sunshine, which naturally was very hurtful to their business: 'We are suffering from the intolerable competition of a foreign rival, placed ... in a condition so far superior to ours for the production of light that he absolutely inundates our national market with it at a price fabulously reduced' (Bastiat 1934: 47, 49). You can't actually put a tariff on sunshine, of course, but you can put higher taxes on people who live in sunny regions, and even if some do leave as a result, most probably won't. Rain can also be valuable. Dry air is a hindrance in spinning yarns, and a rule of thumb in the late-nineteenth-century textile industry had it that Lancashire's damp climate provided a cost advantage roughly equivalent to a 10 per cent tariff (seminar by Timothy Leunig of Oxford University, Montreal, March 1996).

5 The Harvard Business School's Michael Porter (1990) wrote a bestselling book, *The Competitive Advantage of Nations*, which tried to explain why successful industrial 'clusters,' as he called them, sprang up where they did. He identified a number of factors common to successful clusters in many different countries – most important, the institutional and policy background had to favour what he called 'continual upgrading' – but he was forced to concede that chance played a greater role in deciding precisely where particular industries flourished than social scientists might like to admit. The danger of research emphasizing the role of historical accident is that it gives encouragement to governments – as if they needed it – to spend lots of money on the quixotic project of trying to generate historical accidents. Thus in commenting on Krugman's ideas, left-wing American economist David Gordon recommends precisely that

'governments should seek to influence the "chance and history" on which our future economic well-being will partly depend' (D. Gordon 1996: 197). After three decades' experience with regional incentives, Canadians are more likely to conclude that the idea that 'if only it gets started, industry can thrive almost anywhere,' is a recipe for public profligacy on a grand scale. This country once had a provincial industry minister who believed that a large part of the world's cucumbers should be grown in Newfoundland. They aren't.

6 Whether the trade-off is correctly perceived is another question. Though it borders on the unpatriotic for a Canadian to suggest that an American with a good health insurance package may receive better health care than the average Canadian under medicare, there is ample evidence of both queuing for services in Canada and greater investment in health care technology in the United States. Canadian health economists often point to our queues and the Americans' rich stockpile of CT scanners, magnetic resonance imagers (MRIs), and kidney-stone crushers as evidence of American inefficiency and waste. The average person, not burdened by so sophisticated an understanding of health care economics, will be forgiven for thinking that it might be better to fall ill in a society where such waste is tolerated.

7 In judging the usefulness of public spending, however, it is important to understand that most public spending does not involve income redistribution – that is, moving money between income classes. The bulk of money paid into general revenues goes back to the very same people who paid the taxes. The net movement of funds from the top of the Canadian income distribution to the bottom is actually quite small – roughly $1 for every $8 spent – which is not all that much more than is observed in the United States. Even if greater redistribution is the secret of our societal success, by targeting more of our spending at lower-income Canadians, we could probably accomplish the same redistribution with a much smaller overall expenditure of funds.

8 It's often argued that the poor and unskilled may be especially immobile, while the high-skilled can pick and choose jobs from around the world. However, national language or accreditation differences may be more important in skilled jobs. There is also the

problem that many high-skilled jobs lead people to develop firm- or region-specific skills that reduce their mobility. In his autobiography, the historian Arthur R.M. Lower recounts the following conversation: '"How long have you been in Winnipeg?" I asked a man at lunch one day. "Twenty-five years," he answered. "How long would you be here after you retire?" I went on. "Twenty-five minutes," he said' (Lower 1967: 160).

CHAPTER 8 False Premise

1 An idea the Americans in fact got from two Scots, David Hume and Adam Smith.
2 Maybe some Canadians really do have government in their genes. In the early nineteenth century this country was in good part populated by refugees from the American Revolution, though whether they were as anti-American as often is made out is another question. 'Several thousand ordinary Loyalists abandoned Nova Scotia to return to the United States'; the Loyalist critique itself was cribbed from the American federalists; and most Quebecers and Nova Scotians declined to join the American revolutionaries for reasons having less to do with 'ideology and political preference than ... geography and the balance of military power.' In sum, 'the Loyalist myth ... (like all nationalist myths, America's included) is only tangentially linked to ... historical reality' (Thompson and Randall 1994: 16, 14, 15). But whatever the Loyalists' true opinions of Americans' preference for liberty over order, they were at the very most one hundred thousand people, and we are now 30 million and mostly not of Loyalist stock.
3 From his cogent affirmation of the power of ideas and the people who write about them: 'The ideas of economists and political philosophers, both when they are right and when they are wrong, are more powerful than is commonly understood. Indeed the world is ruled by little else. Practical men, who believe themselves to be quite exempt from any intellectual influences, are usually the slaves of some defunct economist. Madmen in authority ...[etc.] I am sure that the power of vested interests is vastly exaggerated compared with the gradual encroachment of ideas ... Soon or late, it is ideas, not vested interests, which are dangerous for good or evil' (Keynes 1936: 383–4).

Notes to pages 86–8 267

Of course, it was in Keynes's interest as an academic scribbler to promote this line. He did in another mood categorize one of his books as 'the croakings of a Cassandra who could never influence the course of events in time' (Keynes 1963: v). Perhaps not *in* time, but certainly *over* time: a small academic controversy broke out in the early 1970s on the question of whether Keynes's (1924) book *The Economic Consequences of the Peace*, a critical account of the Versailles Treaty negotiations in 1919, had caused the Second World War (see Moggridge 1974: 70).

CHAPTER 9 Governing Misperceptions

1 In 1993 their GDP was U.S.$24,744 per capita, while ours was Can.$24,750 or, using the 1993 exchange rate, U.S.$19,181. In fact, in 1993 our exchange rate was probably a little below its 'purchasing-power parity,' so in terms of what we could actually buy our incomes probably went a little further than U.S.$19,181, though not so far as U.S.$24,744.
2 We may be wrong. In 1995, 63,000 Canadians were lawyers, or 2.1 out of every one hundred Canadians, which was 60 per cent of the American ratio, up from below 50 per cent in 1986. We are currently producing lawyers more quickly than the United States, no doubt partly because, like them, we have adopted a written bill of rights (Easton and Lippert 1996: 26).
3 The 80th's predecessor, the majority Republican 79th Congress, had acquiesced in Harry Truman's request to draft striking railway workers into the army in May 1946, though the threat never had to be carried out, since the union broke under the pressure of public opinion (McCullough 1992: 505–6). This remarkable assertion of government authority happened in what we Canadians think of as a *laissez-faire* society. My own favourite example of Americans' penchant for over-regulation, drawn from the experience of living in Manhattan for nine months, was the sign hanging from a low overpass on Franklin Delano Roosevelt Drive on the East River: 'Overheight vehicles stop.' Well, yes, of course. At one point during my stay I received a notice from some or other city agency informing me that if children under ten years of age were living in my apartment, my landlord was

required to install – at his expense – protective bars in all windows, so as to prevent the kids from falling. And even if there were no kids in the apartment, I still had the option of requiring that bars be installed, again at the landlord's expense. Is it any wonder that rental housing is scarce in New York? (See Watson 1991).
4 There are good data on spending by individual governments, since they kept books. But measures of GDP aren't very reliable. In the pre-Keynesian age, before the 1930s, governments were not in the habit of measuring annual output, so estimates have had to be constructed after the fact, which greatly reduces their reliability. Moreover, in federal countries with lots of lower-level governments – the United States, for instance, which for most of the last century has had at least thirty state governments and several score thousand municipal governments – there aren't good data on overall public spending, since, except for a very few years, no one has gone back and added all the governments' spending together, taking care to net out grants from one level of government to another, so as not to count any dollars twice.
5 In fact, the last Canadian figure is for 1926.

CHAPTER 10 The American 'Governmental Habit'

1 *The Governmental Habit* is the title of a 1977 book by Jonathan R.T. Hughes, on which this chapter relies heavily. See also its second edition, Hughes 1991.
2 A decision in which that era's infatuation with its own technological sophistication played an important role: 'It cannot be too strongly insisted upon that the right of continuous transportation from one end of the country to the other is essential in modern times,' wrote the majority in one crucial case (cited in Hughes 1991: 13).
3 From section 8 of the constitution: 'No tax or duty shall be laid on articles exported from any State ... No preference shall be given by any regulation of commerce or revenue to the ports of one State over those of another; nor shall vessels bound to, or from, one State, be obliged to enter, clear, or pay duties in another.' Section 8 also empowers Congress to 'regulate commerce with foreign nations, and among the several States' – a sentence that could usefully be inserted

in our own constitution the next time amendments to it are considered.
4 As one contractor put it, 'You take a [government] clerk that gets $1,000 a year salary, and offer him $2,000 to get certain information in his office, and there is a temptation for him to break a lock and get it' (Berton 1970: 242).
5 There was even a pair of scandals associated with the railways, not unlike John A. Macdonald's CPR fiasco. In fact, both the Canadian and American railway scandals broke within a year of each other and were investigated in 1873. Though an American president was never caught wiring a railway magnate saying: 'I must have another ten thousand; will be the last time of calling; do not fail me; answer today,' as Sir John A. did just before the 1872 election, the Credit Mobilier scandal was serious enough, 'becoming a major issue in four Presidential elections, and involving a dozen Congressmen, a Secretary of the Treasury, two Vice-Presidents, a leading Presidential contender, and one man [James Garfield] who was later to become President' (Fogel 1960: 17). Government funds transferred to the Union Pacific after the completion of every twenty-mile segment of rail had then been paid to the Credit Mobilier, the general contractor set up by several directors of the Union Pacific to build the railway. A congressional investigation eventually concluded that, as a result of this system of laundering, the railway's directors, the construction company, and the contractors, who were often the same people, made excessive profits. Whether because of this or not, the Union Pacific went into receivership in 1893.

A separate congressional investigation censured two members of the House of Representatives for their part in what it concluded had been an attempt to prevent an inquiry into the Credit Mobilier's profitability. One of the two, who was both a brother of the Union Pacific's president and, very conveniently, a member of the House of Representatives Committee on Railroads, had sold Credit Mobilier stock on very favourable terms to, among others, the sitting vice-president; the man who became Ulysses S. Grant's running-mate in 1872; and Representative James Garfield, who made $329 on the deal – not bad in an era in which the average annual earnings of non-farm employees were $489 (United States, Bureau of the Census, 1989: Series D735).

In the more tolerant ethical climate of that era, this did not prevent Garfield from becoming president in 1880. 'We wanted capital and influence,' the censured Congressman said, 'influence not on legislation alone, but on credit, good, wide, and a general favourable feeling' (quoted in Trottman 1966: 83). A biographer has concluded that 'he was probably quite as honest as the Congress which passed judgment on him' (Trottman 1966: 83).

Political mores have changed, of course. Politicians who profit directly from the expenditures they authorize now go to jail. It is now the politicians who pay, rather than receive, the bribes, and they do so with taxpayers' own money. Directing public funds to ad agencies or ridings that have been particularly helpful to the party in power is thus regarded as normal political behaviour. If the politicians who have engineered such expenditures subsequently are re-elected, this is considered mainly as evidence of their political astuteness.

6 An even larger puzzle, of course, is why the railway policies of the 1880s, let alone a misreading of such policies, should influence any Canadian policies of the 1970s, 1980s, or 1990s.

CHAPTER 11 'The Most Rugged Surviving Individualists'

1 Owram quoting Andrew Haydon in 1899 (Owram 1986: 4).
2 By contrast, a much more generous pension scheme for parliamentarians had been introduced the year before: *plus ça change ...*
3 Earlier Innis had argued that the new national concern with full employment might become 'a racket on the part of the central provinces for getting and keeping what they can' (Owram 1986: 272). Salvation might come from what many would regard as an unexpected source, however, for though 'the lack of unity which has preserved Canadian unity threatens to disappear ... fortunately, we are sufficiently divided in regions, races and religion to resist [the] demand for centralization' (Innis 1945: 133, xii).
4 Pickersgill countered the first objection by arguing that 'the inclusion of fishermen was no more unsound actuarially than the inclusion of seasonal workers had been several years earlier' – which is precisely

the point. The second objection was got round by concocting the legal fiction that the fishermen were employed by the companies that bought their fish (Pickersgill 1994: 419) – a fiction still not granted to farmers, though they are just as legitimately 'employed' by those to whom they sell their produce.

CHAPTER 12 The American Lead

1 To my knowledge, a phrase first used by economist Thomas Courchene.
2 A delay that Owram attributes not so much to Canadian intellectual backwardness or isolation as to the fact that urbanization and industrialization came later here. The 1931 census was the first in which more Canadians were categorized as urban than rural (Urquhart and Buckley 1983: Series A67–69).
3 To be precise, Washington offered a 90 per cent rebate of a federal tax introduced for this purpose if a firm belonged to an approved state system of unemployment insurance. The federal government also absorbed the costs of administering the system (Hughes 1991: 175). Ottawa's plan involved direct payments by the federal government to citizens. Even this belated response to the Depression probably would have been impossible had not Maurice Duplessis lost the 1939 Quebec provincial election to the Liberal Adélard Godbout, who was much more willing to deal with Ottawa and became a one-legislature premier as a result.
4 He also predicted, however, that if after the war it proved to be 'the ineluctable pull of history, Mr. King will adjust himself to it, if he is still in office. If the negation of Liberalism is necessary, the Liberal Party will call it a new and up-to-date Liberalism' (Hutchison 1943: 90). As it happened, many Liberals came naturally to the New Deal. Lester Pearson writes in his memoirs about how in 1932 he was 'intensely interested in President Roosevelt's New Deal ... and in the energetic and imaginative action being taken there about which we were getting enthusiastic reports from our Canadian minister in Washington' (Pearson 1972a: 79). The minister, William Herridge, R.B. Bennett's brother-in-law, is generally credited with having per-

suaded Bennett to introduce his own New Deal in 1935. Pearson tells a funny story about how, as a young hand in Ottawa, he drafted a more or less openly socialist speech for Bennett, which must have caused some confusion for both its reader and its listeners when a tired prime minister delivered it without having first read through it.

5 Addressing Seymour Martin Lipset's contention that we have always had a stronger left and a more active public sector, they say, in understatedly Canadian fashion: 'This conclusion is inconsistent with the histories of the two countries: until the 1950s, Canada was America's backward neighbor in both regards. Historian Robert Bothwell's conclusion that "Lipset's contrast of a classically Liberal U.S. society with a ... Tory Canadian counterpart is somewhat overdrawn" is a gentle way of suggesting that Lipset's argument is incomplete' (Thompson and Randall 1994: 241). Which is itself a gentle way of saying that it is wrong.

6 In other areas there seems not to have been much to choose between the two countries: both provided extensive assistance, including health care, for victims of industrial accidents; both provided unemployment insurance to low-income workers, with payments varying in Canada according to previous contributions and in the United States to previous earnings; finally, both countries helped out with funeral expenses (ILO 1950).

7 Wisconsin was also the inspiration for 'the Wisconsin idea' – the vision, influential in university reformist circles in the 1910s, 'of the political economist as an expert closely tied to social policy.' The Wisconsin reference was to 'the alliance that had developed between the University of Wisconsin and progressive reformers in the state government' (Owram 1986: 67).

8 Schlesinger's thesis, inherited from his historian-father, is that America moves between reform and revision on roughly a twenty-year cycle. By this schedule, the 1990s were supposed to be a period of reform (by which, of course, is meant greater government interventionism), a prediction that looked reasonable with the election of a Democratic president in 1992 but apparently went off the rails with the mid-term congressional elections of 1994, which gave control of both houses of Congress to the Republicans for the first time since the late 1940s (see Schlesinger 1986).

CHAPTER 13 Canadian Free Enterprise

1 Now it would be: in 1993 transfers to persons were 31.2 per cent of overall government spending.
2 In fact, the *Adventures* are set in the United States, though Leacock must have had ample opportunity to observe similar behaviour in turn-of-the-century Montreal.
3 An expansion made easier no doubt by the fact that until 1914 U.S. banks could not operate international branches (Thompson and Randall 1994: 66).
4 Gwyn also notes: 'In *Fortune*'s list of the top five hundred international industrial companies, Canada ranks only in twelfth place with just six firms making the list,' though we have seventeen of the top 500 service corporations, most of them financial institutions, which puts us sixth (Gwyn 1995: 77). What he doesn't explain is why, since we have the world's twelfth-largest economy, twelfth in industry isn't a satisfactory score and sixth in services a dramatic overachievement.

CHAPTER 14 The Unimportance of Being Different

1 'According to the polls,' says Richard Gwyn (1995), '97 per cent of Canadians want to continue to be Canadian ... Not a scrap of evidence exists that Canadians want to become Americans' (54).
2 The rates in Saskatchewan, Alberta, and British Columbia – 3.8, 3.4, and 3.6, respectively – while also higher than Minnesota's and North Dakota's, were lower than those in Montana, Idaho, and Washington, where they were 4.7, 4.9, and 4.7, respectively. Yukon and the Northwest Territories had a higher murder rate – 16.9 per 100,000 – than Alaska, where the rate was 11.6 per 100,000 (Kopel 1992: 159n).
3 In per-capita terms, however, our rate of police shootings is one-third the American, where there is roughly one per day (Kopel 1992: 162).
4 The Civil War itself involved an assertion of government power – Lincoln's refusal to allow secession – that at least one Canadian prime minister (Trudeau) declared would not occur here, despite our supposedly greater appreciation of the virtues of more powerful government.

5 The other great American failing in many Canadians' eyes – the lack of 'free' health care for all – obviously does result from their lesser use of government. To provide equal or at least satisfactory health care for everyone probably does require that the state pay. Pay is all it need do, however; it need not provide the health care itself. Requiring that people with normal incomes carry insurance, and giving people with inadequate incomes the means to buy it, would satisfy the desire for universal coverage without involving government in the day-to-day management of health care.
6 Gwyn (1995) does concede that on affirmative action 'much that was happening here was also the product of the *zeitgeist*, or spirit of the times, particularly the public temper south of the border, where affirmative action was being enforced rigorously and comprehensively and where Bill Clinton's new cabinet would turn out to be the most "diverse" ever (even while containing more lawyers than ever before).' He argues that the also-imported doctrines of 'historical disadvantage' and 'equality of results' are inappropriate for Canada (149, 174).

CHAPTER 15 Distinct Society?

1 Though the way it is defined here, 'upper income' encompasses a broad range – anyone who makes more than twice the poverty level. There may be more Americans than Canadians at the very top end of this upper-income range, as Canadian prejudices presumably would have it.
2 Most Canadians probably don't realize the extent of the redistribution effected by the tax and transfer system. In 1995, before income taxes and cash transfers from governments, the average family in the top fifth of the income distribution made $21 for every $1 earned by the lowest fifth of families. After taxes and transfers, that was down to $5 for every $1. From $21 to $5 is pretty aggressive levelling. Moreover, per family member, top-fifth families ended up with only $3.50 for every $1 that bottom-fifth families netted (Statistics Canada, *The Daily*, 12 May 1997).
3 Which we can assume to be roughly 3.09 million. In 1986 there were 26.2 million Canadians, and the source being used (Blank and Han-

ratty 1993) argues that 11.8 per cent were poor, which is 3.09 million. But 3.09 million times $770 equals $2.38 billion. The conversion from U.S. to Canadian dollars that follows uses 1986's average exchange rate of U.S.$1 = Can.$1.389, or Can.$1 = U.S.$0.72.
4 An obvious thought is that it's going into health care, but recall that the U.S. public sector, despite the absence of universal, comprehensive, public health insurance, spends only 1.5 points of GDP less on health care than ours does. Ours spends 7.1 per cent of GDP, theirs 5.6, per cent (see Tholl 1994: Tables 7 and 9).
5 The effect of the Harris cuts was to move Ontario down one place, to twelfth, behind Vermont (Walker and Emes 1996: Table 1).
6 Perlin (1997) also finds 'little difference in attitudes towards trade unions in the two countries' (92).
7 Our high gun ownership rate and low – compared to the United States – murder rate creates problems for advocates of gun control. Between 1984 and 1994 only 32.2 per cent of Canadian murders were committed with firearms, while 29.2 per cent were committed with knives, though there is as yet no organized knife-control movement (Buckner 1995: 565–6). It is worth noting that when television was introduced into the United States, Canada, and South Africa, murder rates jumped, though ownership of firearms did not change appreciably (Kopel 1992: 413).
8 University graduates of British/Irish origin 'constitute the only category in which Canadians are more supportive of minority cultural maintenance than Americans are; the proportions are 54 and 42 per cent' (Reitz and Breton 1994: 31); that cultural group is probably more than proportionately influential in the Canadian, or at least the English-Canadian media, as a glance at the masthead of the *Globe and Mail* or the *Financial Post* will confirm. In the electronic media, 'Gzowski' may be the exception that proves the rule. Names such as Mansbridge, Robertson, Wallin, Matheson, Duffy, and Pringle originate in the traditional majority group. Our semi-official view of ourselves as a mosaic rather than a melting pot may be a result of its excessive weight in our affairs.
9 In a Toronto field trial conducted in 1984, 'whites received three times as many job offers as blacks ... [while] blacks were five times more likely than whites to be told that a job had been filled when a

subsequent white applicant was invited for an interview' (Reitz and Breton 1994: 83).
10 In his recent review of Canadian and American poll results on political values, George Perlin (1997) concludes that there is 'little evidence of differences either in underlying values or in approaches to public policy' between the two countries. He finds one important exception: 'Canadians, collectively, seem more willing than Americans to use government in an active role to pursue both economic and social objectives' (103). The evidence for this is that whereas in 1987 only 24 per cent of American respondents said 'the government should see to it that every person has a job and a good standard of living,' 44 per cent of English Canadians and 73 per cent of French Canadians thought it should. (Unfortunately, the U.S. question referred to 'the government in Washington,' so the results are not directly comparable; Perlin 1997: Table 3.A6, n5.) Canadians are also more committed to the concept of publicly-provided health care as an absolute right, though 'this is the only piece of evidence that supports the hypothesis that Canadians would be more disposed than Americans towards the principle of universality of social programs' (Perlin 1997: 93).
11 He does not explain why, if we gave up the high taxes that go with egalitarianism and collectivism, we would not become as rich as the Americans.
12 They also allowed us to stock up on American munitions and aircraft, which America's Neutrality Laws would not have permitted had we declared war immediately (Thompson and Randall 1994: 150).

CHAPTER 16 Cement for a Nation?

1 *Lament*'s Galahad, however implausible this seems from a late-century perspective, is John Diefenbaker, whom Grant portrays as the last Canadian political hero – a nice contrast, as mentioned above, with the judgment of the Albertans Bercuson and Cooper, who, writing thirty years later, consider Diefenbaker the first prime minister in the 'modern incompetent' tradition. By contrast, the villain of Grant's *Lament* is Lester Pearson, the 'ambitious diplomat' whose government now is best remembered for introducing medicare,

which polls tell us most Canadians consider our defining difference from the Americans. (In his memoirs, Pearson [1972b] himself mentions medicare precisely once [244], though the volume covering his period as prime minister was in large part put together by committee after his death.) Universal health insurance was still just a campaign promise when Grant wrote in 1965, however, and the now largely forgotten black spot that in his eyes damned Pearson irredeemably was the Liberal leader's winter 1962–3 change of mind about whether Canada should accept nuclear warheads for its Bomarc missiles – the same decision that drove a constitutional lawyer named Pierre Elliott Trudeau into the NDP for a time, even as Grant left the NDP over its decision to support the Liberals in bringing down Diefenbaker's government.

2 'I think very few sophisticated people today would say they believed in progress,' a CBC interviewer said in a question in 1985, and Grant did not object (Cayley 1995: 75).

3 As Grant said, 'Most people are not intended for sustained thought' (quoted in Cayley 1995: 57).

4 Though obviously even liberals concede that if one person's freedom bumps up against another's, accommodation somehow must be made.

5 Since at least some of those most recently in charge of the political party called 'Tory' did not share this critique, while many of those called 'Liberal' do, use of the lower-case 't' is intentional.

6 'When he thought of his own family, he was forced to conclude that industrialism was a blessing. Without machines Sheila would be a slave to the daily chores of life' (Christian 1993: 166).

7 Though they may not: at the time of the democratic uprising in China in 1989 much was made of how the fax machine and backpack satellite transmitter now made totalitarianism impossible. Unfortunately, the totalitarians possessed more effective, if also more primitive, technologies – namely, tanks, truncheons, and bullets. Other twentieth-century inventions, the radio and tape recorder, were instrumental in disseminating the fourteenth-century fundamentalist, anti-progressive philosophy of the Ayatollah Khomeini in the 1970s, thus helping lead the way to his Islamic revolution (Hobsbawm 1994: 501). By contrast, the new communications technologies,

especially the electronic window on Western living standards, generally are given considerable credit for the democratic revolution in the Soviet Union. So perhaps the message on whether the new media lead directly to tyranny is mixed.

8 Or does living half as meaningfully twice as long constitute double punishment – expiative suffering, in fact, as in the contest in which first prize was one week, and second prize two weeks, in Buffalo?

9 In the rest of Canada the corresponding numbers were 88.2 deaths per 1,000 in 1921 and only 9.6 in 1981 (Nagnur 1986: Table C1). Of 100 male children born in Canada in the years 1920–2 fewer than 85 reached 20 years of age and fewer than 58 made it to 65. In 1980–2, almost 98 could expect to reach age 20, and almost 75 age 65 (Nagnur 1986: Table C4).

10 In the 1930s some Canadian welfare agencies would not allow funds for the purchase of tooth powder. In the 1990s, by contrast, Canadians were debating whether welfare recipients should be allowed to own video-cassette recorders, and not only did no province prohibit this, but no province's laws or regulations even addressed the question. Moreover, 60 per cent of families with incomes less than $10,000 a year owned one. 'Gone are the days,' writes Peter Shawn Taylor, 'when only people without running water were considered poor' (Taylor 1996: 26).

11 It remained so well into this century. 'What a luxury a bath is a morning like this,' Canadian millionaire Joseph Flavelle wrote to his wife during a heat wave in the summer of 1916: 'One remembers the army of working men and women who must put on the same underwear as yesterday' (Bliss 1978: 333). In his recollection of Montreal in the interwar years, William Weintraub (1996), tells how 'during a July heat wave, outside the Schubert Bath, the body odour from perspiring blue-collar workers lined up to get in was legendary ... It was an aroma familiar to all of the city's sixteen public baths, all in poor districts where hot water was at a premium' (186).

12 Or, as Eric Hobsbawm (1994) has put it: 'What once [was] luxury [has become] the standard of comfort' (264).

13 Measured in 1986 dollars, GDP per capita was $11,037 in 1965, $20,444 in 1994 (Statistics Canada 1995: Table 1; Department of Finance 1995: Reference Table 1).

14 Quite apart from these practical questions there is the hard moral question whether it would be right for us to allow others – i.e., the Americans – to live meaningless, materialist, liberal lives and then ourselves take advantage of the technologies that the sacrifice of their souls produced. Of course, we face that dilemma now, since the American health care system which most Canadians find so abhorrent morally produces many of the technological miracles our no doubt much fairer system no longer generates on its own but does not hesitate to borrow (see Porter 1990). As the subject is philosophy, perhaps an extreme comparison will be permitted: in relying on technology produced in the American for-profit health regime, our moral dilemma is like that faced by scientists who wish to use data from Nazi experiments on human beings, or, to choose an example that the anti-abortionist Grant might have preferred, by doctors who could treat Parkinson's disease using fetal tissue acquired in abortions. The method of acquisition is morally repugnant, but the material acquired is so useful.
15 Fully 33.3 per cent of all exports are within the same firm, while another 32.6 per cent are from the subsidiaries of one transnational to those of another (United Nations 1995: 193).
16 'He too experienced the exhilaration of freedom ... He knew the practical worth of modern technology every time Sheila washed the clothes in her machine or the doctor gave antibiotics to one of their sick children ... How could he persuade his compatriots to turn away from the science of mastery, particularly if they no longer understood the significance of redemptive suffering?' (Christian 1993: 250).
17 Catholic Quebec *had* been different, though the more liberal form of Catholicism that attended the Quiet Revolution meant that it would not be different for long: 'With this kind of Catholicism, industrialized Quebec would hardly be distinguishable from the rest of North America ... With such a moral heart, Quebec will soon blend into the continental whole and cease to be a nation except in its maintenance of residual patterns of language and personal habit' (Grant 1965: 83). In the mid-1990s, even as 60 per cent of French-speaking and at least nominally Catholic Quebecers vote for at least nominal nationhood, this seems to be exactly what has happened. Grant almost certainly would not regard contemporary Quebec as any more distinct a soci-

ety than English Canada, even if Quebec before the Quiet Revolution had been. As Eric Hobsbawm (1994) has observed, Quebec nationalism 'emerged as a significant force precisely when Quebec ceased to be the "distinct society" it had so patently and unmistakably been until the 1960s' (429).
18 In mid-1944 he told Prime Minister King: 'After the war we must protect our best market to the extent of helping the U.K. rebuild its economy' (Muirhead 1992: 16). Muirhead has Howe finally souring on the British relationship only in early 1950, mainly because of chronic British reluctance to buy Canadian goods, and because, should the trade not recover, 'we should be vulnerable indeed with all our eggs in the U.K. basket' (Muirhead 1992: 44–5). Still, as late as June 1952 Howe stressed the importance of British trade links in the House of Commons (Muirhead 1992: 86).
19 The book's popularity has made Bennett a reported $5 million and allows him to command U.S.$40,000 a speech on the lecture circuit and live in what he calls 'the beach house that virtue built' (Kelly 1995: 30). Virtue and profit evidently are not always inconsistent.

CHAPTER 17 The Rising Cost of Civilization

1 Which is not to say that the good people of Sidney, Ontario, did not benefit when their bowling alley was renovated with infrastructure funds or that the citizens of North York did not appreciate better lighting on their ball field.
2 A good argument for the GST is that it catches people adept at avoiding income and payroll taxes.
3 Like many middle-aged university professors, he made a decent salary, one that put him in the top 10 per cent of the income distribution. He was hardly a plutocrat, however, though he was taxed like one.
4 Subtract these numbers from 1.0 and you get their 'marginal' and 'average' tax rates in effect in 1993.
5 Similarly, the reason for the spike near $30,000 of income has to do with the fact that UI and Canada Pension Plan premiums and low-income GST credits fade out around this level (Dahlby 1994: 54–5).

6 Which is what you'd expect from a progressive system, one that taxes higher incomes at steeper rates: if overall tax rates rise with income, the first dollars a worker makes aren't taxed as much as the last dollars, so his or her overall or average tax rate will be lower than the tax rate on the last dollar of income. Turning that upside down, he or she gets to keep more out of the first dollars earned than the last dollars, so the overall retention rate will be higher than the last-dollar retention rate.

7 And yet it still ran a deficit because interest payments on its debt were now $40 billion a year instead of the $20 billion they had been ten years earlier.

8 Anyone who was a taxpayer ten years ago got more in public services than he or she paid in taxes. The people who did best under this system are people who have died since the mid-1980s. They got all the extra spending benefits and now escape the taxes. They do have the misfortune of being dead, however. New taxpayers, Generation X-ers, get the short end of the tax stick. They are paying today and will pay tomorrow for public services other people consumed yesterday.

9 Imagine! A country that worries about hewing wood and drawing water subsidizes employment in its fishery and forest sectors.

10 It's possible that, having tried life with fewer videos, you decide that you like it. But the usual assumption in economics is that people (or their spouses) are the best judges of such matters. And even if they're not wholly competent to make such decisions for themselves, why suppose that the minister of finance knows any better?

11 If you are addicted to videos, the tax won't cause you to rent fewer of them, and therefore there isn't any excess burden from taxation, since your behaviour hasn't been changed. Because diabetics will pay anything to get their insulin, a tax on insulin would be very efficient, in that it would bring about a minimal change in behaviour. Of course, most people, and especially diabetics, would consider such a tax very unfair. First you get diabetes, then the government uses you as a tax cow. In the same way, Margaret Thatcher's poll tax, which with slight exceptions was the same for everyone regardless of income, was a non-distorting tax: you couldn't escape it by changing your economic behaviour. You could only escape by leaving the

United Kingdom. But, efficient or not, it struck most people as not very fair and eventually was withdrawn, though not until after Mrs. Thatcher had left office, a departure hastened by the tax's unpopularity.

12 If it's exactly equal to what he or she adds, there's no advantage in hiring this worker. The cost of doing so is exactly equal to the gain from doing so. If what the worker adds is *less* than what he or she is paid, only the government would think of hiring him or her. A private firm wouldn't, since it would lose money by doing so.

13 Table 17.2 includes three entries that say 'not defined.' They aren't defined because Dahlby was calculating how much excess burden there is for each extra dollar of revenue raised by raising the relevant tax rate. In these three cases, however, increasing the income tax surcharge didn't raise tax revenues; it lowered them, which means that as far as this form of tax is concerned, Manitoba, Nova Scotia, and Prince Edward Island are 'on the wrong side of the Laffer Curve.' Named after its inventor, American economist Arthur Laffer, the curve traces tax revenues on a vertical axis against tax rates on the horizontal. Only two tax rates produce no tax revenue – zero and 100 per cent – so the curve's endpoints are predetermined. At some rate in between, tax revenue must peak. Beyond the peak, raising tax rates actually lowers tax revenues. The Laffer curve therefore looks (at least roughly) like an upside-down U. Being on the right-hand leg of the U is not smart. In that region – 'the wrong side of the Laffer Curve' – tax revenues could be raised by *lowering* tax rates. When Dahlby assumes that a 10 per cent increase in tax rates gives rise to a 2 per cent rather than a 1 per cent reduction in effort, he finds that hiking income surtaxes to raise revenue is futile in every single province: they are all now on the wrong side of the Laffer curve. To raise more revenue, every province would have to *lower* tax rates. When Ronald Reagan proposed just that in 1980, George Bush called it 'voodoo economics,' and when David Stockman, Reagan's budget director, built it into his forecasts it provided budget predictions so fantastical that they eventually cost Stockman his job. It may have been economic fiction in the United States in the early 1980s but in Canada in the early 1990s, 'voodoo economics' was rapidly becoming a fact of life.

CHAPTER 18 The Psychic Costs of Government

1 Thanks to the supposedly pro-business Mulroney Tories' 1986 Competition Act, which the supposedly anti-business Liberals had dithered about since 1969 but never passed. Cartels have been illegal in Canada since 1889 – we got our anti-trust legislation, which we call anti-combines legislation, at exactly the same time as the Americans – though ours turned out to be 'ceremonial legislation which threatened no one' (Bliss 1978: 231). Because our laws provided jail sentences for the white-collar crime of dominating a market, prosecutors hardly ever got convictions. In almost eight decades the government had never won a contested merger case and had prevailed in only one major contested monopoly case (Green 1990: 309).
2 The railways that went bankrupt would not have been built in the first place had governments not subsidized them.
3 Fraser writes: 'An old story, still current on the prairies, tells of the farmer who woke one morning to find his ripe crop ruined by blight. After a long silence he said to his wife: "Well, God damn the C.P.R."' (B. Fraser 1967: 314–15).
4 He also believed that interregional bickering was not altogether a bad thing. Referring to the wartime accretion of powers by Ottawa he observed: 'Fortunately we are sufficiently divided in regions, races, and religion to resist ... [these] demands for centralization' (Innis 1945: xii).
5 This is in 1994 dollars. The principal beneficiary of this transfer has been Quebec, to the tune of $167 billion, though all other provinces except Ontario have also gained. In per capita terms, Alberta's contribution has been a little over $2,000 a year, with PEI, the biggest winner, receiving almost $4,000 a year. In per capita terms, the transfer to Quebec has averaged $803. The calculations include the value of energy transferred from Alberta by Ottawa's policy of pricing oil at less than world market prices from the mid-1970s to the mid-1980s (Mansell and Schlenker 1995: Table 1).
6 There is a long tradition of catering to regional needs. In the early days of the First World War, contracts to manufacture artillery shells were 'spread across the country in response to government pressure to provide jobs in the West; the West's claim for war orders was

based on the high percentage of men it was sending to the front, not on economics ... It may have made political sense to ship forgings from Ontario to be machined into shells in British Columbia and then shipped back again – incurring the highest labour costs in Canada and four thousand miles' worth of freight charges – but there was no economic justification for placing these orders' (Bliss 1978: 252, 249).

7 A point once cited in his own defence by John Diefenbaker, one of our less successful ditherer-prime ministers (Bliss 1994: 206).

8 This is shameless second-guessing, since its author steadfastly supported the FTA, NAFTA, the Meech Lake Accord, and, alas, the hopelessly ill-advised Charlottetown Accord. But experience that does not teach is mere time-filling.

CHAPTER 19 Virtually Canadian

1 As a result of foreign investment, tens of thousands of us also have had the experience of dealing directly with superiors in the home office in the United States. Not that many fewer – since Canadian investments in the United States are now two-thirds the value of American investments in Canada – deal with American employees in Canadian operations south of the border. In the early 1990s we boasted 1,447 head offices of our own, though not all had subsidiaries in the United States. The United States had 2,966 head offices, far fewer than the usual ten-to-one ratio would predict (United Nations 1995: Table 1.2).

2 There is a history of this sort of thing: between the wars Canadian censors snipped 'closeups of the Stars and Stripes and movies in which the U.S. Army won the [First] world war' (Thompson and Randall 1994: 123).

3 So far, the machines don't come close. Since 1990 Hugh Loebner, a philanthropist, businessman, and self-described 'Utopian engineer,' has offered the $100,000 Loebner Prize to encourage them – or rather their programmers – to become more intelligent (Loebner Prize 1996; Loebner 1996). In the first run of the competition, in 1992, human questioners had to restrict their inquiry to narrow topics agreed on in advance. Even so, the machines did very poorly. Only in one cate-

Notes to pages 220-7   285

gory, 'whimsical conversation,' were five human judges unable to decide whether they were conversing with machines or people. 'The randomness of whimsy,' concluded the *Scientific American*'s correspondent, 'springs as readily from a silicon chip as from a human mind' (Dewdney 1992). Well, yes, but randomness of thought may not be the truest test of intelligence. Since 1995, inquiry in the competition has been unlimited and the machines have done worse still, though a prize of $2,000 has been given each year to the programmer who produced the machine the judges considered 'most human.'

4 Though on meeting Vincent Massey, Calvin Coolidge, a New Englander, did ask the new Canadian minister to Washington whether his home town of Toronto was anywhere near Lake Ontario (Thompson and Randall 1994: 106).

5 In his book *On Being Canadian*, written half a century ago, Vincent Massey provided a similar list: 'A constable of the Royal Canadian Mounted Police – and Canada has no better symbol; a sheaf of Marquis wheat; Canadian landscape painting; a beaver-pelt; a silvered church spire in French Canada; a bar of nickel; a bush-pilot; a pair of moccasins; the Wolfe-Montcalm monument at Quebec; a tube of insulin; a totem pole; a calèche; a cake of maple sugar; a Hudson's Bay blanket; the song "Alouette"; a hockey stick; the Canadian Boat Song; a pair of snow-shoes; a roll of birch-bark; a silver fox; a canoe; a Canada goose; a grain elevator; a lacrosse stick; a boom of logs; a buffalo; the Quebec Citadel; a maple tree; the opening of Parliament in winter' (Massey 1948: 31).

6 In parts of eastern Europe the waiting time for a phone hook-up is ten years or longer. In Mozambique only one person in 300 has phone service (Wysocki 1997: A1).

7 Already, the U.S. National Archives in Washington, DC, has roughly five billion documents in storage, while other federal repositories have 19 million cubic feet more, enough, spread end to end in boxes, to stretch across the United States. There will soon be lots of electronic information, as well. The amount of information stored in print everywhere in the world is estimated to be 200 'petabytes' – a petabyte being a quadrillion bytes and a quadrillion being 10 to the power 15. By the year 2000 the amount of information accumulated on-line is expected to be two and a half times that, with more coming

every day. The U.S. government, for instance, decided in 1995 that it would archive all its e-mail (Murphy 1996b: 22).

8 As the historian Paul Johnson (1997) has put it: 'History shows, again and again, that it is the unexpected that happens. Powerful trends disappear disconcertingly and suddenly into the sands of time. New developments shoot up from nowhere, without warning, to the consternation of the wise. Horrible monsters aburptly stride centre stage and change the play fundamentally. So do unknown heroes. Civilized life is threatened or saved, by a deus ex machina no-one had an inkling of five or ten years before. Who, at the beginning of the eleventh century, would have forecast the renewal of the church and the crusades, or at the beginning of the twelfth the creation of the university, or at the beginning of the thirteenth the birth of parliament, or at the beginning of the fourteenth the Black Death, or at the beginning of the fifteenth the discovery of the new World, or at the beginning of the sixteenth the Reformation: The Industrial Revolution, the French Revolution, the arrival of such transforming forces as steam power, electricity, nuclear energy – all these seemed obvious and inevitable after they had happened but no-one expected them, (19).

9 Some of us do make a living, often quite a good living, trying to foretell the future path of interest rates. The impressive sums for which such musings can be sold suggest that we are better at this brand of soothsaying than the average person. Then again perhaps this is one of the (assuredly very rare) cases in which the market fails.

10 When, just after the Second World War, the Canadian government commissioned one of the world's best-known demographers to forecast the country's population growth, her estimate was that as a mature, urban-industrial nation whose population therefore would grow slowly, Canada could expect to have 14 million people by 1971 and 15 million by the end of the century, after which its population would begin to decline (Owram 1994: 107). She was wrong by a factor of precisely two.

11 Technological determinism isn't absolute, however. Satellites can provide many different signals, which can lead to audience fragmentation, while, within rapidly expanding limits prescribed by the capacity of servers, millions of web-surfers can check out the same web site, thus leading to uniformity of experience even in an individ-

ualistic medium. The landing of an American robot on Mars in July 1997 led to a world-record number of hits, as millions of people around the world visited NASA's web site to view incoming pictures.
12 A convenient fact that favours its use in testing the purchasing power of currencies; see Pakko and Pollard 1996.

CHAPTER 20 Do Countries Still Make Sense?

1 Remember, however, that not everyone did have a television: I vividly recall the day we got ours.
2 One that is available, a disc barely four inches across, weighing almost nothing, holds 3,500 literary works, including all of Shakespeare as well as unabridged major works from 204 other writers, including Dickens, Shelley, Burke, Locke, Hobbes, Blake, Euripides, the Grimms, Joyce, Keats, Kipling, and even Lucy Maud Montgomery (see *Library* ... 1994).
3 And the cost has been falling. In the summer of 1995 it was $120. In the fall of 1997, a disc containing all Canadian and American phone numbers, plus several million other data permits, could be had for only $83.
4 And by 1981 80.2 per cent of Canadian households did (Sarlo 1996b: Table 4).
5 A (ahem) virtual certainty usually ignored by the advocates of large governments, who often seem to suggest that if taxation should fall below 40 per cent of people's total income, their sense of community would be utterly destroyed. If as a species we are driven to meet, then we probably would devise ways of gathering even if we did away with government entirely, which not even we neoconservatives are suggesting.
6 Whether it *should* be made to work on such a scale is another question, since electronic balloting seems most likely to increase the number of uninformed votes. One virtue of representative democracy is that citizens don't have to spend their time reading long, complicated bills. They can specialize in other things while the people they have elected do their politics for them. If we get a referendum of the week, however, participation rates may fall off drastically, which

means that only the highly motivated get to decide things. It should not be assumed that they will make consistently wise decisions.
7 A consideration that would be important even if there were no government-sponsored redistribution across regions, in which case the redistribution would take place as people moved, either temporarily or permanently, out of low-employment regions to higher-employment regions
8 Social scientists talk about 'the sharing community,' defined as the domain over which people are willing to share (see Simeon and Janigan 1991). Canada may be becoming less of a sharing community than it has been: people outside Quebec certainly are not shy about telling pollsters that they are tired of sharing with Quebec, even if that sentiment is belied by the generous outpouring of donations after almost biblical floods devastated Quebec's most strongly separatist region in the summer of 1996. But for the time being, the numbers suggest that Canadians apparently feel much more comfortable sharing among themselves than with people from other countries.
9 The passage was drafted for him by Secretary of State William Henry Seward (Sandburg 1968: 35).

References

Abrahamsson, Bernhard J. (1980) *International Ocean Shipping: Current Concepts and Principles.* Boulder, Col.: Westview Press.
Bank of Canada (1996) *Bank of Canada Review.* Winter 1995–96. Ottawa: Bank of Canada.
Banting, Keith, Hoberg, George, and Simeon, Richard, eds. (1997) *Degrees of Freedom: Canada and the United States in a Changing World.* Montreal: McGill-Queen's University Press.
Banting, Keith, and Simeon, Richard (1997) 'Changing Economies, Changing Societies,' in Banting, Hoberg, and Simeon, eds. (1997), 23–70.
Barlow, Maude, and Robinson, David (1995) 'Another Take on the Effects of Free Trade.' Letter to the *Globe and Mail*, 15 Dec. 1995.
Bastiat, Frédéric (1934) *Economic Fallacies.* Ottawa: R.J. Deachman.
Baumol, William J. (1967) 'Macroeconomics of Unbalanced Growth: The Anatomy of Urban Crisis' *American Economic Review*, 57 no. 3 (June 1967) 415–26.
Baumol, William, J., Blackman, Anne Batey, and Wolff, Edward N. (1989) *Productivity and American Leadership: The Long View.* Cambridge, Mass.: MIT Press.
Beach, Charles M., and Slotsve, George A. (1996) *Are We Becoming Two Societies? Income Polarization and the Myth of the Declining Middle Class in Canada.* Toronto: C.D. Howe Institute.
Bénéton, Philippe (1985) 'Trends in the Social Policy Aims of the United States (1960–1980),' in Girod, Laubier, and Gladstone, eds. (1985), 71–90.

Bercuson, David, and Cooper, Barry (1994) *Derailed: The Betrayal of the National Dream.* Toronto: Key Porter.
Berton, Pierre (1970) *The National Dream: The Great Railway, 1871–1881.* Toronto: McClelland and Stewart.
Bhagwati, Jagdish, and Hudec, Robert E. eds. (1996) *Fair Trade and Harmonization: Prerequisites for Free Trade?* Volume I. *Economic Analysis.* Cambridge, Mass.: MIT Press.
Bhagwati, Jagdish, and Srinivasan, T.N. (1996) 'Trade and the Environment: Does Environmental Diversity Detract from the Case for Free Trade?' in Bhagwati and Hudec, eds. (1996), 159–223.
Bishop, John H. (1996) 'Is the Market for College Graduates Headed for a Bust? Demand and Supply Responses to Rising Collge Wage Premiums' *New England Economic Review* (May/June) 115–38.
Blackburn, McKinley L., and Bloom, David E. (1993) 'The Distribution of Family Income: Measuring and Explaining Changes in the 1980s for Canada and the United States,' in Card and Freeman, eds. (1993), 233–65.
Blank, Rebecca M., and Hanratty, Maria J. (1993) 'Responding to Need: A Comparison of Social Safety Nets in Canada and the United States,' in Card and Freeman, eds. (1993), 191–231.
Bliss, Michael (1978) *A Canadian Millionaire: The Life and Business Times of Sir Joseph Flavelle, Bart. 1858–1939.* Toronto: Macmillan.
– (1987) *Northern Enterprise: Five Centuries of Canadian Business.* Toronto: McClelland and Stewart.
– (1994) *Right Honourable Men.* Toronto: HarperCollins.
Blomqvist, Åke, and Brown, David M. eds. (1994) *Limits to Care: Reforming Canada's Health System in an Age of Restraint.* Toronto: C.D. Howe Institute.
Blumenthal, Sidney (1996) 'Our Next Prime Minister,' *New Yorker,* 20 May 1996, 4–5.
Boadway, Robin (1995) 'The Constraints of Global Forces Are Exaggerated,' *Policy Options Politiques.* 16 no. 5, 11–16.
Board of Inquiry into Cost of Living in Canada (1915) *Report of the Board, Volume II.* Ottawa: King's Printer.
Borjas, George J. (1993) 'Immigration Policy, National Origin, and Immigrant Skills: A Comparison of Canada and the United States,' in Card and Freeman, eds. (1993), 21–43.

Bothwell, Robert, Drummond, Ian, and English, John (1987) *Canada: 1900–1945*. Toronto: University of Toronto Press.
Breton, Albert, and Scott, Anthony (1978) *The Economic Constitution of Federal States*. Toronto: University of Toronto Press.
Brown, David M. (1994) 'No Sense of Direction: Public/Private Compensation Differentials,' in Harris, Dymond, and Robertson (1994), 77–117.
Bryce, Robert (1986) *Maturing in Hard Times: Canada's Department of Finance through the Great Depression*. Montreal: McGill-Queen's University Press.
Buckner, Taylor (1995) 'Comment on Neal Boyd's "Bill C-68: Simple Problem, Complex Soutions,"' *Canadian Journal of Criminology*, 37 no. 1, 565–6.
Burke, Edmund (1986) *Reflections on the Revolution in France*. London: Penguin.
Button, Graham, ed. (1995) 'The Billionaires,' *Forbes*, 156 no. 2 (17 July 1995), 110–223.
Cameron, Stevie (1994) *On the Take: Crime, Corruption, and Greed in the Mulroney Years*. Toronto: Macfarlane, Walter and Ross.
Cameron, Duncan, and Watkins, Mel, eds. (1993) *Canada under Free Trade*. Toronto: James Lorimer & Co.
Campbell, Bruce (1993) 'Continental Corporate Economics,' in Cameron and Watkins, eds. (1993), 21–40.
Canada (1955) *Mothers' Allowances Legislation in Canada*. Memorandum No. 1, Social Security Series, Revised Edition. Ottawa: Research Division: Department of National Health and Welfare.
– (1996) *Public Accounts of Canada* Part II, Volume II. Ottawa: Supply and Services Canada.
Caplan, Gerald, Kirby, Michael, and Segal, Hugh (1989) *Election: The Issues, the Strategies, the Aftermath*. Scarborough, Ont.: Prentice-Hall.
Card, David, and Freeman, Richard B., eds. (1993) *Small Differences That Matter: Labor Markets and Income Maintenance in Canada and the United States* (Chicago: University of Chicago Press)
Card, David, and Riddell, W. Craig (1993) 'A Comparative Analysis of Unemployment in Canada and the United States,' in Card and Freeman, eds. (1993), 149–89.

Cayley, David (1995) *George Grant: In Conversation.* Concord, Ont.: House of Anansi.
Chandler, Alfred, Jr (1977) *The Visible Hand: The Managerial Revolution in American Business.* Cambridge, Mass.: Belknap Press of Harvard University.
Chrétien, Jean (1985) *Straight from the Heart.* Toronto: Key Porter Books.
Christian, William (1993) *George Grant: A Biography.* Toronto: University of Toronto Press.
Clark, Joe (1994) *A Nation Too Good to Lose: Renewing the Purpose of Canada.* Toronto: Key-Porter Books.
Colombo, John Robert (1992) *The Canadian Global Almanac 1992: A Book of Facts.* Toronto: Global Press.
Compton's Interactive Encyclopedia (1994) Version 2.01VW, Compton's NewMedia, Inc.
Cook, Ramsay (1996) 'Founding Peoples or Sovereign Nations?' *Beaver,* 76 no. 3 (June/July), 14–20.
Cooper, Barry (1992) 'Did George Grant's Canada Ever Exist?' in Umar, ed. (1992), 151–64.
Corak, Miles, and Pyper, Wendy (1994) 'The Distribution of UI Benefits and Taxes in Canada,' *Canadian Economic Observer* (Dec. 1994), 3.1–3.15.
Correctional Service of Canada (1994) *Basic Facts about Corrections in Canada: 1993 Edition.* Ottawa: Minister of Supply and Services.
Courchene, Thomas J. (1994) *Social Canada in the Millennium: Reform Imperatives and Restructuring Principles.* Toronto: C.D. Howe Institute.
Courchene, Thomas J., and Neave, Edwin H. (1997) *Reforming the Canadian Financial Sector: Canada in Global Perspective.* Kingston, Ont.: John Deutsch Institute for the Study of Economic Policy.
Creighton, Donald (1976) *The Forked Road: Canada, 1939–1957.* Toronto: McClelland and Stewart.
Dahlby, Bev (1994) 'The Distortionary Effect of Rising Taxes,' in William B.P. Robson and William M. Scarth, eds., *Deficit Reduction: What Pain, What Gain?* Toronto: C.D. Howe Institute, 43–72.
Damus, S. (1992) *Canada's Public Sector: A Graphic Overview.* Ottawa: Economic Council of Canada.
Department of Finance (1995) *Economic Reference Tables: August 1995.* Ottawa: Department of Finance.
Derthick, Martha, and Quirk, Paul J. (1985) *The Politics of Deregulation.* Washington, DC: Brookings Institution.

Dewdney, A.K. (1992) *Scientific American*, 266 no. 1 (Jan. 1992), 30–1.
dodgers.com: http//www.dodgers.com/newfield.html.
Dominion Institute (1997) 'Youth History Survey.' Angus Reid Group, mimeo, May.
Drache, Daniel (1993) 'The Future of Trading Blocs,' in Cameron and Watkins, eds. (1993), 264–76.
Drucker, Peter F. (1995) 'Really Reinventing Government.' *Atlantic Monthly*, 275 no. 2 (Feb.), 61.
Dunning, John H. (1970) *Studies in International Investment*. London: George Allen & Unwin Ltd.
Easterbrook, Gregg (1995) 'Here Comes the Sun,' *New Yorker*, 10 April 1995, 38–43.
Easton, Stephen, and Lippert, Owen (1996) 'Civil Law in the United States: An Expensive Precedent for Canada?' *Fraser Forum* (June 1996), 25–6.
Economist (1990) 'What Now? A Survey of the Soviet Union,' 20 Oct., 1–22 following 66.
- (1996a) 'Kenneth Clarke's Triumph,' 23 Nov. 63.
- (1996b) 'Over-Regulating America: Tomorrow's Economic Argument,' 27 July, 19–21.
- (1997) 'The Tap Runs Dry,' 31 May, 21–3.
Edelstein, Michael (1994) 'Foreign Investment and Accumulation, 1860–1914,' in Floud and McCloskey, eds. (1994), 173–96.
Eichengreen, Barry, ed. (1986) *The Gold Standard in Theory and History*. New York and London: Methuen.
Eichengreen, Barry, and Lindert, Peter (1989) *The International Debt Crisis in Historical Perspective*. Cambridge, Mass.: MIT Press.
Emery, J.C. Herbert, and McKenzie, Kenneth J. (1996) 'Damned If You Do, Damned If You Don't: An Option Value Approach to Evaluating the Subsidy of the CPR Mainline,' *Canadian Journal of Economics*, 29 no. 29 255–70.
Engel, Charles, and Rogers, John H. (1995) 'How Wide Is The Border?' *American Economic Review*, 86 no. 5 (Dec.), 1112–25.
English, John (1992) *The Worldly Years: The Life of Lester Pearson, 1949–1972*. Toronto: Vintage Books.
Feileke, Norman S. (1995) 'The Uruguay Round of Trade Negotiations: An Overview,' *New England Economic Review* (May/June), 3–14.

Fletcher, Joseph (1992) *Canadian Attitudes toward Competitiveness and Entrepreneurship*. Ottawa: Department of Industry, Science, and Technology.
Floud, Roderick, and Donald McCloskey, eds. (1994) *The Economic History of Britain since 1700.* Volume 2. *1860–1939.* Cambridge: Cambridge University Press.
Fogel, Robert William (1960) *The Union Pacific Railroad: A Case in Premature Enterprise.* Baltimore, Md.: Johns Hopkins Press.
Foster, Angus (1995) 'Brazilian Dream Gets Another Chance,' *Financial Post,* 7 Dec. 1995, 14.
Francis, Diane (1993) *A Matter of Survival: Canada in the 21st Century.* Toronto: Key Porter Books Limited.
Fraser, Blair (1967) *The Search for Identity: Canada, 1945–67.* Toronto: Doubleday & Co.
Fraser, Graham (1989) *Playing for Keeps: The Making of the Prime Minister, 1988.* Toronto: McClelland and Stewart.
Freeman, Kenneth D., Oum, Tae H., Tretheway, Michael, and Waters, W.G. (1987). *The Growth and the Performance of the Canadian Transcontinental Railways 1956–1981.* Vancouver, University of British Columbia, Centre for Transportation Studies.
Freeman, Richard (1996) 'Labour Market Institutions and Earnings Inequality,' *New England Economic Review* (May/June), 157–68.
Friedman, Milton (1989) 'Evidence Shows the "Internationalized" Economy Is Nonsense,' *Globe and Mail,* 6 May. B2.
Frye, Northrop (1982) *Divisions on a Ground: Essays on Canadian Culture.* Toronto: Anansi.
Gallup Canada Inc. (various dates) *The Gallup Poll.*
Gentilcore, R. Louis (1993) *Historical Atlas of Canada.* Volume II. *The Land Transformed 1800–1891.* Toronto: University of Toronto Press.
George, Peter J. (1968) 'Rates of Return in Railway Investment and Implications for Government Subsidization of the Canadian Pacific Railway: Some Preliminary Results,' *Canadian Journal of Economics,* I no. 4, 740–62.
Girod, Roger, de Laubier, Patrick, and Gladstone, Alan, eds. (1985) *Social Policy in Western Europe and the US, 1950–80: An Assessment.* London: Macmillan, in association with the International Institute for Labour Studies.

Globe and Mail (1989), 'CMA's Thibault Seeking Cuts in Spending on Social Programmes,' March, B13.
Globerman, Steven, with Carter, Deborah (1988) *Telecommunications in Canada*. Vancouver: Fraser Institute.
Goldberg, Michael A., and Levi, Maurice D. (1994) 'A Portfolio View of Canada,' *Canadian Public Policy*, 20 no. 4, 341–52.
Gordon, David (1996) *Fat and Mean: The Corporate Squeeze of Working Americans and the Myth of Managerial 'Downsizing.'* New York: Martin Kessler Books.
Gordon, Roger H., and Bovenberg, A. Lans (1996) 'Why Is Capital So Immobile Internationally? Possible Explanations and Implications for Capital Income Taxation,' *American Economic Review*, 86 no. 5 (Dec.), 1057–75.
Granatstein, J.L. (1986) *Canada 1957–67: The Years of Uncertainty and Innovation*. Toronto: McLelland and Stewart.
– (1994) 'Canadian Social Policy: From Laissez-Faire to Safety Net to ...?' in Granatstein and Åkerman, eds. (1994), 123–35.
Granatstein, J.L., and Åkerman, Sune, eds. (1994) *Welfare States in Trouble: Historical Perspectives on Canada and Sweden*. North York, Ont: Swedish-Canadian Academic Foundation, York University.
Grant, George (1965) *Lament for a Nation: The Defeat of Canadian Nationalism*. Reprint 1991. Ottawa: Carleton University Press.
Green, Christopher (1990) *Canadian Industrial Organization and Policy*. 3rd ed. Toronto: McGraw-Hill Ryerson.
Guest, Dennis (1980) *The Emergence of Social Security in Canada*. Vancouver: University of British Columbia Press.
Gwyn, Richard (1995) *Nationalism without Walls: The Unbearable Lightness of Being Canadian*. Toronto: McClelland and Stewart.
Harris, R. Cole, ed. (1987) *Historical Atlas of Canada*. Volume I. *From the Beginning to 1800*. Toronto: University of Toronto Press.
Harris, Richard, with Cox, David (1983) *Trade, Industrial Policy, and Canadian Manufacturing*. An Ontario Economic Council Study. Toronto: University of Toronto Press.
Harris, Richard G. (1993) 'Globalization, Trade, and Income,' *Canadian Journal of Economics*, 26 no. 4, 755–76.
Hart, Michael, with Dymond, Bill, and Robertson, Colin (1994) *Decision*

at Midnight: Inside the Canada–US Free-Trade Negotiations. Vancouver: UBC Press.
Hartt, Stanley (1992) 'Sovereignty and the Economic Union,' in Hartt et al. (1992) 3–30.
Hartt, Stanley, de Mestral, A.L.C., McCallum, John, Loungnarath, Vilaysoun, Morton, Desmond, and Turp, Daniel (1992) *Tangled Web: Legal Aspects of Deconfederation.* Toronto: C.D. Howe Institute.
Helliwell, John F. (1995) 'Do National Borders Matter for Quebec's Trade?' Draft paper for presentation at the Annual Meetings of the Canadian Economics Association, Université du Québec à Montréal, 2 June.
Helliwell, John F. (1996) 'Do National Borders Matter for Quebec's Trade?' *Canadian Journal of Economics* 29 no. 3, 507–22.
Helliwell, John F., and McCallum, John (1995) 'National Borders Still Matter for Trade,' *Policy Options Politiques,* 16 no. 5, 44–8.
Higgs, Robert (1987) *Crisis and Leviathan: Critical Episodes in the Growth of American Government.* New York: Oxford University Press.
Hobsbawm, Eric (1994) *Age of Extremes: The Short Twentieth Century, 1914–1991.* London: Michael Joseph.
Hodges, Andrew (1996) *The Alan Turing Home Page.* http:// www.wadham.ox.ac.uk/ ~ahodges/Turing.html.
Hughes, Jonathan R.T. (1977) *The Governmental Habit: Economic Controls from Colonial Times to the Present.* New York: Basic Books.
– (1983) *American Economic History,* Dallas, Tex.: Scott, Foresman & Company.
– (1991) *The Governmental Habit Redux: Economic Controls from Colonial Times to the Present.* Princeton, NJ: Princeton University Press.
Hutchison, Bruce (1943) *The Unknown Country.* Toronto: Longmans, Green & Company.
Ignatieff, Michael (1993) *Blood and Belonging: Journeys into the New Nationalism.* Toronto: Penguin Books.
Innis, Harold (1945) *Political Economy in the Modern State.* Toronto: Ryerson Press.
International Labour Office (ILO) (1950) *International Survey of Social Security.* Geneva: ILO.
Irwin, Leonard Bertram (1968) *Pacific Railways and Nationalism in the*

Canadian-American Northwest, 1845–1873. First published 1939. New York: Greenwood Press.
Jansson, Bruce S. (1988) *The Reluctant Welfare State: A History of American Social Welfare Policies.* Belmont, Calif.: Wadsworth.
Johnson, Paul (1997) 'Future Shockers,' *Saturday Night* (June), 15–19.
Jorgensen, Dale W., and Landau, Ralph, eds. (1993) *Tax Reform and the Cost of Capital: An International Comparison.* Washington, DC: Brookings Institution.
Kelly, Michael (1995) 'Letter from Washington: The Man of the Minute,' *New Yorker*, 17 July, 26–30.
Kent, Tom (1988) *A Public Purpose: An Experience of Liberal Opposition and Canadian Government.* Montreal: McGill-Queen's University Press.
Kenwood, A.G., and Lougheed, A.L. (1992) *The Growth of the International Economy 1820–1990.* London: Routledge.
Keynes, John Maynard (1924) *The Economic Consequencies of the Peace.* London: Macmillan.
– (1926) *The End of Laissez-Faire.* London: Hogarth.
– (1936) *The General Theory of Employment, Interest and Money.* London: Macmillan.
– (1963) *Essays in Persuasion.* First pub. 1932. New York: Norton.
Klevorick, Alvin K. (1996) 'Reflections on the Race to the Bottom,' in Bhagwati and Hudec, eds. (1996), 459–67.
Kolko, Gabriel (1970) *Railroads and Regulation, 1877–1916.* New York: Norton.
Koller, Frank (1993) 'An Interview with Lee Kuan Yew,' *Inroads* (spring 1993), 101–90.
Kopel, David B. (1992) *The Samurai, the Mountie and the Cowboy: Sould America Adopt the Gun Controls of Other Democracies?* Buffalo, NY: Prometheus Books for the Cato Institute.
Krugman, Paul R. (1989) *Exchange-Rate Instability: The Lionel Robbins Lectures.* Cambridge: Mass.: MIT Press.
– (1991) *Geography and Trade.* Cambridge, Mass.: MIT Press.
– (1996) 'Global Economy: Déjà Vu' *Harper's Magazine* (May), p. 22.
Leacock, Stephen (1914) *Arcadian Adventures with the Idle Rich.* Toronto: Bell and Cockburn.
Levi, Maurice K. (1997) 'Are Capital Markets Internationally Integrated?,' in Courchene and Neave, eds. (1997) 63–86.

Library of the Future: 3rd Edition (1994). Irvine, Calif.: A World Library Product.

Lipset, Seymour Martin (1990) *Continental Divide: The Values and Institutions of Canada and the United States.* New York: Routledge.

Loebner, Hugh G. (1996) *Hugh G. Loebner Home Page.* http://info.acm.org/~loebner/ homepage.htmlx.

Loebner Prize (1996) *Home Page of the Loebner Prize.* http://info.acm.org/~loebner/ loebner-prize.htmlx.

Lohrmann, Reinhard (1994) 'International Migration in the Nineties: Trends and Prospects,' in International Social Security Agency (1994) *Migration: A Worldwide Challenge for Social Security,* Geneva: ISSA 9–30.

Lower, Arthur R.M. (1967) *My First Seventy-Five Years.* Toronto: Macmillan.

McCalla, Robert J. (1994) *Water Transportation in Canada.* Halifax: Formac.

McCallum, John (1993) 'National Borders Matter: Regional Trade Patterns in North America.' *McGill University Department of Economics Working Paper 12/93.* Montreal: mimeo.

McCallum, John, and Helliwell, John F. (1995) 'The Extraordinary Trade-Generating Powers of the Canadian Economic Union (CEU)' mimeo.

McCullough, David (1992) *Truman.* New York: Simon & Schuster.

McLaughlin, Gordon (1995) 'The King of the Gurus: Drucker Eats His Young,' *Financial Post,* 25 March, 17.

McQuaig, Linda (1995) *Shooting the Hippo: Death by Deficit and Other Canadian Myths.* Toronto: Viking.

McVey, Wayne, Jr., and Kalbach, Warren E. (1971) *The Demographic Bases of Canadian Society.* Toronto: McGraw-Hill.

– (1995) *Canadian Population.* Toronto: Nelson Canada.

Maddison, Angus (1991) *Dynamic Forces in Capitalist Development: A Long-run Comparative View.* Oxford: Oxford University Press.

Mansell, Robert, and Schlenker, Ronald (1995) 'The Provincial Distribution of Federal Fiscal Balances,' *Canadian Business Economics,* 3 no. 2 (winter), 3–19.

Markusen, Ann Roell (1983) *Profit Cycles, Oligopoly, and Regional Development.* Cambridge, Mass: MIT Press.

Martin, Paul, Hon. (1994) *National Defence: Budget Impact.* Ottawa: Department of Finance; Feb. 1994.

– (1995) *Budget Speech.* Ottawa: Department of Finance, 27 Feb. 1995.

- (1997) *Budget Plan.* Ottawa: Department of Finance, 18 Feb.
Massey, Vincent (1948) *On Being Canadian.* Toronto: J.M. Dent & Sons.
Mauser, Gary (1990) 'A Comparison of Canadian and American Attitudes towards Firearms,' *Canadian Journal of Criminology,* 32 no. 4, 573-89.
Morgan, Kathleen O'Leary, Morgan, Scott, and Quinto, Neal, eds. (1995) *State Rankings 1995: A Statistical View of the 50 United States.* Lawrence, Kansas: Morgan Quinto Press.
Morton, Desmond (1983) *Years of Conflict 1911-21.* Toronto: Grolier.
- (1994) *A Short History of Canada,* 2nd rev. ed. Toronto: McClelland and Stewart.
Morton, Peter (1996) 'U.S. Reaches to Canada to Strike Telemarketers,' *Financial Post* 12 June, 1.
Muirhead, Bruce (1992) *The Development of Postwar Canadian Trade Policy: The Failure of the Anglo-European Option.* Montreal: McGill-Queen's University Press.
Murphy, Cullen (1996a) 'Hello, Darkness' *Atlantic Monthly,* 277 no. 3 (March), 22-4.
- (1996b) 'Backlogs of History' *Atlantic Monthly,* 277 no. 5 (May) 20-20.
Nagnur, Dhrwa (1986) *Longevity and Historical Life Tables, 1921-81 (Abridged).* Statistics Canada Cat. No. 89-506. Ottawa: Minister of Supply and Services.
Naylor, Tom (1975) *The History of Canadian Business 1867-1914.* Volume I, *The Banks and Finance Capital.* Toronto: James Lorimer & Company.
Newman, Peter C. (1968) *The Distemper of Our Times.* Winnipeg: Greywood Publishing.
- (1995) *The Canadian Revolution, 1985-1995: From Deference to Defiance.* Toronto: Viking.
Noll, Roger, and Owen, Bruce M., eds. (1983) *The Political Economy of Deregulation: Interest Groups in the Regulatory Process.* Washington, DC: American Enterprise Institute.
Ohmae, Kenichi (1991) *The Borderless World: Power and Strategy in the Interlinked Economy.* New York: HarperCollins.
Organization for Economic Co-operation and Development (OECD) (1995). *Revenue Statistics of OECD Member Countries, 1965-94.* Paris: OECD.
Orwell, George (1989) *Down and Out in Paris and London.* First pub. 1933. London: Penguin.

Owram, Doug (1986) *The Government Generation: Canadian Intellectuals and the State, 1900–1945.* Toronto: University of Toronto Press.
- (1994) 'Demographic Patterns in a New World Nation,' in Granatstein and Åkerman, eds. (1994), 101–21.
Pakko, Michael R., and Pollard, Patricia S. (1996) 'For Here or to Go? Purchasing Power Parity and the Big Mac,' *Federal Reserve Bank of St. Louis Review,* 78 no. 1 (Jan./Feb.), 3–21.
Pearson, Rt. Hon. Lester (1972a) *Mike: The Memoirs of the Right Honourable Lester B. Pearson.* Volume I. *1897–1948.* Toronto: University of Toronto Press.
- (1972b) *Mike: The Memoirs of the Right Honourable Lester B. Pearson.* Volume III. *1957–1968.* Toronto: University of Toronto Press.
Perlin, George (1997) 'The Constraints of Public Opinion: Diverging or Converging Paths?' in Banting, Hoberg, and Simeon, eds. (1997), 71–149.
Perry, David B. (1996) 'Fiscal Figures: Changes in Government Spending Patterns,' *Canadian Tax Journal,* 44 no. 2, 578–92.
- (1996) 'Fiscal Figures: The Evolution of Federal Personal Income Taxes in Canada,' *Canadian Tax Journal,* 44 no. 1, 260–6.
Peters, Hans J. (1993) *The Maritime Transport Crisis.* Washington, DC: World Bank.
Pickersgill, Jack (1994) *Seeing Canada Whole: A Memoir.* Toronto: Fitzhenry & Whiteside.
Picot, G., Zin, L. and Beach C. (1995) 'Recent Trends in Employer Payroll Taxes' *Canadian Economic Observer* Sept. 3.1–3.24.
Pole, J.R. (1978) *The Pursuit of Equality in American History?* Berkeley: University of California Press.
Porter, Michael (1990) *The Competitive Advantage of Nations.* New York: Free Press.
Rand McNally (1996) *Rand McNally TripMaker: 1996 Edition.* Skokie, Ill.: Rand McNally New Media.
Reich, Robert (1991) *The Work of Nations: Preparing Ourselves for 21st-Century Capitalism.* New York: Alfred A. Knopf.
Reitz, Jeffrey G., and Breton, Raymond (1994) *The Illusion of Difference: Realities of Ethnicity in Canada and the United States.* Toronto: C.D. Howe Institute.
Le Répertoire des subventions et aides gouvernementales (1993). Montreal: Les Éditions Édipro.

Riddell, W. Craig (1993) 'Unionization in Canada and the United States: A Tale of Two Countries,' in Card and Freeman, eds. (1993), 109–47.
Robin, Martin (1992) *Shades of Right: Nativist and Fascist Politics in Canada, 1920–1940.* Toronto: University of Toronto Press.
St-Hilaire, France (1996) *For Whom the Tax Breaks.* Montreal: Institute for Research on Public Policy.
Sandburg, Carl (1968) *Abraham Lincoln: The War Years, 1861–1864.* New York: Dell.
Sapir, André (1996) 'Trade Liberalization and the Harmonization of Social Policies: Lessons from European Integration,' in Bhagwati and Hudec, eds. (1996), chap. 15.
Sarlo, Christopher (1996a) 'A Comment,' in Beach and Slotsve (1996), 161–75.
– (1996b) *Poverty in Canada.* 2nd ed. Vancouver: Fraser Institute.
Schlesinger, Arthur M., Jr. (1966) *The Bitter Heritage: Vietnam and American Democracy, 1941–1966.* New York: Fawcett Crest.
– (1986) *The Cycles of American History.* Boston: Houghton Mifflin.
– (1995) 'Camelot Revisited,' *New Yorker* 5 June, 33.
Simeon, Richard, and Janigan, Mary, eds. (1991) *Toolkits and Building Blocks: Constructing a New Canada.* Toronto: C.D. Howe Institute.
Sirois, Charles (1996) 'Canada and the Globalization of Communications' *Canadian Corporate Report,* 30 April, 65–71.
Skidmore, Max J. (1995) 'Social Security in the United States,' in John Dixon and Robert P. Scheurell, eds. *Social Security Programs: A Cross-Cultural Perspective* (Westport, Conn.: Greenwood Press), 17–33.
Slemrod, Joel (1996) 'Tax Cacophony and the Benefits of Free Trade,' in Bhagwati and Hudec, eds. (1996), chap. 6.
Slutsky, Samuel (1995) 'High Taxes Speed Brain Drain to U.S.,' *Financial Post,* 7 Feb., 24.
– (1996a) 'Flat Tax Blocked by Reality,' *Financial Post,* 25 June, 28.
– (1996b) 'Cyberspace May Defeat Taxman,' 2 July, 19.
Smith, Denis (1995) *Rogue Tory: The Life and Legend of John G. Diefenbaker.* Toronto: Macfarlane, Walter & Ross.
Sopolsky, Harvey M., Crane, Rhonda J., Newman, W. Russell, and Noam, Eli M. (1992) *The Telecommunications Revolution: Past, Present and Future.* New York: Routledge.
Stanford, Jim (1993) 'Investment,' in Cameron and Watkins, eds. (1993), 151–72.

Stark, Steven (1995) 'Too Representative Government,' *Atlantic Monthly*, 273 no. 5, 92–106.
Statistics Canada (1995) *Universities: Enrolment and Degrees, 1990*. Cat. No. 81–204. Ottawa: Statistics Canada.
– (1978) *Historical Compendium of Education Statistics from Confederation to 1975*. Cat. No. 81–568. Occasional. Ottawa: Statistics Canada.
– (1995) *Canadian Economic Observer Historical Statistical Supplement 1994/95*. Ottawa: Statistics Canada.
– (1996) *Infomat: A Weekly Review*, 7 June, 5.
Tanzi, Vito (1995) *Taxation in an Integrating World*. Washington. DC: Brookings Institution.
Taylor, Peter Shawn (1996) 'Melancholy Babies,' *Saturday Night* (May), 23–8.
Tholl, William G. (1994) 'Health Care Spending in Canada: Skating Faster on Thinner Ice,' in Blomqvist and Brown, eds. (1994), 53–89.
Thompson, John Herd (1985) *Canada 1922–1939: Decades of Discord*. Toronto: McClelland and Stewart.
Thompson, John Herd, and Randall, Stephen J. (1994) *Canada and the United States: Ambivalent Allies*. Montreal: McGill-Queen's University Press.
Thurow, Lester (1992) 'Is Telecommunications Truly Revolutionary?' in Sopolsky et al. (1992) 1–50.
Trottman, Nelson (1966) *History of the Union Pacific: A Financial and Economic Survey*. First published 1923. New York: Augustus M. Kelly.
Turing, Alan M. (1950) 'Computing Machinery and Intelligence' *Mind* (Oct.).
Turner, Frederick (1995) 'The Freedom of the Past: On the Advantage of Looking Backward,' *Harper's Magazine*, 290 no. 1739 (April), 59–62.
Umar, Yusuf K., ed. (1992) *George Grant and the Future of Canada*. Calgary: University of Calgary Press.
United Nations (1993) *World Population Prospects: The 1992 Revision*. New York: United Nations.
– (1995) *World Investment Report 1995: Transnational Corporations and Competitiveness*. New York: United Nations.
– (1995) *Statistical Abstract of the United States*. Washington, DC: Deparment of Commerce, Bureau of the Census.

References 303

United States, Bureau of the Census (1989) *Historical Statistics of the United States: Colonial Times to 1970*. White Plains, NY: Kraus International Publications.
Urquhart and Buckley (1983) *Historical Statistics of Canada*. 2nd ed., ed. F.H. Leacy. Ottawa: Statistics Canada and Social Science Federation of Canada.
Valaskakis, Kimon (1995) *The Delusion of Sovereignty: Would Independence Weaken Quebec?* Montreal: Robert Davies.
Waite, P.B. (1996) 'Quebec's Laurier ... Canada's Prime Minister,' *Beaver* 76 no. 4 (Aug./Sept.), 10–71.
Walker, Michael, and Emes, Joel (1996) 'Are Canadians Less Compassionate than Americans?' *Fraser Forum* (April), 5–17.
Watson, William (1987) 'Things That Weren't on the Table' *Fraser Forum* (Nov./Dec.), 3–4.
– (1988) *National Pastimes: The Economics of Canadian Leisure*. Vancouver: The Fraser Institute.
– (1990) 'Pushing the Trade Deal? Say It Ain't So, Premier,' *Financial Post*, 9 March, 13.
– (1991) 'Rules Aplenty Keep Americans in Order,' *Financial Post*, 1 Feb., 11.
Webber, Carolyn, and Wildavsky, Aaron (1986) *A History of Taxation and Expenditure in the Western World*. New York: Simon and Schuster.
Weintraub, William (1996) *City Unique: Montreal Days and Nights in the 1920s and '50s*. Toronto: McClelland and Stewart.
Westley, Margaret W. (1990) *Remembrance of Grandeur: The Anglo-Protestant Elite of Montreal*. Montreal: Editions Libre Expression.
White, Bob (1993) 'Why Mexico?' in Cameron and Watkins, eds. (1993), 243–520.
Wilkins, Mira (1989) *The History of Foreign Investment in the United States to 1914*. Cambridge, Mass: Harvard University Press.
Williams, Marjorie (1995) 'The Ironman Cometh,' *Vanity Fair* (May), 112–70.
Wonnacott, Paul (1987) *The United States and Canada: The Quest for Free Trade*. Washington, DC: Institute for International Economics.
Wysocki, Bernard, Jr (1997) 'Development Strategy: Close Information Gap,' *Wall Street Journal*, 7 July, A1.

Index

Adams, Bryan, 221
agricultural revolution, 164–5
Air Canada, 198, 199, 209
American Economic Association, 49
American Economic Review, 49, 50
Americans' ignorance of Canada, 219–20
Anne of Green Gables, 221
Articles of Confederation (U.S.), 78, 94
asymmetric information, 75; as explanation for capital immobility, 50
Atlantic Monthly, 98
Atlantic provinces, excessive government in, 201–2
Austro-Hungarian Empire, 215
Avonlea, 234
Axworthy, Lloyd, 186

Bach, Johann Sebastian: George Grant's love for, 160
Bain, George, 222
Bank Act, 206
Bank of Canada, 93
Bank of Montreal, 123
Bank of the United States, 92
Banting and Best, 221; not known to Canadian students, 243

Barlow, Maude, 16
Bastiat, Frédéric, 264
Bennett, R.B., 114, 115, 128, 271, 272
Bennett, William, 174, 280
Bennett's New Deal, 115
Bercuson, David, 44, 116, 118, 276
Bernardo, Paul, 226
Berra, Yogi, 79
Berton, Pierre, 221, 241
Beveridge Report, 110, 116
Bill 101 (Quebec), 221
Black, Conrad, 220
Blake, William, 287
Bliss, Michael, xi, 99, 127, 258
Bluenose, 221
Blumenthal, Sidney, 88
Boadway, Robin, 60
Bonhomme Carnaval, 221
Borden, Robert, 113
borders, effect on Canada–U.S. trade flows, 51–6
Bothwell, Robert, 272
Bracken, John, 243; and family allowances, 110
Brainiac, 211
Brébeuf and Lalemant, 221

306 Index

Breton, Albert, on the costs of governance, 247-51
Breton, Raymond, 153-5
Bristol Aerospace, 208
British Labour party, 62
Broadbent, Ed, 257
Bronfman, Charles, 126
Bronfman, Edgar Miles, Sr, 126
Brookings Institution, 16
Brothers Grimm, 287
Brown, George, 95
Buchanan, James, 206
Buchanan, Pat, 159, 225
Burke, Edmund, 227, 254, 287
Bush, George, 31, 282

Calgary Stampede, 221
Cameron, Neil, xii
Cameron, Stevie, 202
Campbell, Bruce, 16
Canada Council, 112
Canadair Ltd, 208, 221
Canada Pension Plan, 45, 117, 181, 280
Canada-United States Autopact, 30, 43, 217
Canada-United States Free Trade Agreement (FTA), ix, 3, 6, 7, 8, 10, 11, 19, 52, 53, 147, 158, 217, 257, 284
Canada-United States social differences: in crime and incarceration, 151; difficulty explaining, 132-6; in educational attainment, 143; in gun ownership, 150-1; in income distribution, 143-5; in labour-management relations, 143; in popularity of unions, 148-9; in racial intolerance, 151-6; in reduction in poverty gaps, 145-6; in views of capitalism, 149-50; in welfare generosity, 146-7

Canada-United States Softwood Lumber Agreement, 252
Canadian-United Kingdom trade, 43, 171
Canadian-United States tax differences, 38-43
Canadian-U.S. trade, 171; growth in, not inconsistent with policy differentiation, 43-5, 51-6
Canadian Centre for Policy Alternatives, 16
Canadian Chicken Marketing Agency, 195
Canadian Council on Child and Family Welfare, 108
Canadian Dairy Commission, 195
Canadian Manufacturers' Association, 14, 84
Canadian nationalists, 260
Canadian National Railways, 99, 198
Canadian Northern, 100
Canadian Pacific Airlines, 198
Canadian Pacific Railway (CPR), 5, 10, 81, 95, 96, 97, 122, 129, 172, 207, 241
Canadian Tire, 54
Canadian Transportation Commission, 198, 200
canals, U.S. subsidies to, 96
capital mobility, exaggerated, 49-50
capital taxation, 9; supposed difficulty of, in globalized world, 57; true incidence not on capital, 60; varies across countries, 58-9
Carleton University, 235
Carr, Emily, 221
Cartier, George-Étienne, 240
Castro, Fidel, 230
Catherwood, Robert, xii
Cayley, David, 163, 176

Index 307

CBC (Canadian Broadcasting Corporation), 82, 88; *Newsworld*, 233; CBC television's monopoly in 1950s, 237
CBS (Columbia Broadcasting System), 238
C.D. Howe Institute, xi
CF-18 contract, 208, 210
Chandler, Alfred, Jr, 100
Charlottetown Accord, 284
Cherry, Zena, 222
child mortality, decline in, 164
Chrétien, Jean, 38, 98; only one per cent of Americans can identify, 219; on the virtues of pragmatism, 78–81
Churchill, Winston, 235, 239, 243
Civilian Conservation Corps (U.S.), 115
Clark, Joe, 78, 98
Clayoquot Sound, 167
Cleveland, Grover, 101
Clinton, Bill, 31, 64, 87, 157, 274
Clinton, Hillary, 157
CNN (Cable News Network), 233
cocooning, 246
Coffey, Paul, 222
Collège militaire royale, 210, 211
Columbus, Christopher, 227
Company of Young Canadians, 137
Concorde, Anglo–French, 167
Confederation, 24, 44, 47, 80, 207, 210, 240, 243, 253
Connors, Stompin' Tom, 221
Coolidge, Calvin, 285
Cooper, Barry, 44, 116, 118, 276
Co-operative Commonwealth Federation (CCF), 116
Coronation Street, 234; George Grant a fan of, 170
Council of Canadians, 16

Courchene, Thomas, 270
Cox, George, 124
Coyne, Andrew, 76
Credit Mobilier scandal, 269
Creighton, Donald, 82, 222
Crosbie, John, 221
Cross, Devon Gaffney, xi
Crow Rate, 80
CRTC (Canadian Radio-television and Telecommunication Commission), 174, 195, 196
CTV (Canadian Television Network), 237
Custer, George, 92

Dahlby, Bev, 180, 182, 193, 282
Darwin, Charles, 140
debt interest, 183–4, 205
Declaration of Independence (U.S.), 77, 93
De Mille, Cecil B., 235
Department of Finance (Canada), 168
deregulation, benefits of, 200
Deutsch, Antal, xii
Dickens, Charles, 287
Diefenbaker, John, 44, 118, 168, 222, 261, 276, 284; and family allowances, 110
'Diefenbuck,' 26
Disney Channel, 225
Doctor Kildare, 238
Dole, Bob, 163
Dominion Institute, 243
Douglas, Roger, 206
Drache, Daniel, 15
Drapeau, Jean, 221
Drew, George, 237; opposes family allowances, 110
Drucker, Peter, 118
Du Bois, W.B., 153

308 Index

Due South, 220, 225
Duffy, Mike, 275
Duplessis, Maurice, 271

Eagleson, Alan, 222
Earth Day, 159
Eaton's, 220
economic rent, 61
economics of federalism, 66-8
Economist, ix, 17, 207
Elizabeth II, 126
emigration from Canada, 47
English, John, 116, 118
equalization formula, 190, 222
Erickson, Arthur, 221
Erie Canal, 96
Euripides, 287
European Community, 30
European Economic Community, 32, 33, 260; lack of tax harmonization in, 35; reasons for policy harmonization in, 34
European Union, 32, 54, 58, 69, 252, 253, 260; trade barriers still significant in, 54-5
Eurosclerosis, 34
Evans, Catherine, 63
Expo 67, 241

family allowances, 212; W.L. Mackenzie King reluctant to introduce, 109
Federal Aviation Administration (U.S.), 200
federal election (1911), 84, 85, 216
federal election (1988), 3, 8, 14, 84, 85
Federal Reserve Act, 93
Ferrante, Angela, xi
Financial Post, 17, 275
fiscal tastes, 67
Flavelle, Joseph, 23, 124, 278
Fogel, Robert, 97, 99

Forbes, Steve, 85
Forbes Magazine, 126
foreign investment: historical dependence of Canadian economy on, 23-4; in *Lament for a Nation*, 168; in nineteenth century, 24; U.S., abroad, 50
Foreign Investment Review Agency, 53
Francis, Diane, 17
Frankel, Jeffrey, 55
Fraser, Blair, 207, 241, 283
Friedman, Milton, 47
Friendly Giant, 220
Frobisher, Martin, 127
Front Page Challenge, 220
Frum, David, 188
Frye, Northrop, 140, 241

Galbraith, John Kenneth, 80, 118
Gallup Poll, 8, 110, 148, 207, 257
Galt, A.T., 258
Garfield, James, 269, 270
Gates, Bill, 63
GATT (General Agreement on Tariffs and Trade), 19, 30, 33, 43
General Motors, 168, 199
George III, 92, 93
Gingrich, Newt, 88
globalization, ix, 10, 57; definition of, 21; not as complete as commonly thought, 46; not new, 21-6; novelty for United States, 23; thought to force policy harmonization, 15-17, 41
Godbout, Adélard, 271
Golden Square Mile, 123, 125
Goldwater, Barry, 160, 230
Gore, Al, 87
Gordon, David, 148, 264
Gould, Glenn, 223

Index 309

Gramm, Phil, 204
Granatstein, Jack, 17, 82, 104, 109, 212
Grand Trunk Railway, 101, 106
Grant, George, 44, 118, 158–77, 206, 220, 228, 229, 234, 242, 276, 277, 279
Grant, Sheila: life made easier by technology, 277, 279
Grant, Ulysses S., 269
Grantham, George, xii
Great Depression, 114, 115, 128
Great Society, 119, 137
green card, 47
Green, Christopher, xi, xii
Gretzky, Wayne, 220, 223
Grey Cup, 220
Grimard, Franque, xii
Group of Seven, 220
GST (Goods and Services Tax), 6, 180, 280
Guest, Dennis, 106, 111
Gulag archipelago, 235
Gutenberg, Johann, 227
Gwyn, Richard, 8, 15, 16, 55, 81, 82, 85, 86, 120, 125, 126, 137, 153, 156, 214, 216, 240, 273, 274
Gzowski, Peter, 221, 275

Harper's, 79
Harris, Mike, 275
Hart, Michael, 22
Harvard Business School, 264
Harvard University, 147
Havel, Vaclav, 230
Haydon, Andrew, 270
Hearne, Samuel, 122
Hearst, Randolph, 23
Heidegger, Martin, 167
Henderson, Paul, 221
Herridge, William, 271
Higgs, Robert, 77, 84, 201

Hobbes, Thomas, 287
Hobsbawm, Eric, 21, 32, 108, 112, 162, 165, 173, 239, 242, 278, 280
Hockey Night in Canada, 238
Hogan, Seamus, xii
Holmes, Oliver Wendell, Jr, 178
Holt, Herbert, 124
Homolka, Karla, 222
Hoover, Herbert, 128
Hopkins, Thomas, 197
Howe, C.D., 118, 171, 176, 261, 280
Hudson's Bay Company, 22, 122, 239
Hughes, Jonathan, 91, 102, 103, 197, 200, 268; and the American 'governmental habit,' 91–103
Hume, David, 160, 266
Hurtig, Mel, 221
Hutchison, Bruce, 115, 116, 156

Ignatieff, Michael, 21, 81, 222, 240–1
Ilsley, J.L., 111
immigration: anti-immigration bias, 152–3; to Canada, 48, 262; controls, 48; at record lows in 1980s and 1990s, 48
income redistribution: impressive degree of, effected through tax system, 274; and mobility, 64–5; most public spending not for, 265
Innis, Harold, 22, 25, 111, 167, 202, 208, 228, 240, 270
Internal Trade Agreement, 262
International Labour Office, 117
International Monetary Fund, 26, 58
International Olympic Committee, 215
international trade, in nineteenth century, 25
interregional jealousy, 207–12
Interstate Commerce Commission (U.S.), 92, 100

Irving, John, 69
Irving, K.C., 220
Jackson, Andrew, 93
Jackson, Jesse, 160
Jacobi, Derek, 218
Johnson, Ben, 221
Johnson, Lyndon, 117, 120, 160
Johnson, Paul, 286
Joyce, James, 287
Juliette, 238
Just Society, 119, 137

Kant, Immanuel, 160
Keats, John, 287
Kennedy, Edward M., 200
Kennedy, John F., 119, 120, 128
Kent, Tom, 112, 118
Keynes, John Maynard, 10, 47, 74, 75, 76, 84, 267
Khomeini, Ayatollah, 277
Kierans, Tom, xi
King, W.L. Mackenzie, 44, 85, 115, 128, 171, 212, 220, 225, 240, 243, 271, 280; and *laissez-faire*, 106–11
Kinsella, W.P., 63, 204
Kipling, Rudyard, 287
Kolko, Gabriel, 101
Krugman, Paul, 24, 25, 264
Ku Klux Klan, 135, 153
Kundera, Milan, 136

labour mobility, may have declined since nineteenth century, 46–8
Laffer, Arthur, and the Laffer curve, 282
Lamarck, Jean-Baptiste, 140
Lament for a Nation, 44, 118, 158–77; prophetically flawed, 159

lang, kd, 220
Lapham, Lewis, 79
Last Spike, 89
Laurier, Wilfrid, 105, 106, 212; as neo-conservative, 105–6
Lavalée, Calixa, 47
lawyers: proliferation of, in Canada, 267; United States ridden with, 87
Leacock, Stephen, 106–7, 123, 222, 273
Leblanc, Alfred, xii
Lemieux, Mario, 221
liberalism: does not explain demise of nation-state, 216–18; George Grant opposes, 158–9
Liberal party of Canada, 271
life expectancy, increase in, 1920–2 to 1980–2, 164
Lincoln, Abraham, 255, 273
Lipset, Seymour Martin, 142, 272
living standards, dramatic increase in, from nineteenth century, 165–6
Locke, John, 160
Loebner, Hugh, and the Loebner Prize, 284
Long, Huey, 118
Los Angeles Dodgers, 17
Lower, Arthur R.M., 266
Ludwig, Daniel, 139

Maastricht Treaty, 34
Macarthur, Duncan, 108, 109
McCallum, John, 253, 262; on the effects of the Canadian–U.S. border on trade flows, 51–6
Macdonald, John A., 22, 78, 95, 123, 206, 212, 243, 269
McDonald's, 232
McGill University, xi, 51, 106
McGovern, George, 160

Mackenzie, Alexander, 95
Mackenzie Brothers, 221
McKinley tariff, 23
Mackinnon, Mary, xii
McLennan, Hugh, 222
McLuhan, Marshall, 167, 228
Macmillan Bloedel, 167
McQuaig, Linda, 205
Maitland, Frederic William, 129
Manning, Preston, 254
Mansbridge, Peter, 275
Mansell, Robert, 211, 252
Maple Leaf flag, 171
market failure, as justification for government intervention, 74–7
Markusen, Ann, 63
Marsh Report, 110, 111
Martin, Paul, 16
Marxism, 160, 206
M*A*S*H, 235
Massey Commission, 112
Massey, Vincent, 285
Matheson, Dan, 275
Mead, Walter Russell, 16
medicare, 40, 45, 64, 265
Meech Lake Accord, 209, 222, 247, 284
Messier, Mark, 223
military spending, 41
Mill, John Stuart, 105
Mills, Russell, xi
Montgomery, Lucy Maud, 287
Montreal Expos, 60
Montreal Stock Exchange, 124
Moodie, Susanna, 221
Moosehead beer, 221
Morton, Desmond, xii, 77, 241, 242
Mother Teresa, 139
mother's pensions, 107–8, 114, 117

Mowat, Farley, 222
Mozart, Wolfgang, George Grant's love for, 162
MTV (Music Television), 232
Muirhead, Bruce, 171, 261, 280
Mulroney, Brian, 3–9, 38, 42, 44, 85, 96, 129, 157, 169, 207, 212, 217, 283
Munro, Alice, 221, 222
Murdoch, Rupert, 23
Murray, Anne, 221

NAFTA (North American Free Trade Agreement), ix, 7, 8, 10, 11, 15, 16, 19, 55, 217, 218, 284
Nash, Knowlton, 221
National Energy Policy, 53, 207, 208
National Health Grants, 111
National Policy, 19, 95, 127
nation-states, costs of governance in, 247
Navigation Acts, 93
Navigation Laws, 94
NBC (National Broadcasting Company), 233, 238
Nietzsche, Friedrich, 174
neoconservatism, 188
New Deal, 88, 114, 115, 271
Newman, Peter, 241
New Yorker, 228
New York Times, 219
Nipissing University, 144
Nixon, Richard, 251

OECD (Organization for Economic Co-operation and Development), 19, 28, 38, 143, 258; lack of convergence of tax rates in, 28–32
Ohmae, Kenichi, 53
old age pensions, 107, 150

Olympic Games, 226, 231
OPEC (Organization of Petroleum Exporting Countries), 196
original six members of the European Common Market, 36, 38; policy harmonization in, 34
Orwell, George, 209, 210
Osgoode Hall, 221
Ottawa Citizen, xi
Owram, Doug, 270, 271; on Canadian political philosophy 1900–50, 104–12

Parti Québécois, 210
payroll taxes, 191–2
Peace Corps (U.S.), 137
Pearson, Lester, 40, 44, 111, 116, 118, 120, 172, 271, 272, 276, 277
Penfield, Wilder, 111
Perlin, George, 148, 149, 151, 275, 276
Perry, Commodore Matthew, 23
Peterson, David, 147
Pickersgill, Jack, 109, 110, 111, 198, 270
Plato, 160, 164
Philip, Prince, 221
Phillips, Robin, 221
Plouffes, Les, 238
Pole, J.R., 119
policy harmonization, 11, 66; extent of convergence, 27–44; factors forcing it, 17–19; lack of, across U.S. states, 36–7; to the highest common denominator?, 65–6
Porter, John, 206
Porter, Michael, 264
poverty gap, 146–7
pragmatism, as the Canadian ideology, 79–80
Prime Suspect, 234

Pringle, Valerie, 275
productivity, price effects of slower growth in the public sector, 184
profits, at all-time lows in the 1990s, 163
progress: unfashionability of, 175, 176; unimportance of, to George Grant, 160
Progressive movement, 113
public accounts of Canada, selected entries from, 187
public-choice school, 83
Purvis, Douglas, 258

Quebec Pension Plan, 181
Queen's Plate, 221
Queen's University, 108, 148
Quiet Revolution, 279

race to the bottom, ix, 57
Radisson and Groseillers, 221
Ragan, Chris, xii
Randall, Stephen, 114, 115, 116, 139, 152, 258
'Rat Pack,' 4
RCMP (Royal Canadian Mounted Police), 218
Reagan, Ronald, 6, 30, 31, 36, 38, 58, 85, 86, 105, 129, 230, 260, 282
Reciprocity Treaty, 94
Reform party, 174, 209
regional-development incentives, 265
regulation, cost of, 197; redistribution implicit in, 195
regulators, captured by regulated interests, 200
Reich, Robert, 64
Reitz, Jeffrey, 153–5
rent-seeking, 202–4

Index   313

Reynolds, Neil, xi
Richards, John, xii
Richler, Mordecai, 221
Riddell, Craig, 148
Riel Rebellion, 89, 221, 240
Robertson, Lloyd, 275
Robinson, David, 16
Robson, William, xii
Rochester Institute of Technology, 197
Rockefeller, John D., 126
Roosevelt, Franklin, 114, 115, 116, 117, 128
Roosevelt, Theodore, 114
Rousseau, Jean-Jacques, 160
Royal Bank of Canada, 51, 124
Royal Canadian Mint, 168

St Hilaire, France, 180
St Laurent, Louis, as non-interventionist, 111–12
St Lawrence Seaway, 207, 208
Sajak, Pat, 232
Samuelson, Paul, 227
Sapir, André, 34
Sarlo, Christopher, 144
Schlenker, Ronald, 211, 252
Schlesinger, Arthur, Jr, 99, 119, 272
Schwanen, Daniel, xii
Scott, Anthony, on the costs of governance, 247–51
Second Bank of the United States, 93
Secord, Laura, 221
Service, Robert, 221
Sesame Street, 225
Seward, William Henry, 288
Sewell, David, xii
Shelley, Percy Bysshe, 287
Siddiqui, Fakri, xi
Simpson, Sir George, 122

Simpson, Jeffrey, 131
Simpson-Sears, 168
Siskel and Ebert, 190
Slemrod, Joel, 34, 59, 263
Smallwood, Joey, 221
Smith, Adam, 21, 160, 266
Smith, Allan, 143
Smith, Donald, 123
Smith, Goldwin, quoted approvingly by Harold Innis, 111
Smith, Michael, xii
Smoot–Hawley Tariff (U.S.), 114
Snow, Adrienne Delong, xi
Social Charter, 34
'social–policy railway,' 112, 113
social security, 117
Solzhenitsyn, Aleksandr, 235
Soviet Empire, 215, 230
Spry, Graham, 82, 147
Stanford, Jim, 258
Stanley Park, 64
Star Trek, 247
Stark, Andrew, xii
Stephen, George, 123
Stockman, David, 282
Stratford Festival, 221
Strauss, Stephen, 82
Sung, Alfred, 221

Tanzi, Vito, 58, 62, 263
tariffs, aggressive use of, by the United States, 93–5
Taschereau, Louis-Alexandre, 115
tax incidence, 60; not on capital, 11, 60
taxes: on corporate profits, 263; current level of, in Canada, 178–80; excess burden of, 188–94
Taylor, E.P., 176
Taylor, Peter Shawn, 278
Teleglobe Inc., 202

Thatcher, Margaret, 30, 31, 34, 36, 38, 79, 85, 260, 281, 282; made United Kingdom safe for taxation, 62
Thibault, Laurent, 14, 15, 19, 84
Thompson, John Herd, 114, 115, 116, 139, 143, 258
Thomson, Kenneth, 126
Thurow, Lester, 25
Tilley, Leonard, 95
Tomlin, Lily, 185
Toronto Blue Jays, 60, 221
Toronto General Hospital, 124
Toronto *Globe*, 95
Toronto *Globe and Mail*, 82, 241, 275
Toronto *Star*, 18
Toronto Stock Exchange, 124
trade liberalization, 26, 33
transportation costs, 18, 239–40
Treasury Board, 168
Trudeau, Pierre, 14, 44, 120, 172, 273, 277
Truman, Harry, 88, 118, 267
Turing, Alan, 218; and the Turing test, 218–19
Turner, Frederick, 160
Turner, John, 3–9, 11, 86, 95, 165

underground economy, 70
unemployment insurance, 114, 185, 280; industrial variation in, 186
Union Pacific Railway, subsidies to, 97–9, 128, 269
United Empire Loyalists, 221, 266; cannibalism among, 166
United Nations, 249
University of Alberta, 180

University of British Columbia, 148, 247, 251
University of Calgary, 209, 252
University of Chicago, 235
University of Toronto, 124, 154, 247
U.S. Bill of Rights, 92
U.S. Civil War, 127, 236, 273

Vancouver Stock Exchange, 221
Velk, Tom, xii
Vimy Ridge, 243
Von Neumann, John, 218
voting with the feet, effect on tax rates, 66–8

Waite, P.B., 212
Walker, Michael, 8
Wallace, Henry, 160
Wallin, Pamela, 275
Watt, James, 227
Wayne and Shuster, 221
Webber, Carolyn, 68, 85
Webster, Jack, 220
Weintraub, William, 278
Westgate, Murray, 221
Wheel of Fortune, 232, 233
White, Bob, 221
White, Vanna, 232
Whitton, Charlotte, 108, 110
Wildavsky, Aaron, 68, 85
Wilson, Charles, 199
Wilson, Michael, 14
Wisconsin idea, 272
WTO (World Trade Organization), ix, 10, 11, 19, 215, 217, 249, 252, 253

Yew, Lee-Kwan, 127

www.ingramcontent.com/pod-product-compliance
Lightning Source LLC
Chambersburg PA
CBHW030219100526

44584CB00014BA/1008